"A MAJOR C ____ ____ ____TION. *Black Families in White America* was the first book to debunk the myths and mythologies surrounding the black family. It delves beneath the surface to portray black families as diverse, healthy, adaptive, and resilient. Billingsley's unique approach allows the reader to understand the delicate balance society has always maintained with black families—by denying opportunity on the one hand, but offering a ray of hope on the other."

> —Joyce A. Ladner, Ph.D.
> Professor, Howard University
> School of Social Work

"A CLASSIC THAT CONTINUES TO OFFER UNIQUE INSIGHTS. *Black Families in White America* enhances our understanding of the causes of the current family crisis, and provides a foundation for developing policies that strengthen rather than weaken black families."

> —Robert B. Hill, Ph.D.
> Author of *Economic Policies and Black Progress*

BLACK FAMILIES IN WHITE AMERICA

Andrew Billingsley

With the assistance of Amy Tate Billingsley

A Touchstone Book
Published by Simon & Schuster Inc.
New York • London • Toronto • Sydney • Tokyo

Touchstone
Simon & Schuster Building
Rockeller Center
1230 Avenue of the Americas
New York, New York 10020

Copyright © 1968 by Simon & Schuster Inc.

First Touchstone Edition, 1988
TOUCHSTONE and colophon are registered trademarks
of Simon & Schuster Inc.
Manufactured in the United States of America

1 3 5 7 9 10 8 6 4 2 Pbk.

Library of Congress Cataloging in Publication Data
Billingsley, Andrew.
    Black families in White America/Andrew Billingsley, with the
assistance of Amy Tate Billingsley.—1st Touchstone ed.

    p.   cm.—A Touchstone Book
    ISBN 0-671-67162-6   Pbk.
    1. Afro-American families. 2. Afro-Americans—Social
conditions—1964–1975. 3. Afro-Americans—Social
conditions—1975–   . I. Title.
E185.86.B5   1988
305.8'96073—dc19   88-16340
                            CIP

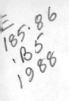

To Mrs. Ellen Towns and Mrs. Inez Duke Tate
Senior members of one black family
in white America

Acknowledgments

Many persons have helped to produce this book. Chief among them is my wife who, were it not for her modesty, should be co-author. I am indebted also to the U.S. Children's Bureau and to the University of California at Berkeley for financial support during the time of the book's preparation. In addition to the facilities of the University of California, I have been aided especially by the librarians at the Moreland collection of the Howard University Library, the Schomberg collection of the New York Public Library, and the Library of Atlanta University.

Among my academic colleagues who gave advice and read portions of the manuscript, I am particularly indebted and grateful to the following professors: Jeanne M. Giovannoni of San Francisco State College, Horace Mann Bond of Atlanta University, Milton M. Gordon of the University of Massachusetts, Howard Freeman of Brandeis University, Margaret Purvine of Rutgers University, and Charlotte Dunmore of Simmons College. Among the groups who gave critical reactions to early drafts of this book are my students at the University of California, the members of the Alain Locke Society, and members of the Christian Duty Club of Oakland, California.

For technical assistance at various stages of the manuscript, I am especially indebted to Jeanette Taylor, Gloria Washington, Flora Orsi, and Leah Smith. I am also indebted to Ruth Davis for her help in research and editing.

Finally, I wish to thank James Clark at Prentice-Hall for encouragement and support during the early stages of the manuscript and Michael Hunter of Prentice-Hall for a most imaginative, understanding, persistent, and responsive performance as editor.

Contents

Preface to the 1988 Edition

In the two decades since the first publication of *Black Families in White America*, enormous changes have occurred among Afro-American families, as among American families generally. Structural changes in family life have been most pronounced. The decline of the traditional European-American nuclear-family norm has been accompanied by the rise of alternative lifestyles including adult singlehood, cohabitation, gay and lesbian relationships, childless couples, divorce, separation, single parents, working wives and mothers, and many other changes as industrial society gives way rapidly to the new information society and as the blue-collar manufacturing economy gives way to the white-collar service economy. The spectacular growth of the black middle class, accompanied by the even more spectacular growth of the black underclass, seems to represent a puzzling paradox. The rapid improvement in the economic status of the black elderly stands in sharp contrast to the expansion of poverty among black children. A proper understanding of these changes and their impact on Afro-American family life requires the kind of broad historical and social systems perspective set forth in *Black Families in White America*.

The vestiges of the African heritage, the experience of slavery, the mixture of cultures, the long shadow of the Southern plantation, the transition to Northern urban communities, the persistence of racism, the impact of the civil rights movement and the public-policy initiatives it produced, all set forth in this book, can be seen to play important roles in an understanding of contemporary Afro-American family patterns. The systems framework, the typology of family structures, the sources of achievement, the role of social class, and the variety and complexity of Afro-American families laid out in this book illuminate efforts to understand, explain, and enhance the status and the future of Afro-American families.

Nor are the book's insights limited to the character of Afro-American families. Increasingly, it is being recognized that structural changes in society impact on a broad cross section of all American families. Still, the poor, less powerful sectors of the population are more vulnerable and suffer more. An editorial in the March 19, 1988, issue of *The New York Times* captures the essence of this new insight. "If America is to give each of its children a fair chance to succeed, it must help troubled, disadvantaged families survive and become self-sustaining. That would save not just one generation but two."

This is an insight, however, that often escapes the best-intentioned professionals, reformers, scholars, and policymakers. In their basic orientation toward enhancing family life in America, they often seek to consider black and white families separately, set the poor aside from the rest, and try to rescue children at the expense of their parents—all the while treating both children and families as though they were isolated from the community and the larger society that surround them.

To its credit, the *Times* editorial reflects a deeper understanding of the American family crisis. It recognizes the broad influence on families of the social system that was the cornerstone of *Black Families in White America*. Thus, in pointing to the need for professionals to (1) build on family strengths instead of focusing only on weaknesses, (2) treat parents as partners in dealing with children rather than as antagonists, (3) provide comprehensive services to families and children rather than relying on fragmented services, and (4) foster the integration between families and strong community-based institutions. The *Times* was echoing the best family studies by black scholars and others over the past two decades along the lines set forth in *Black Families in White America*.

According to this systems perspective, it is false and misleading to argue whether government policies *or* community-based self-help initiatives are required for the strengthening of Afro-American family life, as it has been fashionable to argue since about 1980. As John Hope Franklin and Eleanor Holmes Norton stated so eloquently on behalf of a group of black scholars in 1987, both the need and the history of both types of initiatives are firmly established in the black experience. Moreover, after the 1984 black Family Summit, sponsored by the nation's two largest black organizations, the NAACP and the National Urban League, there has been a plethora of community-based black self-help initiatives by most of the national black organizations and their affiliates. Prominent among these have been black churches, the strongest institutions in the black community, under the leadership of the Congress of National Black Churches, founded expressly to coordinate the social outreach programs of the seven major historic black denominations. Black women's organizations, under the leadership of Dorothy Height and the National Council of Negro Women, have also sponsored a series of family-focused self-help initiatives. Working in tandem with these organizations and spearheading the public-policy agenda has been the Children's Defense Fund under the leadership of Marian Wright Edelman.

An appreciation of this basic approach to understanding and enhancing Afro-American family life, the centerpiece of this book, will provide effective guidance to the nation's family professionals, scholars, and policymakers during the years ahead as the technological revolution continues to exert enormous pressures on all families, pushing them out of their historic patterns and forcing them to adapt new patterns for survival. In this period, poor, powerless, and oppressed minorities will continue to serve as barometers for the more privileged sectors of society, which sooner or later will feel the impact of these changes as well. Already it can be seen that the greatest manifestations of these structural changes—working mothers, divorce, single parenthood, unemployment, and poverty, all driven by changes in the technological base of society—are beginning to show that they are no respecters of color, creed, or social class. The crisis in child care alone substantiates this perspective. Thus, an appreciation of how Afro-American families cope with these changes will be of enormous value to the evolution of a national family policy in America that will benefit all families.

Preface

The family is the most basic institution of any people, the center and source of its civilization. Within the intimate context of the family, individuals develop their concepts of themselves, their values, and their worth in relation to the others in their world. Yet the family is not an independent unit of society. It is not the causal nexus of social behavior. It is highly interdependent with a great number of other institutions in the larger society, and dependent on many of those institutions for its definition, its survival, and its achievement. The Negro family, then, cannot be understood in isolation or by concentration on its fragments, or on particular forms of family life, or by concentration on its negative functions. The Negro family can best be understood when viewed as a varied and complex institution within the Negro community, which is in turn highly interdependent with other institutions in the wider white society. This is the central theme of *Black Families in White America*.

This book is essentially descriptive in nature. We describe some of the major dimensions of Negro family life, so that some of the problems and potentials associated with different patterns can be more clearly understood and more accurately perceived. We also seek to trace the implications of those approaches which may be taken by Negroes themselves, by other individuals and organizations interested in Negro life and affairs, as well as by the governmental agencies whose responsibility it is to provide leadership in the development of a viable interracial, pluralistic, and democratic society.

Part 1

BLACK FAMILIES
IN PERSPECTIVE

Chapter 1

A Social Systems Approach to the Study of Negro Family Life

In a sense, the title of this book should be *Black Families in Black and White America*, a title which would reflect both the theoretical perspective and the value position being advanced here. Theoretically, we urge that the Negro family might appropriately be viewed as a social system inextricably bound up with and heavily influenced by the major institutions of the larger society. At the same time we argue that Negro families would function much more productively if the Negro experience were more adequately reflected in the dominant values and programs of the larger society.

Negro families have been mistreated, ignored, and distorted in American scholarship in part because of the absence of general theories guiding studies of American families. Such theoretical frameworks, we argue, might help to overcome or expose the limitations of the Anglo-European conformity type biases which still pervade most contemporary public discussions of Negro family life in this country. Unfortunately, social scientists and other students of group life, as well as the mass media, have helped to perpetuate this ignorance and distortion. This point has been made recently by Ralph Ellison,[1] when asked by a group of young Negro writers to comment on how they might more truly reflect the complexity of the human condition, using the Negro experience as a theme.

He responded that the Negro writer would never see his subject if he accepted the stereotype of the Negro family as a broken one and a matriarchy, or of Harlem as "piss in the halls and blood on the stairs." Such clichés, he went on, may have a basis in reality, but they vastly oversimplify the complexity of the Negro condition, denying " 'that

[1] Ralph Ellison, "A Very Stern Discipline," *Harper's Magazine* (March, 1967), pp. 76–95.

3

something else' which makes for our strength, which makes for our endurance and our promise."

As harsh and accurate as is Ellison's view of the general treatment of Negro families, it is not a universal view, nor is the condition he describes a necessary part of the sociological perspective. A number of social scientists are beginning to approach the Negro experience with new lenses and to view it and describe it in its own right, and in much of its variation and complexity.

In this chapter, then, a particular theoretical orientation is advanced as a framework for viewing Negro families. This orientation emphasizes both the interdependence of these families with other levels of society and the variability among Negro families.

The Negro Family as a Social System

Four major concepts provide the essential elements of this perspective: (1) social system, (2) ethnic subsociety, (3) family structure, and (4) family function. Each of these major concepts refers to a stream of social science theory which has been developed and tested primarily in relation to other social phenomena than the family. The four are, however, highly compatible and suggestive for a study of Negro family life precisely because Negro families have been so conspicuously shaped by social forces in the American environment.

The concept of a social system has been elaborated most fully by Talcott Parsons and his associates and collaborators.[2] A system is an organization of units or elements united in some form of regular interaction and interdependence. The key words in this definition are *units, organization, interaction,* and *interdependence.* According to Parsons, a social system is an aggregation of persons or social roles bound together in a pattern of mutual interaction and interdependence. It has boundaries which enable us to distinguish the internal from the external environment, and it is typically imbedded in a network of social units both larger and smaller than itself. The Negro family as a social system is diagramed in Figure 1.

Principal among the subsystems of the larger society which have a direct impact on family life are the values, the political, the economic, the educational, the health, and the communications subsystems. Negroes

---

[2] Talcott Parsons, *The Social System* (New York: The Free Press, 1951); and Talcott Parsons and Robert F. Bales, *Family, Socialization and Interaction Process* (New York: The Free Press, 1955).

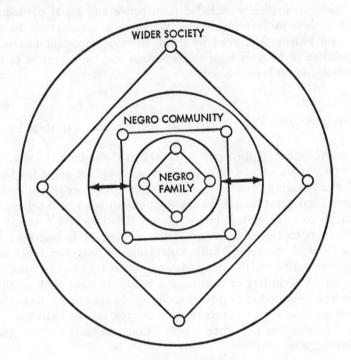

FIGURE 1
The Negro Family as a Social System

The Negro family is imbedded in a network of mutually interdependent relationships with the Negro community and the wider society.

The Negro family includes within itself several subsystems: that of the Husband-Wife, and those of Mother-Son, Mother-Daughter, Father-Son, Father-Daughter, Brother-Sister, Brother-Brother, Sister-Sister, and some- times the Grandmother-Mother-Daughter subsystems, to mention only the most common.

The Negro community includes within itself a number of institutions which may also be viewed as subsystems. Prominent among these are: schools, churches, taverns, newspapers, neighborhood associations, lodges, fraternities, social clubs, age and sex peer groups, recreation associations, and small businesses, including particularly, barber shops, beauty parlors, restaurants, pool halls, funeral societies, and various organized systems of hustling.

The wider society consists of major institutions which help set the con- ditions for Negro family life. Chief among these are the subsystem of values, the political, economic, education, health, welfare, and communi- cations subsystems.

have been systematically excluded from active and equal participation in each of these major subsystems of the larger society, yet all the while have been heavily influenced by them. Another important fact is that the exclusion of Negroes from the definition and the resources of these subsystems has not been uniform.

THE NEGRO COMMUNITY AS AN ETHNIC SUBSOCIETY

In many respects in this country, as well as throughout the world, the Negro people are viewed as a group, a category, set apart from other peoples and sharing conditions, attributes, and behavior in common. On the other hand, great variations of conditions, attributes, and behavior are obvious in so large and diverse a people. The concept of ethnic sub-society helps capture the nature of this duality. It is borrowed from Milton Gordon's theoretical work *Assimilation in American Life*,[3] and is highly consistent with the social systems conception just described. An ethnic group, according to Gordon, is a relatively large configuration of people with a "shared feeling of peoplehood." In our society, these groups are commonly bound by our conceptions of race, religion, national origin, or some combinations of these factors. "Common to the ethnic group," Gordon suggests,

> is the social-psychological element of a special sense of both ancestral and future-oriented identification with the group. These are the "people" of my ancestors, therefore, they are my people, and will be the people of my children and their children. With members of other groups I may share political participation, occupational relationships, common civic enterprise, perhaps even an occasional warm friendship, but in a very special way, which history has decreed, I share a sense of indissoluble and intimate identity with *this* group and not *that* group within the larger society and the world.[4]

This conception of ethnic group seems to capture not only the reality of existence for the Negro people but the new sense of awareness of identity and peoplehood which is becoming increasingly legitimated in black communities throughout the country.

But if Negroes are an ethnic group bound together not only by common

[3] Milton Gordon, *Assimilation in American Life* (New York: Oxford University Press, Inc., 1964). Future quotations from this source reprinted by permission of Oxford University Press, Inc.
[4] Gordon, p. 29.

definition and treatment on the part of the larger society, but also by a common sense of peoplehood, they are not a uniform group. Ethnic subsociety is a concept which reflects some of the dimensions of variation within the ethnic group. The Negro community as an ethnic subsociety is diagramed in Figure 2. Gordon has stressed three social dimensions

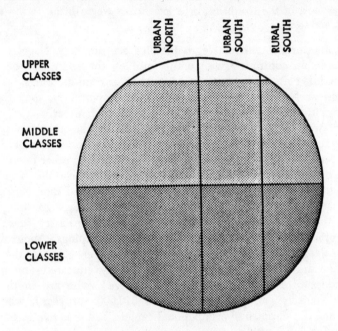

FIGURE 2
The Negro Community as an Ethnic Subsociety

Negro families are located variously in the social spaces created by the intersections of social class, North-South, and urban-rural residence.
This figure is conceptual and does not reflect the exact social and geographic distribution of the Negro population. In 1966, roughly one-half of all Negro families lived in the urban North, one-fourth in the urban South, and still another quarter lived in the rural South. We also estimate that roughly half of all Negro families may be considered lower class, about 40 per cent middle class and about ten per cent upper class. If we consider family income as an index of social class, it may be observed that in 1966, 56 per cent of Negro families earned less than $7,000, 32 per cent earned between $7,000 and $10,000 and 12 per cent earned over $10,000. There is a high, though by no means perfect, correlation among income, education, and occupation of family head.

which help to capture some of the variation within ethnic groups, namely,

> social class, rural or urban residence, and region of the country lived
> in . . . Thus a person is not simply a white Protestant, he is simultane-
> ously a lower-middle class white Protestant, living in a small town in the
> South, or he is an upper-middle class white Catholic living in a metro-
> politan area of the Northeast, or a lower-class Negro living in the rural
> south and so on. . . .[5]

For our purposes, then, Negro families are not only Negroes to be
compared and contrasted with white families, they may also be upper
class, middle class, or lower class, with urban or rural moorings, and with
Southern or Northern residence, and, most importantly, they may be
meaningfully compared and contrasted with each other.

In modern times, social class has come to be the most powerful of
these three dimensions which help to define the conditions of life for
Negro families. Social class among Negroes, as among other peoples, is a
complex phenomenon which explains only a part of social life. The Negro
community is much more complex and highly stratified than is generally
appreciated. There are, in general, three social class groupings—the
upper, the middle, and the lower classes. Within each of these three
major groupings, however, are additional subgroupings. About 10 per
cent of Negro families may be considered upper class in the sense
that they are headed by men who are highly educated (often with
advanced professional degrees beyond college), who are in the high
income brackets (ranging upward from $10,000 per year), who have
secure and developmental occupational careers, and who live in adequate
and comfortable housing.

Within this upper class group, however, are two upper classes rather
than one. The first and perhaps most traditional Negro upper class is
composed of the "old families." These are families with long histories of
privilege, achievement, and social status. They reached the top of the
social status ladder by building on the head start provided in previous
generations. Members of this old upper class often had parents who were
middle or upper class, with higher than the Negro average in education,
income, and property holdings, often dating back over several generations. These include families headed by doctors, judges, businessmen,
high government officials, and the like, who got to the top over several
generations. Prominent among these old families, for example, are those
of the three highest Negro officials in the federal government: Senator

[5] Gordon, p. 47.

Edward Brooke, Supreme Court Justice Thurgood Marshall, and Secretary of Housing and Urban Development Robert Weaver.

At the same time, there are other and slowly increasing numbers of Negro upper class families, headed by men who made it to the top in one generation, whose parents and grandparents before them were poor. Their achievement is based not on a long history of family status, but on ability and societal supports. Prominent among this new upper class, for example, are Mayor Richard Hatcher of Gary, Indiana, and Mayor Carl B. Stokes of Cleveland. There are, of course, more and perhaps better prototypes of these two upper classes outside the political system than within it, though the political leaders are more conspicuous at the present time.

Negro middle class families are more familiar. They account for perhaps 40 per cent of all Negro families. There are, however, three distinct groupings. There are the upper middle class families, the solid middle class, and the precarious middle class. These are distinguished by educational, income, and occupational achievement, but also by styles of family life, and by the security of their hold on middle class status.

Finally, there are the lower classes, where perhaps half of all Negro families are located. Again, however, there are several groupings, which may be distinguished by the occupational history and security of their heads as well as by education, income, and the like. Starting from the top of the lower class, then, we may identify the "working nonpoor," the "working poor," and the "nonworking poor." The first group of families is headed by men who have a stable and secure niche in the unionized industrial sector of the economy. They are likely to be semi-skilled on the basis of on-the-job experience. The largest group of lower class families, however, may be described as the working poor. Their heads work in unskilled and service occupations with marginal incomes, which often range downward from $3,000 per year. The final group of lower class families is the one about which most information appears in the literature and in the public press. Comprising about a quarter of all lower class Negro families, it is largely peopled by men and women who are unemployed or intermittently employed, supported by relatives and friends or by public welfare.

The importance of social class does not mean, as a number of social scientists still hold, that middle class Negro families have more in common with middle class white families than they do with lower class Negro families. Some liberal social reformers even hold that lower class Negro families have more in common with lower class white families than they do with middle class Negro families. Such naive analyses—on which programs are often based—are possible because of a failure to make distinctions between different types of identity people share.

The concept ethnic subsociety helps to call attention to such distinctions.

> Succinctly, then, one may say that the ethnic group is the locus of a sense of *historical identification*, while the ethclass [the intersection of ethnicity and social class] is the locus of a sense of *participational identification*. With a person of the same social class but of a different ethnic group, one shares behavioral similarities but not a sense of peoplehood. With those of the same ethnic group but of a different social class, one shares the sense of peoplehood but not behavioral similarities. The only group which meets both these criteria are people of the same ethnic group *and* social class.[6]

Although it may well be that social class divisions among Negroes are relatively less rigid or circumscribing of behavior than among other groups, they nevertheless provide a distinct basis of differentiation which helps to condition Negro family life in ways we shall consider in some detail in later sections of this book.

A Sense of Peoplehood

Middle class Negro families, then, do share certain similarities with middle class white families. They share some, though not nearly all, the privileges, opportunities, resources, and amenities of their middle class white counterparts. When, rarely, they also share neighborhoods, schools, and other common ground on a basis of sustained interaction and equality, they are also likely to share what Gordon refers to as "participational identification." They are not as likely, however, to share a common sense of peoplehood. They have very different histories, very different statuses in society, and very different levels of economic security. They consequently do not share the "historical identification" which middle class Negroes share with other middle class Negro families, including these in the lower classes. It is with other middle class Negro families, however, that these two senses of identity are combined and fortified. They are, indeed, in the same boat.

While Negroes have always been aware of this historical connection with each other and with Negroes in other parts of the world, we have not always been free to recognize it, make it explicit, define it, and build on it. We have been brainwashed by the sea of whiteness which surrounds us and defines us. It was not until after World War II, when

---

[6] Gordon, p. 53.

strides toward increasing freedom for Negroes were made both in this country and in Africa, that the Negro people again took up the theme, at one time advanced by Marcus Garvey, that black people have a common history, a common set of relations with the white world, and a common destiny. And it was not until twenty years later that the general society began to take note, mainly in negative terms, of this search for identity on the part of the Negro people. Now in every major community in the country, upper and middle class Negroes are turning in dozens of ways toward an explicit recognition of the common destiny shared by the Negro people. There is no important civil rights or protest activity that does not have substantial participation and leadership by the more privileged Negroes. And the country was surprised to find such substantial support among middle class Negroes for the ghetto uprisings of 1965, 1966, and 1967 in more than 100 major cities.

But again, this activity is only the surface of the iceberg. The process of identification is much more widespread than that. It reflects itself in such quiet ways as Negro families moving back into the ghetto or refusing to move out. Most communities have some form of continuing dialogue among Negroes about their common condition, destiny, and potential for change. The writings of Frantz Fanon along with those of Malcolm X and W. E. B. DuBois, particularly his *Souls of Black Folk*, frequently serve as the focus of discussion groups devoted to such dialogue. One such group in California which does not confine itself to these writings, and often produces original essays and position papers, is the Alain Locke Society. It is not an organization, has no members, dues, by-laws, or constitution. Rather, it defines itself as a Seminar. A much larger and more highly organized group is Men of Tomorrow, which recently devoted its annual retreat to the theme of the role of middle class Negroes in efforts to improve conditions of Negroes in the ghetto.

Negro physicians, social workers, teachers and other professionals are beginning to take special recognition of and special initiative on behalf of low income Negro families and children. At the University of Massachusetts, which probably has a higher proportion of Negro faculty members than most other universities, a group of Negro faculty members came together and designed a program for the recruitment and education of Negro students. A similar movement is under way at the University of California. In Berkeley, as in other cities, a group of Negro public school teachers came together and designed a special summer program for Negro children, combining a healthy amount of regular academic work with special learnings about the cultural heritage of the

Negro people. The program, which had the active support of the school system and the community, was officially titled "TCB." For the general community this meant "teaching, creating, building," but for the Negro community it meant "takin' care of business."

In financial ways, too, this racial consciousness or ethnic solidarity is manifesting itself. In 1967, for the first time, a group of the wealthiest Negroes in the nation came together in New York to consider how their money, their positions in the Negro community, and their influence in the larger society might be put into more effective efforts for improving the condition of underprivileged Negroes. In Chicago, a struggling United Negro Appeal, patterned after the highly successful United Jewish Appeal, is gaining ground. Some of the larger efforts on the part of the more privileged Negroes to express their connection with the Negro experience in society were reflected in the renaissance in Negro art and drama during the three years between 1965 and 1968. Most major cities now have at least one Negro theater group where there was none before. Art galleries, book stores, Negro history courses, small business enterprises, mass meetings which deliberately exclude white people— sometimes even when whites help provide financial support—are springing up in Negro communities all over the country.

The most impressive examples of racial solidarity occurred during 1967 in the political arena. The election of Negro mayors in Cleveland and Gary was made possible only by the unprecedented collaboration of Negroes from all sectors of the community. Block voting along ethnic lines is not unusual in American politics. What is unusual about these two elections is that, for the first time, Negroes voted in larger proportions than white voters and, for the first time, Negro block voting went for a Negro instead of a white candidate for mayor. A similar effort of a Negro candidate for mayor in Memphis did not, however, meet with the same degree of ethnic solidarity present in Cleveland and Gary.

In Cleveland, for example, Mayor Stokes' margin of victory in the primary was 18,000 votes and he received only 16,000 white votes. It was solidarity among Negro voters which made this victory possible. In reality, however, many of the Negroes voted for Stokes precisely because he had an interracial campaign with important and substantial white support. Thus, white liberals, students, businessmen and the press made a major contribution to Negro ethnic solidarity and achievement working within the framework of the Negro community. The major leadership, however, came from middle class Negroes working in a new burst of collaboration with lower class Negroes.

Not all middle class Negro families are yet able or willing to see the connections they share with all other Negroes. Many still hold to the view that they are more middle class than Negro, and are still seeking to convince the white middle class of that fact. The process is fraught with what Kenneth Clark calls "fantasies" on both sides.

> A common fantasy is to deny one's own identification with the racial dilemmas: "I have no racial problem." Yet to the extent to which either the Negro or white believes this and behaves accordingly, the psychological distance between Negro and white is increased even if it may, on the surface, appear to be otherwise.[7]

It is amazing how little middle class white people know about the conditions of life and the sensibilities of the middle class Negroes with whom they are in daily contact. This is a by-product of the fantasy of denial which often pervades these interracial contacts. It often happens that when middle class Negroes seek to disengage themselves from this fantasy, identifying more closely with the Negro experience, it causes a great deal of consternation among their white colleagues. Many find it possible to adjust to the new reality, while others shake their heads in disbelief, withdraw their contributions from SNCC, stop pushing for integration in their own institutions, and argue long and hard for law and order, and against "reverse segregation." It is an irreverent and irrelevant response to the situation, but wholly understandable under the circumstances. Social change is often painful, and ethnic solidarity is a powerful force for change which the country has come to accept from other ethnic groups. Its gradual but distinct and growing reawakening among Negroes has tremendous potential for disrupting old alliances and shattering old stereotypes of friend and foe alike. At the same time, however, it has even greater potential for contributing to the reconstruction of Negro family and community life and for the development of a more viable pluralistic and democratic society.

All of these recent behavioral manifestations of participational identification among Negroes indicate an intensification of those dimensions of ethnic similarity which set any people apart as a distinct subsociety. Nonetheless, there remain those dimensions of variation, such as social class, which stimulate great diversity among Negro people. It is in both these dimensions, similarity and difference, that the utility of the concept of ethnic subsociety rests as an integral part of the framework for the study of Negro family life.

The data in Table 1 help to clarify the relevance of the several ele-

---

[7] Kenneth B. Clark, *Dark Ghetto* (New York: Harper & Row, Publishers, 1965), p. 226.

TABLE 1

NEGRO FAMILIES WITH CHILDREN HEADED BY MEN
[BY FAMILY INCOME AND URBAN-RURAL RESIDENCE]
(1960)

	Total %	Under $3,000 %	$3,000 & over %
All Negro Families	79	64	93
Rural Residence	86	82	95
Urban Residence	77	53	92
All White Families	94	78	97
Rural Residence	96	88	98
Urban Residence	93	62	96

ments of the ethnic subsociety for family structure. The table shows that each of these major variables has some impact on the structure of family life, but social class as represented by total family income is by far the major influence. Thus among Negro families as a whole, there is an important rural-urban difference, with 86 per cent of rural families with children and 77 per cent of urban families with children being headed by men. If we look at family income alone, we also note a difference with 64 per cent of families in the low income group and 93 per cent of families in the higher income group being headed by men. But among Negro families earning $3,000 or above, there is virtually no difference between rural and urban families in the proportion of male heads. Difference between ethnic groups are maintained within each subgroup, but they are diminished considerably by social class. Thus, among urban families earning $3,000 and over, for example, 92 per cent of Negro families with children and 96 per cent of white families with children were headed by men, whereas among the low income groups, these proportions were 53 per cent and 62 per cent respectively.

It is important to stress, however, that social class does not obliterate the differences between Negroes and whites, not even on so simple a dimension as the sex of the family head. There are several reasons for this. Perhaps most important is the fact that even when the two groups, Negroes and whites, are in the same income range, they do not have the same incomes. Middle class Negro families do not have the resources available to them that middle class white families do. And lower class Negro families are considerably poorer than lower class white families. Negro families earning above $3,000, for example, will have considerably lower average earnings than white families in the same range. Negro families will cluster toward the lower end of the range and white families will cluster toward the upper end. In a similar manner, levels of education, occupational security, and opportunity are not equal for middle class Negroes and whites. The same is true at the lower class levels.

Even with comparable education, however, Negroes do not have the same occupational opportunities, and even with similar occupations, they do not have the same incomes, and even if they could be equated on all these measures, they have different statuses and histories in this country. Considering all these factors, the wonder is that there is so little difference between Negroes and whites in the proportion of families with male heads. That is the phenomena which deserves to be explained. Or perhaps neither the white-Negro difference nor the male head-female head dichotomy are sufficient for an understanding of the structure of Negro family life. It is considerably more complex and dynamic, adaptive and resilient than can be captured by such simplistic descriptions.

Another problem with the two types of family approach is that such characterization tends to treat female-headed families as if they were a Negro phenomenon, despite the fact that there were roughly four million white single-parent families and about one million Negro single-parent families in 1966.[8]

In addition, as Elizabeth Herzog has observed, such characterization tends to treat female-headed families as "nonfamilies"[9] and supports the view that the government or somebody should do something to put all Negro children into families with male heads. Furthermore, this way of characterizing family structure distorts and exaggerates the prevalence and the consequences of the "matriarchy" among Negro families. Perhaps the most important limitation of this two-way description is that it obscures rather than clarifies the range and variety of Negro family structure.

For an understanding of the structure of Negro family life, then, it seems important to take into consideration not only the sex of the family head but also the relationship of each household member to the head.

THE STRUCTURE OF NEGRO FAMILY LIFE

It is very common to observe that there are two types of family structure in America: male-headed families and female-headed families. Such

[8] U. S. Census Bureau, "Social and Economic Conditions of Negroes in the United States," *Current Population Reports*, Series P-23, No. 24 (October 1967), p. 68.
[9] Elizabeth Herzog, "Is There a Breakdown of the Negro Family?" *Social Work*, II, No. 1 (January 1966), 3–10.

characterization is almost always followed by the assertion or assumption that male-headed families are stable whereas female-headed families are unstable, and that the latter are more than twice as common among Negroes as among whites.

This manner of characterizing the structure of Negro family life has a number of inadequacies. First, it underestimates the variations among Negro families living under different basic conditions.

On the basis of such conditions, three general categories of families may be identified: primary families, extended families, and augmented families. A family is commonly defined as a group of persons related by marriage or ancestry, who live together in the same household. Nuclear families are confined to husband and wife and their own children, with no other members present. Extended families include other relatives or in-laws of the family head, sharing the same household with the nuclear family members. Augmented families include members not related to the family head who share the same household living arrangements with the nuclear family. Each of these three categories of families will be considered in some detail. Roughly two thirds of all Negro families are nuclear families, a quarter are extended families and a tenth are augmented families.

Further, within the framework of these three categories, twelve different types of family structure may be specified. In addition, this typology allows for the elaboration of subtypes within several of these twelve types of family structure. The basic typology of Negro family structures appears in Table 2.

Nuclear Families

Among nuclear families, three specific types of family structure may be observed. Type I, the *incipient nuclear family,* is composed of husband and wife living together in their own household with no children. Nearly a fifth of all Negro families, or roughly a million families, are of this type. They are young married couples who have not yet had time or economic security to start their family, older couples who have not been able or willing either to have their own children or to adopt others, and still older couples whose children have grown up and left the home. This type also includes a few families whose minor children have been placed in foster homes or institutions because of illness or other incapacity of one or both parents. The largest single subgroup in this category consists of those husbands and wives who do not have children of their own for a variety of reasons. These families are generally economically

TABLE 2
NEGRO FAMILY STRUCTURE

	Household Head		Other Household Members		
Types of Family	Husband & Wife	Single Parent	Children	Other Relatives	Non-relatives
Nuclear Families					
I: Incipient Nuclear Family	X				
II: Simple Nuclear Family	X		X		
III: Attenuated Nuclear Family		X	X		
Extended Families					
IV: Incipient Extended Family	X		X	X	
V: Simple Extended Family	X		X	X	
VI: Attenuated Extended Family		X	X	X	
Augmented Families					
VII: Incipient Augmented Family	X				X
VIII: Incipient Extended Augmented Family	X			X	X
IX: Nuclear Augmented Family	X		X		X
X: Nuclear Extended Augmented Family	X		X	X	X
XI: Attenuated Augmented Family		X	X		X
XII: Attenuated Extended Augmented Family		X	X	X	X

viable because both partners work, except during illness, old age, or widespread unemployment. Incipient nuclear families, then, are a large, important, and complex aspect of the structure of Negro family life. Yet they are almost completely ignored in studies of Negro families. They offer an important potential for the care of children in the Negro community, though there is some indication that among many Negro families those with some children already may be more willing to take in other children than those without children of their own.

A second type of family is the *simple nuclear family*. This family type consists of husband and wife and their own or adopted children living together in their own household with no other members present. This is the traditional type of family structure in America and Europe. Among students of the family, it is considered the ideal and most universal family form.

It might be instructive to note, however, that while this nuclear family arrangement is the ideal and the model against which all other families, particularly Negro families, are compared, it does not encompass the majority—even among white families. A study by Paul C. Glick found that in 1953 only 28.6 per cent of household units consisted of a husband and wife and their own minor children.[10] And a study in 1965 in Richmond, California, by Alan Wilson found that 45 per cent of white families and 49 per cent of Negro families consisted of husband, wife, and their own children.[11] Thus the "ideal" family pattern, the simple nuclear family, may not be any more common among whites than it is among Negroes. Nationally, about 36 per cent of all Negro families, or more than 1½ million families, are of the simple nuclear type.[12]

A third type of family structure is the *attenuated nuclear family*. This type of family structure has either a father or a mother—but not both— living together with minor children in the parent's own household with no other persons present. Commonly referred to as a broken family, this is an important type of family structure in the United States. Its most frequent form is mother and children living together.

Of the more than 2¼ million attenuated nuclear families in the United States in 1965, 733,000 were Negro families, constituting about 16 per

[10] Paul C. Glick, *American Families* (New York: John Wiley & Sons, Inc., 1957), p. 2.

[11] Alan Wilson, "Western Contra Costa County Population, 1965: Demographic Characteristics" (unpublished paper, 1966, Survey Research Center, University of California, Berkeley), p. 16.

[12] This typology is based on data taken from the U. S. Bureau of the Census, U. S. Census of Population, 1960, *Families*, PC(2)-4A-P-1, Table 1 (Washington, D. C.: U. S. Government Printing Office, 1965).

cent of all Negro families. The vast majority of these familes (689,000) were headed by females, while 44,000 were headed by males who were not married and not living with other relatives.[13] A wide variety of families are encompassed within this type. Ten specific subtypes may be derived, depending on whether the single parent is male or female and whether he or she is (a) single, (b) married with an absent spouse, (c) legally separated, (d) divorced, or (e) widowed.

When we speak of attenuated families, then, and when others speak of one-parent families or broken families, we are not referring to a unified entity, for the attenuated family encompasses a wide variety of subtypes, with different meanings, different causes, and different consequences for its members. The concept of attenuated families is designed to minimize some of the invidiousness associated with other terms and to be simply descriptive, suggesting as it does, that somebody important to the family constellation is missing.

Extended Families

In all three types of nuclear families described above, the members live together in their own house, every member being related to the head of the household either by marriage or by birth. In the second major category of family structures, other relatives are introduced into this nuclear household, making of it an extended family.

The types of extended families include: (a) the *incipient extended family*, consisting of a married couple with no children of their own who take in other relatives; (b) the *simple extended family*, consisting of a married couple with their own children, who take in other relatives; and (c) the *attenuated extended family*, consisting of a single, abandoned, legally separated, divorced, or widowed mother or father living with his or her own children, who takes into the household other relatives. Each of these patterns exists in appreciable numbers among Negro families. To know which of the subtypes of extended family is under consideration would help to clarify the generalizations which can be made, for these subtypes differ greatly in their causes and their consequences for their members and for society.

It is also possible to distinguish extended families by examining who is being taken into the primary family. Thus it may make a great deal of difference whether the relative coming to live with a nuclear family is a six-year-old nephew, or an 87-year-old aunt.

[13] U. S. Bureau of the Census, U. S. Census of Population, 1960, *The Negro Population* (Washington, D. C.: U. S. Government Printing Office, 1965).

There are, then, four classes of relatives who can and often do come to live with Negro families. These are (a) minor relatives, including grandchildren, nieces, nephews, cousins, and young siblings under eighteen; (b) peers of the primary parents, including, particularly, siblings, cousins, and other adult relatives; (c) elders of the primary parents, including, particularly, aunts and uncles; and finally, (d) parents of the primary family heads. The structure of authority, to mention only one aspect of family life, may shift considerably, depending on the status of the relative coming to live in the family.

In 1965 nearly 15 per cent of all Negro families had one or more minor relatives living with them who was not their own child, and better than a quarter of all Negro families had a relative living with them who was eighteen or over.[14] Many of these families had more than one relative living with them, and some had more than one level or status of relative living with them. Among the husband and wife families with children of their own, for example, fully 26.7 per cent had one or more additional relatives living with them in their house. A majority of the female-headed attenuated families and a third of the male-headed attenuated families also had another relative living in the home.

There is a further basis for differentiating subtypes of extended families. Some relatives who come to live with a family come alone. They become, then, *secondary members* of the family. Other relatives come with their spouse or their children. These become *subfamilies*. There are, then, *incipient subfamilies*, or husband and wife pairs who come to live in the household of their relatives; *simple nuclear subfamilies*, consisting of husband, wife, and their small children, who live with another family; and *attenuated subfamilies*, consisting of one parent and his or her children, living in a relative's household. Furthermore, it is very common for two families of siblings or other relatives to share the same household.

Among the 4.4 million Negro families in 1965, there lived a total of 248,000 subfamilies. Altogether, 210,000 of these subfamilies had their own children under eighteen. (The average number of children in each subfamily was 2.6.) The heads of these subfamilies were relatively young, with 34.7 per cent under twenty-five years of age and 67.3 per cent being under thirty-five. But many were obviously peers, elders, and parents. Fully 22.6 per cent were thirty-five to forty-four years old and 10.1 per cent were forty-five years old or over.

The subfamilies seem to consist mostly of young families living with relatives before they are able to make it on their own. The median age

[14] *Ibid.*

of heads of these subfamilies was 29.2, compared with a median age of 43.3 for primary family heads. Altogether, among the 248,000 subfamilies in 1965, 43 per cent were married couples—the majority with children of their own; roughly 15 per cent were incipient subfamilies with no children of their own; 30 per cent were simple nuclear subfamilies; and another 57 per cent were attenuated subfamilies, the majority headed by females.

Augmented Families

It would not be appropriate to conclude this discussion of structures and substructures in Negro family life without adding a third major category of families. These are families which have unrelated individuals living with them as roomers, boarders, lodgers, or other relatively long-term guests. Since these unrelated persons often exert major influence in the organization of Negro families, this group of families is referred to as "augmented families." While the number of augmented families is unknown, it is obviously substantial. In 1965 there were nearly a half million Negro persons living with family groups with whom they were not related by marriage, ancestry, or adoption. Of these, 326,000 were men and 173,000 were women. They were mostly adults; 80 per cent of the men and 70 per cent of the women were eighteen years of age and over, and nearly a third were fifty-five years of age and over.

In every Negro neighborhood of any size in the country, a wide variety of family structures will be represented. This range and variety does not suggest, as some commentaries hold, that the Negro family is falling apart, but rather that these families are fully capable of surviving by adapting to the historical and contemporary social and economic conditions facing the Negro people. How does a people survive in the face of oppression and sharply restricted economic and social support? There are, of course, numerous ways. But surely one of them is to adapt the most basic of its institutions, the family, to meet the often conflicting demands placed on it. In this context, then, the Negro family has proved to be an amazingly resilient institution.

FUNCTIONS OF NEGRO FAMILY LIFE

All families are expected to meet certain responsibilities placed on them by the wider society and to provide for the basic needs of their members.

The degree to which the family is able to meet these responsibilities and needs is a measure of family functioning. There is a general tendency in discussions of Negro families to focus on a very limited number of family functions—specifically, on the manner in which families are *not* functioning adequately. While this limitation is both understandable and necessary for specific studies, it often contributes to the distortions and excessively negative characterizations of Negro family life. In a general work such as this, then, it seems desirable to approach the discussion of family functioning in the broadest possible framework.

Some family functions are essentially instrumental in character, serving to maintain the basic physical and social integrity of the family unit—e.g., the provision of food, clothing, shelter, and health care. Other functions are more expressive in character, designed to maintain and enhance the socio-emotional relationships and feelings among family members. Still other functions involve an inextricable mixture of instrumental and expressive qualities.

These functions are highly interrelated with each other, and their effective execution depends not only on the structure of the family, but also on the structure of the society and the place of the family in that social structure. The place of Negro families in the wider society, and in the Negro community viewed as an ethnic subsociety, varies greatly; consequently, the ability of Negro families to meet the requirements of society and the needs of their members also varies across a wide spectrum.

According to Talcott Parsons, the distinction between instrumental and expressive functions is relative rather than absolute.

These distinctions are . . . defined in terms of amount and mode of influence on the functioning of the family as a social system. . . . The instrumental-expressive distinction we interpret as essentially the differentiation of function, and hence of relative influence, in terms of "external" vs. "internal" functions of the system. The area of instrumental function concerns relations of the system to its situation outside the system, to meeting the adaptive conditions of its maintenance of equilibrium, and "instrumentally" establishing the desired relations to desired goal objects. The expressive area concerns the "internal" affairs of the system, the maintenance of integrative relations between the members, and regulation of the patterns and tension levels of its component units.[15]

Figure 3 shows a conceptual view of the functions of Negro families.

[15] Parsons and Bales, p. 46.

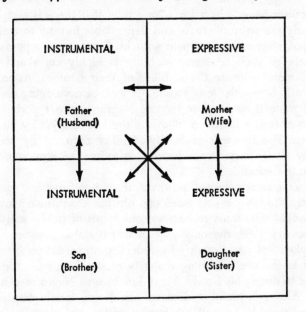

FIGURE 3
Functions of the Negro Family

Adapted from Parsons and Bales, Family Socialization and Interaction Process, *p. 46. Reprinted by permission of The Macmillan Company. The arrows are designed to stress the interchange of roles so common among Negro families of both high and low status.*

Instrumental Functions

Chief among the instrumental functions of families is the economic function. Society expects families to sustain themselves economically through the efforts of their own members. This requirement is also consistent with the needs of family members for food, clothing, and shelter. Another important demand society places on families is that they maintain their physical and social boundaries. Families are expected to be stable, which implies that no member should leave the family prematurely, except for a good cause. For the senior members of the family, death is the only recognized good cause. The junior members are often expected to stay with the family until they get married.

These two very important instrumental functions of the family are highly interrelated in ways that are both complimentary and conflicting.

Social workers have known for a long time that there is nothing like a good steady job with adequate and dependable income to make a man get married, stay married, remain with his family, and support it, while the absence of such economic viability is highly correlated with the refusal of men to insure the stability of their families. Attorneys who have recently begun the long-avoided process of developing and expanding legal protections for low income Negroes have reported vivid illustrations of family break-up following the loss of a job by the husband and father. The function of family stability required by society and desired by family members is impossible unless the economic functions of the family are fulfilled.

Under some circumstances, however, these two functions conflict with each other. Nowhere is this more conspicuous than among low income Negro families who must rely on various forms of public assistance. As late as January 1968, the only way in which stable families victimized by unemployment could qualify for federally supported public assistance payments in the overwhelming majority of states was for the husband and father to desert his family. Many low income Negro men have done just that. Although many students of the Negro family consider this a highly irresponsible act and attribute it to the historical tendencies toward matriarchy, it might be more appropriately viewed as a highly responsible, innovative, and painful act in the face of two impossible demands. Eighteen states do make it possible for simple nuclear families to qualify for AFDC payments when the husband is unemployed, but they have done so only recently, and many of them are very restrictive. (They are all among the richest states, with not a single southern state among them.)

Some students of the family hold that the responsibilities of economic well-being, education, and health have passed from the family to larger societal institutions. The family, however, must still mediate the relations between its members and these institutions and prepare its members to understand and manipulate these institutions if they are to function effectively. The family cannot, of course, perform its instrumental functions effectively unless these major economic, education, and health institutions function adequately and with respect to the needs of families. This is a particular problem for low income Negro families, for most of these institutional arrangements have been developed according to the needs and response patterns of middle class white families. Only in recent years have we come to see the essential cultural rigidities and dysfunctions built into our institutional framework. Although many families, including low income Negro families, function amazingly well in the face of the most intransigent institutional obstacles, in general the family will not be able to meet the instrumental needs of its members or its responsibilities to the larger society until this institutional framework is reconstructed. Even then, however, some families will be better able to do so than others.

It is sometimes said by students of the family that husbands and fathers play a preeminent role in the meeting of instrumental functions, while women are assigned the more expressive functions. This view, however, provides far too simplistic a framework for examining the functioning of Negro families. As we have just seen, the dramatically increased economic hazards faced by the Negro ethnic subsociety, and the consequences of the caste system have a direct bearing on the difficulty and complexity of carrying out the major instrumental functions of the Negro family. The white breadwinner's security of employment and his reliance upon community systems in fulfilling the functions of providing stability and basic needs to family members are denied the Negro breadwinner. Thus the simple model which allocates instrumental functions to the father cannot be expected to describe all of the adaptations required for the Negro family in its struggle for survival. Indeed, as we shall see later, even in the area of economic functioning, as well as in other instrumental areas, Negro women play a very active role, and Negro families vary across a wide spectrum on the nature of male-female role relationships in family life.

It is not at all uncommon for Negro men to engage in expressive functions with respect to the maintenance of family solidarity and to help with child rearing and household tasks.[16] Researchers have found Negro men to be more helpful around the house than a sample of white men, but they have chosen to give this fact a negative reading. These men are considered to be henpecked or under the domination of their strongly matriarchal wives. In the absence of a theoretical framework to provide interpretation of such findings, one is hard put to substantiate such reasoning. According to our view, this behavior may be more appropriately interpreted as another example of the strong tendency toward mutual aid and a reflection of the pragmatic qualities in Negro family life. The reverse situations, in which Negro wives and mothers often play a predominant role in the execution of instrumental functions, are better known. Older children often play the role of the principal adult members, and boys and girls often take on role behavior generally considered,

[16] Robert C. Stone and F. T. Schlamp, "Family Life Styles Below the Poverty Line: A Report to the State Social Welfare Board from the Institute for Social Science Research" (San Francisco State College, 1966).

in the larger society, to be proscribed because of their sex. In some low
income Negro families of the attenuated variety, older daughters sometimes take on aspects of the role of husband and father.

Expressive Functions

Prominent among the expressive functions of the family is the provision
of what Robert Winch calls "psychic security," [17] and what Robert Blood
calls "the mental health function of the family." [18] This is the kind of
atmosphere which generates a sense of belonging, of self-worth, self-
awareness, and dignity. Another important function of the family is the
provision of companionship. Still a third is the generation and propa-
gation of the various forms of love.

Students of the American family traditionally have been concerned
more with expressive functions than instrumental ones. But students of
the Negro family have focused almost exclusively on instrumental functioning. The general family literature, for example, is replete with studies
of marital adjustment, happiness, and parent-child relationships. Negro
family studies, on the other hand, tend to focus on the ability of the
families—or more specifically, the inabilities of families—to provide their
members with the more basic necessities of life. It is an understandable
difference of focus, for instrumental functions are a precondition for the
proper execution of expressive ones, and the difficulties for Negro families in the first area have been legion and are the subject of a great deal
of social concern. However, a general understanding of family life demands a more systematic consideration of the wide range of functions
required of families, and the differentiation which exists *among* Negro
families make such studies both possible and necessary.

Instrumental and expressive functions, even when distinct, are highly
interrelated. The middle class Negro man who goes off to work every
day is meeting the instrumental needs of his family. Failure to do this
will threaten their economic and fiscal integrity. When he kisses his wife
and children before he leaves and when he returns, he is meeting their
expressive needs. Failure to do these, or to provide some functional
equivalent, may also have similar consequences. Furthermore, if he loses
his job, or if he has to have two jobs because he cannot earn enough on
one, which is quite common among middle class Negro families, the

[17] Robert F. Winch, *The Modern Family*, rev. ed. (New York: Holt, Rinehart &
Winston, Inc., 1963), p. 295.
[18] Robert O. Blood and Donald M. Wolfe, *Husbands and Wives: The Dynamics
of Married Living* (New York: The Free Press, 1960), p. 175.

strain developing from the impairment in the instrumental functions may have adverse effects on the more expressive functional relationships in the family.

A graphic illustration of the interrelatedness of instrumental and expressive functions for a low income family is provided by Lee Rainwater:

> When the field worker first came to know them, the Wilsons seemed to be working hard to establish a stable family life. The couple had been married about three years and had a two-year-old son. Their apartment was very sparsely furnished, but also very clean. Within six weeks the couple had acquired several rooms of inexpensive furniture and obviously had gone to a great deal of effort to make a livable home. Husband and wife worked on different shifts so that the husband could care for the child while the wife worked. They looked forward to saving enough money to move out of the housing project into a more desirable neighborhood. Six weeks later, however, the husband had lost his job. He and his wife were in great conflict. She made him feel unwelcome at home and he strongly suspected her of going out with other men. A short time later, they had separated.[19]

In this case, the family situation was too complex and the data too limited to establish simple cause and effect relationships. It is clear, however, that both father-mother roles and instrumental-expressive functions were at variance with more traditional expectations.

Instrumental-Expressive Functions

By far the most important set of family functions in America center around the trilogy of sex, reproduction, and child rearing. These are both instrumental and expressive in quality. They are also highly interrelated, although the ability to separate these three functions from one another is a mark of achievement which varies appreciably with the position of the family in the ethnic subsociety. Middle and upper class Negro families, for example, make a greater distinction between sex and reproduction than do families in the lowest socioeconomic classes. Sex among Negroes has not been systematically studied, though some observers think that for the lower class, sex, like religion, is an island of freedom, one of the few areas of life not thoroughly dominated by the white society.

The socialization of children remains, perhaps, the most exclusive domain of the family. It is within the intimate circle of the family that the child develops his personality, intelligence, aspirations, and, indeed, his

---

[19] Lee Rainwater, "Crucible of Identity: The Negro Lower-Class Family," *Daedalus* (Winter 1966), p. 193.

moral character. Even here, however, the family does not act alone, but as a subsystem of the wider society. Parsons has made this point rather explicitly:

> . . . we must never forget that the nuclear family is *never*, most certainly not in the American case, an independent society, but a small and highly differentiated subsystem of a society. This fact is crucially relevant to our interests at two points. First, the parents, as socializing agents, occupy not merely their familial roles, but these articulate, i.e., interpenetrate, with their roles in other structures of the society, and this fact is a necessary condition . . . of their functioning effectively as socializing agents, i.e., as parents, at all. Secondly, the child is never socialized only for and into his family of orientation, but into structures which extend beyond this family, though interpenetrating with it. These include the school and peer group in later childhood and the family of procreation which the child will help to form by his marriage, as well as occupational roles in adulthood.[20]

It is often assumed, particularly by liberal intellectuals and sometimes by social scientists and social workers, that what is required of Negro families in our society is essentially the same as what is required of white families. According to this view, it is not the demands made on the family, but the ability of the family to meet these demands which distinguishes Negro family life. If, however, the Negro people are viewed as an ethnic subsociety, it can be appreciated that while there are basic similarities in the requirements of all families in America, there are particular requirements for Negro families, which grow out of three factors: (a) the peculiar historical development, (b) the caste-like qualities in the American stratification system which relegates all Negroes to inferior status, and (c) the social class and economic systems which keep most Negroes in the lower social classes.

For the Negro family, socialization is doubly challenging, for the family must teach its young members not only how to be human, but also how to be black in a white society. The requirements are not the same.

Negro families must teach their children very early in life, sometimes as early as two years of age, the meaning of being black. "Every Negro child I know," says Robert Coles, "has had to take notice in some way of what skin color signifies in our society." [21] A Negro mother in Jackson, Mississippi, put it this way:

---

[20] Parsons and Bales, p. 35.
[21] Robert Coles, *Children of Crisis* (Boston: Little, Brown and Co., 1964), p. 62.

When they asks all the questions, they ask about their color too. They more than not will see a white boy or girl and it makes them stop and think. They gets to wondering, and then first thing you know, they want to know this and that about it, and I never have known what to say, except that the Lord likes everyone because He makes everyone. . . . I tell them that no matter what it's like around us, it may make us feel bad, but it's not the whole picture, because we don't make ourselves. . . . When they ask me why colored people aren't as good as whites, I tell them its not that they're not as good; it's that they're not as rich. Then I tell them that they should separate being poor and being bad, and not get them mixed up.[22]

She also needs to teach them to separate being *black* and being bad, which is the real problem and much harder to separate.

In many respects, high income Negro families who live in white suburbs in the North are at the other socioeconomic extreme from low income Negro families who live in the rural South. They often must face the same kinds of problems, however, in teaching their children how to grow up black in a white society. Some face it with resignation. "All you can do is make your children understand that some people are just not going to like them," one middle class suburban Negro mother told Mel Watkins of the *New York Times*.[23]

You can tell them that some people are ignorant or something like that, but they still have to get used to it. You can't hide them from reality. We've had the same experience. We had to learn to live with it—they will too.

Another mother takes a similar approach. Her daughter came home from school one day crying because a white boy had refused to hold her hand during a school game because she was "colored." The daughter wanted to know what that meant.

I sat down and tried to explain that sometimes Negroes are called colored. You see, I wanted her to know that often that kind of thing happens. It's a handicap being a Negro in America and you have to learn to live with a handicap. If the child doesn't know this, she'll get hurt. What else can you tell them?

Still other middle class Negro families take a laissez-faire approach to the problem. An attorney observed:

---

[22] *Ibid.*, pp. 63–64.
[23] The following quotations are from Mel Watkins, "White Skins, Dark Skins, Thin Skins," *New York Times Magazine* (December 3, 1967), pp. 126–39. Reprinted by permission of Mel Watkins.

We've found it best to more or less leave our children to themselves. Left alone—given enough security—they'll determine where the lines are drawn and how to react to them. We've never really talked to our children about racial problems.

Another father spoke in the same vein:

There's no need to tell your children how some people feel about the Negro, they know it, man. It seems a parent should try to minimize the child's concern over it. I wouldn't advise my children unless they got into serious trouble.

It does not take much sophistication to imagine that children with parents who hold these laissez-faire attitudes seldom, if ever, talk with their parents about the dilemmas they encounter growing up black. They learn this silence at a very early age.

Still other black suburbanites take a more activist role in dealing with the problem. "Of course my son has had difficulties," said another father, himself a school teacher,

and each time we've tried talking with him afterwards. Let's face it, there is an undercurrent of bigotry here, and it's not that far from the surface. We've tried to show our son the difference between his value as a person and the distorted view people may have of him. He was eight when we moved here. We were the first Negroes in any of these buildings. A lot of times he'd come in crying from school or from playing in the courtyard outside. Someone would have told him something like— "we don't play with niggers" or "coons stink." I'd tell him children often use bad names or say things that aren't true, but he'd have to understand that they needed to do this. It really had nothing to do with him. I think this helped. He's been able to cope with it. I'm not sure, but I think the well-adjusted Negro has to have a clearer picture of himself. The society, too. There aren't any dreams he can rely on.

Hopefully the dreams may be only deferred. It is a constant challenge for Negro parents, at all levels of the ethnic subsociety, to teach their children how to be human and American and black and proud. Even educated middle class parents who read avidly do not find much help with this problem from psychology books or treatises on child rearing. The books have been written for white parents, to deal with other problems. "The best advice I've had," said one mother, "has been passed along by word of mouth, talking with other Negro parents."

Negro children must be taught not only to distinguish themselves from whites and to accept themselves, but, even more crucial to their survival, they must be taught to deal with white people. There are, of course, a variety of ways both of teaching and doing this; but hatred and fear are often basic mechanisms of survival which go into the socialization of lower class Negro children. Another Negro mother expressed this problem vividly:

> I guess we all don't like white people too much, deep inside. You could hardly expect us to after what's happened all these years. It's in our bones to be afraid of them, and bones have a way of staying around even when everything else is gone. . . . So if you want your kids to live long, they have to grow up scared of whites; and the way they get scared is through us; and that's why I don't let my kids get fresh about the white man even in their own house. . . . So I make them store it in the bones, way inside, and then no one sees it.[24]

It is becoming increasingly difficult for Negro parents to teach their children to hide the hate and fear "way inside." For, in addition to the tremendous toll it takes of the personality of these young people as they grow older and as times change swiftly, the hatred and fear are beginning more and more to explode in patterns of behavior which are no less healthy, though perhaps more immediately destructive than the more gradual effects of self-hatred.

The dilemmas facing the Negro parent in rearing their children in the face of these conflicting demands are deep and intricate. How, indeed, are the ravages of self-hatred to be avoided when a parent may state to a child "It is not you who are bad," but when, for the child's own physical and psychic safety, the obvious corollary, "It is *they* who are bad," cannot be taught? How does a parent impart a moral code to a child when they are surrounded by a socio-legal system which also upholds much of this same code, while violating at every turn their basic human rights?

How Negro parents have resolved these dilemmas is a virtually untouched field of study. While Negro parents have informally shared their experiences with one another, the startling neglect of such important areas of expressive functioning in Negro family life finds us without information which is vital to understanding not only the Negro family, but also a very rich part of the human experience.

SUMMARY

In this chapter, we have sought to make a case for a social systems approach to the study of Negro family life. Viewing the family as a social

[24] Coles, p. 66.

system with external and internal subsystems, and viewing the Negro people as an ethnic subsociety with strong features of common historical identity and participational conditions, it is possible to see not only that the structures of Negro family forms are highly varied, but also that carrying out the functions of family life for Negroes is highly problematic and unique. The interdependence of the family unit with the other important levels and institutions of society has resulted in an intricate network of influences upon both the instrumental and expressive functions in the Negro family, as well as upon the complex interaction between these functions. Inattention to any part of these complex phenomena by students of the Negro family can lead only to an incomplete and inaccurate picture. The results of such oversimplification have given us the kind of distortion we have noted, the kind Ellison criticized for dismissing the Negro family as "matriarchal in form with the mother dominating and castrating the males."

One implication of this point of view is that whatever ails the Negro family is a reflection of ailments in the society at large. The cure for those ills, therefore, is not likely to be found in any single and simple solution. At the same time, however, this approach also makes it possible to observe some of the positive attributes of the Negro people and suggests that a comprehensive and successful effort to include the Negro people into the society as equals, using the same ingenuity and dedication as have been used to exclude them, might benefit the whole society.

We have also set forth in this chapter a general, theoretical approach to the study of Negro family life in America. Drawing on the theoretical works of Talcott Parsons, Milton Gordon, and others, we have urged that the Negro family be viewed as a social system, imbedded within a network of both smaller and larger subsystems located both within the Negro community and in the wider society. We have described the Negro community as an ethnic subsociety created, maintained, and defined by both historical and contemporary social conditions, to which it responds and seeks to adapt. At the same time, we have emphasized the mediating influences of social class and urbanization on Negro family life.

Thus, both the variety and dynamic quality of family structures, and the extent to which families are able to function adequately in meeting the needs of their members and the demands of society are heavily influenced by—and may be viewed as adaptions to and reflections of— forces in this wider social network. The Negro family, we argue, can best be understood, appreciated, and reformed within the context of some such general, theoretical framework as the one we advance.

The discussion has drawn supportive and illustrative data from a variety of sources, including particularly the United States Census, the social science literature, and unpublished reports, as well as our own studies, experience, and observations. It is infused throughout with our own values and commitment to a democratic and pluralistic society, and our view that such a society works best if it has the substantial, sustained, active, and relatively equal participation of all its major ethnic groups in all its major institutions. It would be difficult to find a major institution in our society which has not systematically excluded this kind of participation by the Negro people.

And yet we live in a society which is highly oriented to social change. The Negro family must have a central place in this process of social evolution. In this respect, our own view is consistent with that expressed so dramatically by Daniel P. Moynihan in his several writings and public appearances. But unlike Moynihan and others, we do not view the Negro family as a causal nexus in a "tangle of pathology" which feeds on itself. Rather, we view the Negro family in theoretical perspective as a sub-system of the larger society. It is, in our view, an absorbing, adaptive, and amazingly resilient mechanism for the socialization of its children and the civilization of its society. This is, of course, a theoretical and philosophical point of view. It is put forward as the basis for the discussion in the rest of this book.

Part 2

BLACK
HERITAGE

MOTHER TO SON *

Well, Son, I'll tell you:
Life for me ain't been no crystal stair.
It's had tacks in it,
And splinters,
And boards torn up,
And places with no carpet on the floor——
Bare.
But all the time
I'se been a-climbin' on,
And reachin' landin's,
And turnin' corners,
And sometimes going in the dark
Where there ain't been no light.
So, boy, don't you turn back.
Don't you set down on the steps
'Cause you finds it's kinder hard.
Don't you fall now—
For I'se still goin', honey,
I'se still climbin',
And life for me ain't been no crystal stair.

                                    Langston Hughes

* From Langston Hughes, *Selected Poems* (New York: Alfred A. Knopf, Inc.,
1959). Copyright 1926 by Alfred A. Knopf, Inc. and renewed 1954 by Langston
Hughes. Also reprinted in Langston Hughes and Arna Bontemps, eds., *The Poetry of
the Negro 1746–1949* (Garden City, N. Y.: Doubleday & Company, Inc., 1953),
pp. 104–5. Reprinted here by permission of Alfred A. Knopf, Inc.

Chapter 2

Historical Backgrounds
of the Negro Family

*To know the possibilities of a race
An appraisal of its past is necessary.*
CARTER G. WOODSON

In their study of the major ethnic groups in New York, Glazer and
Moynihan concluded their discussion of the Negro family with the
observation that: "The Negro is only an American, and nothing else. He
has no values and culture to guard and protect." [1] This statement could
not possibly be true. And yet, it represents the prevailing view among
liberal intellectuals who study the Negro experience from the outside.
Nat Hentoff, who holds a different view, has pointed out that not one
of the critical reviewers of Glazer and Moynihan's book took them to
task for this generalization.[2] The implications of the Glazer-Moynihan
view of the Negro experience are far-reaching. To say that a people
have no culture is to say that they have no common history which has
shaped them and taught them. And to deny the history of a people is to
deny their humanity.

If, on the other hand, the Negro people constitute in some important
respects an ethnic subsociety with a distinct history, what are the essential
elements of this history? Three facts stand out above all others. The first
is that the Negro people came to this country from Africa and not from
Europe. The second is that they came in chains and were consequently
uprooted from their cultural and family moorings. The third is that
they have been subjected to systematic exclusion from participation and
influence in the major institutions of this society even to the present time.

[1] Nathan Glazer and Daniel P. Moynihan, *Beyond the Melting Pot* (Cambridge,
Mass.: The M.I.T. Press and The Harvard University Press, 1963), p. 51.
[2] Nat Hentoff, "The Other Side of the Blues," in *Anger and Beyond: The Negro
Writer in the United States*, ed. Herbert Hill (New York: Harper & Row, Publishers,
1966), p. 76.

37

Because of these three factors, "the Jews, Irish, Italians, Poles or Scandinavians who see no difference between their former plight and that of Negroes today are either grossly uninformed or are enjoying an unforgiveable false pride." [3]

At the same time, it needs saying that the Negro experience has not been uniform. It has varied according to time, place, and other conditions. The consequences of these experiences have also been varied and complex. Furthermore, not all the history of the Negro people has been negative. There is much in the historical backgrounds of the Negro people which has helped them survive in the face of impossible conditions. This history has produced a most resilient and adaptive people with a strong appreciation for the realities of existence, as reflected in the ability of Negroes to "tell it like it is," and to "get down to the nitty-gritty" in talking about their life circumstances, at least among their friends, if not always when among their enemies. (Perhaps the increasing ability of Negroes of all social classes to speak out to the wider society about their conditions and "tell it like it is" also indicates a feeling, or at least a precarious hope, that we are indeed among friends.)

In this chapter, we will set forth some highlights of the historical backgrounds of the Negro people which have helped to shape both the structure and the functioning of Negro families. The family is at once the most sensitive, important, and enduring element in the culture of any people. Whatever its structure, its most important function is everywhere the same—namely, to insure the survival of its people.

Two aspects of Negro history will be considered, their African backgrounds and the impact of slavery. Each of these topics could and should be the subject of full-length books. We can only sketch some of the highlights to show their relevance for a more general understanding of Negro families, and a more comprehensive strategy for the reconstruction of Negro family and community life.

African Backgrounds

Negroes, under the tutelage of white Americans, have long viewed their African background with a sense of shame. To be called an African when I was growing up in Alabama was much worse than being called a

---

[3] Harold L. Sheppard and Herbert E. Striver, *Civil Rights, Employment, and the Social Status of American Negroes* (Kalamazoo, Mich.: The W. E. Upjohn Institute for Employment Research, June, 1966), p. 47.

"nigger." And, to be called a "black African" was a sign of extreme derision.

Later, when I was a student in a Negro college, we were more sophisticated, but we were no less ambivalent about our heritage. The two or three African students on campus were isolated. They were viewed and treated with great disdain, while the two or three white students were the objects of adulation. The African students represented the deep, dark past, while the Caucasians represented the great white hope of the future. In spite of vast changes which have occurred in the world since World War II, with respect to Africa and its place in the world, large numbers of Negroes still feel just a twinge of inferiority associated with their African heritage. How could it be otherwise, considering the sources of our knowledge about ourselves and our past? Yet the image is changing radically and rapidly. Negroes are taking seriously the questions posed by Lincoln Lynch, formerly of the Congress on Racial Equality: "It is a question of who are we, and where do we come from, and where are we going?"

A careful reading of history and ethnographic studies reveals a pattern of African backgrounds which are ancient, varied, complex, and highly civilized. The evidence suggests that far from being rescued from a primitive savagery by the slave system, Negroes were forcibly uprooted from a long history of strong family and community life every bit as viable as that of their captors. It was a very different type of society from the European-oriented society in the new world.

Several general features of African family life showed great viability. First, family life was not primarily—or even essentially—the affair of two people who happened to be married to each other. It united not simply two people, but two families with a network of extended kin who had considerable influence on the family, and considerable responsibility for its development and well-being. Marriage could neither be entered into nor abandoned without substantial community support. Secondly, marriage and family life in pre-European Africa, as among most tribal people, was enmeshed in centuries of tradition, ritual, custom, and law. "When the Arabs swept into North and West Africa in the Seventh Century," writes John Hope Franklin, "they found a civilization that was already thousands of years old." [4] Thirdly, family life was highly articulated with the rest of the society. The family was an economic and a religious unit which, through its ties with wider kinship

[4] John Hope Franklin, *From Slavery to Freedom* (New York: Alfred A. Knopf, Inc., 1956), p. 11.

circles, was also a political unit. Family life, then, was strong and viable, and was the center of the African civilization. "At the basis even of economic and political life in Africa was the family, with its inestimable influence over its individual members." [5]

Patterns of Family Life

The most striking feature of African family and community life was the strong and dominant place in family and society assigned to and assumed by the men. This strong, masculine dominance, however, far from being capricious authoritarianism, was supported, guided, and limited by custom and tradition, which also provided a substantial role for the women. The children were provided a quality of care and protection not common in modern societies, for they belonged not alone to their father and mother, but also, and principally, to the wider kinship group.

Family life in West Africa was patterned along several dimensions, including descent, type of marriage, type of family (nuclear, extended), residential pattern, and patterns of child care and protection.

There were three basic patterns of descent or kinship in Africa. The most common was patrilineal descent, in which kinship ties are ascribed only through the father's side of the family. The next most common pattern was matrilineal, in which kinship was reckoned through the mother's side of the family. A third pattern present in only a small part of Africa, mostly in the southern portion of the continent, was double descent, in which kinship was reckoned through both the male and female. This pattern, the only one recognized in America, was virtually unknown in the part of West Africa from which American Negroes came.

The Ibo of Eastern Nigeria, the Yoruba of Western Nigeria, and their neighbors the Dahomeans were patrilineal societies.[6] The Ashanti of Ghana were matrilineal.[7] The Yako people (of Nigeria) practiced double descent.[8]

[5] *Ibid.*, p. 28.

[6] Melville J. Herskovits, *Dahomey: An Ancient West African Kingdom* (New York: J. J. Augustin, 1938), I; and Francis I. Nzimiro, "Family and Kinship in Ibo Land: A Study in Acculturation Process" (Ph. D. dissertation, University of Cologne, 1962).

[7] Melville J. Herskovits, *The Myth of the Negro Past* (Boston: Beacon Press, 1958); Robert A. Lystad, *The Ashanti: A Proud People* (New Brunswick, N. J.: Rutgers University Press, 1958); and Meyer Fortes, "Kinship and Marriage Among the Ashanti," in *African Systems of Kinship and Marriage*, eds. A. R. Radcliffe-Brown and Daryll Forde (New York: Oxford University Press, Inc., 1950), pp. 207-51. Future quotations from this source reprinted by permission of Oxford University Press, Inc.

[8] Daryll Forde, "The Yako of Nigeria," in A. R. Radcliffe-Brown, *op. cit.*

Lineage carried with it distinct rights and obligations. Certain responsibilities of relatives for the care of the family, and especially the children followed the ascription of lineage, as did legal rights and inheritance. In the patrilineal societies, only one's father's relatives were legally and socially responsible for one's welfare. Inheritance was confined to the father's line. Even in patrilineal situations, however, certain informal courtesies were extended to the mother's relatives. Marriage among mother's relatives was generally forbidden, and other relatives often took on major responsibilities in helping with the care of children even though not legally required to do so.

Even in double descent societies there were norms providing for orderly functioning. According to Daryll Forde, the Yako managed rather well.

> The rights and obligations which derive from matrilineal kinship do not formally conflict with those derived patrilineally. . . . Matrilineal kinship should take precedence over patrilineal in the inheritance of transferable wealth, especially livestock and currency . . . and payments made to a wife's kin at the time of her marriage. . . . On the other hand, patrilineal rights and obligations . . . largely relate to the use of land and houses and to the provision of cooperative labor.[9]

Marriage in Africa was rarely an informal matter between two consenting partners and their relatives. Ceremony and exchange of property were important aspects of an elaborate process which consisted of two basic types: those marriages based on the initiation of the two consenting partners and those based on the initiative of their parents and kin.[10] In either case, both the relevant partners and their parents had to give their consent. While there were more than a dozen specific forms which mating and marriage took in one West African tribe alone, they nevertheless followed these two basic patterns. Those initiated by the principals were less elaborate than those initiated by their parents.

A central feature of marriage in West Africa, as among other non-Western peoples, was the bride price, the requirement of some property or material consideration on the part of the bride to legitimize the marriage contract. The bride price might be paid in goods, money such as native beverages, foodstuffs, livestock, and the like. Or it might be paid in the form of services, such as the bridegroom agreeing to help his prospective father-in-law in the fields, or bringing firewood for his mother-in-law. Thirdly, the bride price might be a payment in kind, in which the

[9] *Ibid.*, p. 306.
[10] George P. Murdock, *Africa: Its People and Their Culture History* (New York: McGraw-Hill Book Company, 1959).

bridegroom delivers to his bride's relatives a sister, daughter, or other female relative in exchange for the one he is taking away from them.

The bride price not only was a symbol of the serious and communal nature of marriage, but also served to compensate the parents for a real loss.

Once a couple was married, there were several possible patterns of residence they might follow. The pattern most common in Europe and America is referred to by anthropologists as "neolocal" residence. This pattern involves both partners leaving their homes and taking up residence together in a household not determined by parental ties. This pattern was present, but not common, in Africa. It was almost nonexistent in that portion of West Africa from which American Negroes came.

Another pattern which also had restricted use in Africa was "duolocal" residence, in which neither partner left his parental home after marriage; both partners continued to live among their relatives while visiting each other for brief periods and perhaps working together in the fields. This was a rare custom in Africa, but in Ghana a few tribes practiced this arrangement for the first few years of marriage. Duolocal residence had certain economic advantages for newlyweds who had not had time to establish their economic viability.

Much more common in Africa was a third residential pattern referred to as "unilocal," in which one partner left his or her home and kin to live with the other, who remained in or near the household of his or her parents. There were three varieties of unilocal residence. One pattern was of matrilocal residence, which involved the man leaving his home and taking up residence with his wife in her family home. This pattern, while common in other parts of the world where matrilineal societies predominate, had very limited currency in West African societies. Common in West Africa was another pattern of unilocal residence referred to as "avunculocal" residence, in which the wife left her home to live with her husband who lived, not in the household of his parents, but in that of his maternal uncle. This happened most often in those matrilineal societies where the man had already left home at the time of adolescence and gone to live with or near his maternal uncle, who was primarily responsible for him. A third pattern was patrilocal, in which the wife went to live in the home and compound of her husband and his relatives. This patrilocal residential pattern corresponds with the patrilineal rule of descent, and was the most common residential pattern for families in all of West Africa.

Of the three basic forms of marriage, monogamy, which unites one man with one woman, was the most common throughout West Africa.

Polyandry, which unites one woman with two or more husbands, was almost unknown in this part of the world. But polygyny, which unites one man with two or more wives, was common, though not dominant, throughout that portion of Africa from which slaves were brought to America. Murdock found, as late as 1957, that polygyny was still practiced and sanctioned in 88 per cent of the 154 African societies he studied.

Household organization followed two basic patterns, the nuclear family and the extended family. These two forms of residence existed side by side. Under the nuclear residential pattern, a man and his wife or wives and their children lived together in his house or compound. Often, each woman, along with her small children, occupied a small hut within the husband's compound. Either the man visited them in turn or they took turns coming to spend two or three nights in his hut while doing the cooking and housekeeping. In the extended family household, two or more families, related to each other, lived in the house or compound of a single head. In a typical patrilocal, polygamous extended family, the household might include a patriarchal head, his several wives, and their children, his older sons and their wives and children, plus his younger brothers and their wives and children.

Among the Dahomeans, for example, a senior man in the community may preside over a compound in which live himself and his wives, his younger brothers and their wives, his grown sons and their wives, and the children of all these women.

> There were many instances where a first wife welcomed her second, and where both joined to make a place for the third. Indeed, a woman who, caring for her husband, wishes to further his position in society will . . . make it possible with her own savings for him to obtain another wife. Similarly, when the four day week assigned to a given wife to cohabit with a common husband comes while she is menstruating, her co-wives arrange their time so that this conflict does not deprive her of her opportunity to be with him. And it is far from unusual for a woman to be kind to her husband's children by other women, and for a man to be as close to his children as to their mother. In essence, the great mass of Dahomean matings, either because of complacency or of human ability to make the best of a situation, are permanent ventures which, in terms of human adjustment, cannot be called failures.[11]

The Care and Protection of Children

The father played a very important role in the care and protection of the children in all these West African societies. The strong bonds that

[11] Herskovits, *Dahomey*, p. 341.

bind both fathers and mothers to their children are suggested by the
experience of the Ashanti:

> In terms of personal behavior and attitudes, there is often no apparent
> difference between the relations of mother and children and those of
> father and children. The warmth, trust, and affection frequently found
> uniting parents and offspring go harmoniously with the respect shown to
> both.[12]

Legally, however, an Ashanti father had no authority over his children.
In this matrilineal society, the children belonged to the mother's family.
Her oldest brother, therefore, carried out the legal responsibilities assigned, in other societies, to the father. Nevertheless, by custom, the
children grow up in their father's house, and it was both his obligation
and privilege to "feed, clothe, and educate them, and later to set them
up in life." [13] The father was responsible for their moral and civic, as
well as their economic training. "If anything, Ashanti fathers (unlike
mothers) tend to be overly strict in exacting obedience, deference, and
good behavior from their children." [14] The following excerpt from Fortes
shows the nature of this relationship:

> Ashanti say that a man has no hold over his children, except through
> their love for him and their conscience. A father wins his children's af-
> fection by caring for them. They cannot inherit his property, but he can
> and often does provide for them by making them gifts of property, land,
> or money during his lifetime or on his deathbed.[15]

The children reciprocate the affection and respect of their father.
Fortes continues:

> To insult, abuse, or assault one's father is an irreparable wrong, one
> which is bound to bring ill luck. While there is no legal obligation on a
> son or daughter to support a father in his old age, it would be regarded
> as a shame and an evil if he or she did not do so.[16]

A father was responsible for the moral behavior of his sons. He, as well
as the mother, must give the consent for his son to marry. He is responsible to find his son a wife and to make sure that the suitor of his
daughter is able to support her.

Among the Ibo, who were patrilineal, the father's authority was so

[12] Meyer Fortes, "Kinship and Marriage Among the Ashanti," *op. cit.*, p. 270.
[13] *Ibid.*, p. 268.
[14] *Ibid.*, p. 268.
[15] *Ibid.*, p. 268.
[16] *Ibid.*, p. 268.

strong that it was felt his curse would render a child useless for life.[17]
Even among the Yako, who recognized double descent, the father was
the paramount authority unless the mother and her small children left
the compound. Then, as in the case of the matrilineal groups, the mother's
brother took up the father's authority.

In all of West African society, whether patrilineal or matrilineal, the
relationship between mother and child was primary and paramount. Until
he was weaned at the age of one or two, a child was almost never without
his mother. "The Ashanti regard the bond between mother and child as
the keystone of all social relations."[18] Among the Dahomeans, in spite
of their patrilineal descent, the relationship between mother and child
was especially strong.

Fortes has described the role of the Ashanti mother:

> An Ashanti woman stints no labour or self-sacrifice for the good of her
> children. It is mainly to provide them with food, clothing and shelter
> that she works so hard, importunes her husband, and jealously watches
> her brother to make sure that he discharges the duties of legal guardian
> faithfully. No demands upon her are too extreme for a mother. Though
> she is loathe to punish, and never disowns a child, an Ashanti mother
> expects obedience and affectionate respect from her children.[19]

The strong attachment to the mother carries over into adulthood for
both men and women:

> Ashanti say that throughout her life, a woman's foremost attachment
> is to her mother, who will always protect and help her. A woman grows
> up in daily and unbroken intimacy with her mother, learns all feminine
> skills from her, and above all, derives her character from her. . . . For
> a man, his mother is his most trusted confidante, especially in intimate
> personal matters. A man's first ambition is to gain enough money to be
> able to build a house for his mother if she does not own one. To be mis-
> tress of her own home, with her children and daughters' children around
> her, is the highest dignity an ordinary woman aspires to.[20]

Herskovitz has observed that among the Dahomeans, children are
much more relaxed with their mother than in their father's presence.
He continues, "An outstanding instance of the closeness of the relationship
between mother and child in this patrilineal society was had in connection with the recording of songs. On one such occasion, he observed

[17] Nzimiro, *op. cit.*
[18] Fortes, p. 262.
[19] *Ibid.*, p. 263.
[20] *Ibid.*, p. 263.

of a chief that "though when he commanded his wives and subordinates, he was imperious and his slightest desire was promptly gratified, he was both gentle and affectionate with his mother." [21]

In a matrilineal society, sole legal authority over a child was vested in his mother's oldest living brother. A man's sister's children, and not his own children, were his legal heirs. The rights and obligations associated with this relationship were especially likely to be brought into play in the case of divorce. The mother's brother then assumed the duties and obligations of a father to the children, in addition to his duties to his own children. In general, however, this relationship was more legal than actual, except in regard to inheritance. In this respect, it was sometimes said that the nephew was the enemy of the mother's brother, waiting for him to die.

The father's sister also assisted in the care and protection of his children. She received respect and affection similar to that offered the father, but the attachment was not so deep as to the father and his brothers. She referred to her brother's children as her own, and would discipline and scold them if necessary. His children felt at home in her house and often ate and slept there. This relationship, while not legally binding, was functional and reciprocal. The father's sister could count on her brother's kindness and helpfulness with her own children. They were, after all, his potential heirs.

> Men say that it is to his sister that a man entrusts weighty matters, never to his wife. He will discuss confidential matters, such as those that concern property, money, public office, legal suits, and even the future of his children, or his matrimonial difficulties with his sister, secure in the knowledge that she will tell nobody else.[22]

In the matrilineal society, the strongest bond, next to that between mother and child, was that between siblings by the same mother.

> An older sibling is entitled to punish and reprimand a younger sibling and must be treated with deference. He is, conversely, obliged to help his younger sisters and brothers if they get into trouble. In all other matters, however, equality and fraternity are the governing norms of siblings. It is often said among the Ashanti, for example, "Your brother or your sister, you can deny them nothing." [23]

Among the Ashanti, the relationship between sisters was particularly close.

[21] Herskovits, *Dahomey*, p. 155.
[22] Fortes, p. 275.
[23] *Ibid.*, p. 273.

Sisters try to live together all their lives. A woman treats her sister's children so much like her own that orphan children often do not know whether their apparent mother is their true mother or their mother's sister. This holds, though to a lesser degree, for the brother's.

Siblings borrowed from each other freely, as if their property were joint. "Borrowing between siblings cannot create debts." The strong relationship between siblings was supported by law and custom.

The pivot of the Ashanti kinship system in its function as a system of legal relationship is the tie between brother and sister. A brother has legal power over his sister's children because he is her nearest male equivalent and legal power is vested in males (even in matrilineal society). A sister has claims on her brother because she is his female equivalent and the only source of the continuity of his descent line (in a matrilineal society).[24]

It is sometimes said that "men find it difficult to decide what is more important to them—to have children or for their sisters to have children." If there is a conflict between the need to care for one's sister's children or producing one's own, men generally concluded, according to Fortes, that "sad as it may be to die childless, a good citizen's first anxiety is for his lineage to survive."

If the position of mother and child was the closest, and that of brother and sister the most fraternal, that between a person and his grandparents was the most revered in all of West African society. In Ashanti, for example, "The grandparents on both sides are the most honored of all one's kinfolk." Their position and status were of the greatest importance for the whole social system, in part because they stood between ordinary citizens and the ancestors. If the ancestors got their status because they stood between man and god, the grandparents got theirs because they stood only a little lower on the ladder of infinity. Among the Yoruba, it was the duty and privilege of grandparents to name newborn children. Among the Ashanti, grandmothers—both maternal and paternal—exercised great influence and responsibility in the care and protection of children. "It is from the grandparents of both sexes that children learn family history, folklore, proverbs, and other traditional lore. The grandparents are felt to be the living links with the past." [25]

Family life in the West Africa of our forebears was heavily influenced by geographic, historical, and cultural conditions in that part of the

[24] *Ibid.,* p. 274.
[25] *Ibid.,* p. 276.

world. A preliterate people, the West Africans nevertheless had a highly complex civilization. Their patterns of family life were closely knit, well organized, highly articulated with kin and community, and highly functional for the economic, social, and psychological life of the people.

Thus the men and women who were taken as slaves to the New World came from societies every bit as civilized and "respectable" as those of the Old World settlers who mastered them. But the two were very different types of society, for the African family was much more closely integrated with the wider levels of kinship and society. The simple transition of millions of persons from Africa to America would in itself have been a major disruption in the lives of the people, even if it had proceeded on a voluntary and humane basis. As we shall see presently, however, this transition was far from simple, voluntary, and humane.

THE IMPACT OF SLAVERY ON NEGRO FAMILY LIFE

The Negro family in the United States began with Anthony and Isabella, who were among the original twenty Negroes landed at Jamestown in 1619, one year before the Mayflower. Later Anthony and Isabella were married, and in 1624 their son William became "the first Negro child born in English America." [26] These first Negroes were treated essentially as indentured servants. However, after 1690 the bulk of Negroes were brought into the country and sold as slaves.

We have shown that the Negroes brought to the United States were the descendants of an ancient and honorable tradition of African family life. While scholars are still in considerable dispute about the relative influence of this heritage on Negro family life today, particularly in the United States, there is no doubt that the breaking up of that tradition by the slave trade has had a major impact on both the form and substance of the Negro family. African slavery, stretching over a period of four centuries and involving the capture of more than 40 million Africans, was, for the European countries, a colossal economic enterprise with effects not unlike those of the discovery of gold. But for the African Negroes, it was a colossal social and psychological disruption.

The transportation of slaves from Africa to the New World completely disrupted the cultural life of the Africans and the historical development of the Negro people. This total discontinuity had a particular impact on

---

[26] Lerone Bennett, Jr., *Before the Mayflower: A History of the Negro in America* (Chicago: Johnson Publishing Co., 1964), p. 30.

the Negro family, because the family is the primary unit of social organization. Some of the ways in which this culture was disrupted may be briefly stated.

First, moving as they did from Africa to the New World, the Negroes were confronted with an alien culture of European genesis. Thus, unlike some of the later migrants, including the Germans, Irish, and Italians, they were not moving into a society in which the historical norms and values and ways of life were familiar and acceptable. Secondly, they came from many different tribes with different languages, cultures, and traditions. Thirdly, they came without their families and often without females at all. In the fourth place, they came in chains. These are all major distinctions between the Negro people and all the other immigrants to this country. Therefore, whatever the nature of the two cultural systems from which they came and to which they arrived, and whatever their capacity for adaptation, they were not free to engage in the ordinary process of acculturation. They were not only cut off from their previous culture, but they were not permitted to develop and assimilate to the new culture in ways that were unfettered and similar to the opportunities available to other immigrant groups.

The Negro slaves in the United States were converted from the free, independent human beings they had been in Africa, to property. They became chattel. This process of dehumanization started at the beginning of the slave-gathering process and was intensified with each stage along the way. It should not be difficult to discern that people who, having been told for 200 years—in ways more effective than words—that they are subhuman, should begin to believe this themselves and internalize these values and pass them on to their children and their children's children. Nor is it difficult to imagine how the history and current status of the Negro people might be different if, for all those 200 years, our ancestors had been paid a decent wage for their labor, taught how to invest it, and provided all the supports, privileges, and responsibilities which the New World offered its immigrants of Caucasian ancestry. Conversely, the process of Negro dehumanization provided superior opportunities, privileges, and status to the white majority at the expense of the black minority, and deeply ingrained within white people a crippling sense of superiority.

These are the dynamics of the slave system which must have been in the mind of President Lyndon Johnson when he spoke so eloquently of the need of our society to "heal our history." But the dehumanizing experience of slavery did not come all at once; it came in stages. "Slavery," says Lerone Bennett, was a black man who stepped out of his hut [in Africa] for a breath of fresh air and ended up ten months later in Georgia with bruises on his back and a brand on his chest.[27]

It was that and more. At every stage of this process, the Negroes became progressively more disengaged from their cultures, their families, and their humanity. This transition from freedom to slavery has been captured graphically in personal accounts of the experience.

One such account comes directly from the pen of an African who was captured and sold into slavery. Olaudah Equiano, who was later known as Gustavus Vassa, was born in Africa in 1745. When he was eleven years old, he was kidnapped, sold into slavery, and transported to the New World. After being sold and resold several times, he finally was given an opportunity by a Philadelphia merchant to work and buy his freedom. He became educated and in 1791 wrote his autobiography. He tells of his early experience with slavery.

The first object which saluted my eyes when I arrived on the coast was the sea, and a slave ship, which was then riding at anchor, and waiting for its cargo. These filled me with astonishment, which was soon connected with terror, when I was carried on board. I was immediately handled, and tossed up to see if I were sound, by some of the crew; and I was now persuaded that I had gotten into a world of bad spirits, and that they were going to kill me. Their complexions too differing so much from ours, their long hair, and the language they spoke (which was very different from any I had ever heard), united to confirm me in this belief.

. . . When I looked round the ship too and saw a large furnace or copper boiling, and a multitude of black people of every description chained together, every one of their countenances expressing dejection and sorrow, I no longer doubted of my fate; and, quite overpowered with horror and anguish, I fell motionless on the deck and fainted.

. . . I was soon put down under the decks, and there I received such a salutation in my nostrils as I had never experienced in my life: so that with the loathsomeness of the stench and crying together, I became so sick and low that I was not able to eat, nor had I the least desire to taste anything.

I now wished for the last friend, death, to relieve me; but soon, to my grief, two of the white men offered me eatables; and, on my refusing to eat, one of them held me fast by the hands, and laid me across, I think, the windlass, and tied my feet, while the other flogged me severely.

. . . I would have jumped over the side, but I could not; and, besides, the crew used to watch us very closely who were not chained down to

[27] *Ibid.*, pp. 30–31.

the decks, lest we should leap into the water; and I have seen some
these poor African prisoners most severely cut for attempting to do so,
and hourly whipped for not eating. This indeed was often the case with
myself.

In a little time after, amongst the poor chained men, I found some of
my own nation, which in a small degree gave ease to my mind. I inquired of these what was to be done with us? They gave me to understand we were to be carried to these white people's country to work for
them. I then was a little revived, and thought, if it were no worse than
working, my situation was not so desperate.[28]

These episodes capture the essence of the several stages of the slave
trade. These consisted first of gathering slaves in Africa, principally as a
result of intertribal warfare, but sometimes by simple barter with the
chiefs. Premium was placed on young males. The disruptive elements in
this practice to family life are apparent. The preponderance of men was
so great until, in later years, it was necessary for the European government to require that at least a third of the slaves sold in the New World
should be female. In spite of this practice, on many of the plantations,
men outnumbered women by nine to one. After capture the slaves were
marched to the seaports, a walk often requiring weeks or months of
travel. While most of the slaves were gathered on the West Coast of
Africa, sometimes they were gathered as many as one thousand miles
inland. These slave marches were essentially human caravans, guarded by
armed men "with the leaders of the expedition carried in hammocks."
The situation has been described by Tannenbaum as follows:

> Little Negro villages in the interior of Africa were frequently attacked
> in the middle of the night, the people were either killed or captured by
> Europeans themselves or . . . by Africans acting [for profit] and the
> victims left alive were shackled with a collar about the neck, men, women
> and children, and driven for hundreds of miles to the coast.[29]

The rate of sickness and death of the Africans along the slave march
was very high. DuBois has said, "Probably every slave imported represented on the average 5 corpses in Africa or on the high seas." [30] On
reaching the coast, the Africans were there sold to the European traders,

---

[28] Milton Meltzer, ed., *In Their Own Words: A History of the American Negro
1619–1865,* copyright © 1964 by Milton Meltzer (New York: Thomas Y. Crowell
Company, 1954; Apollo Edition, 1967), pp. 3–5. Reprinted by permission of Thomas
Y. Crowell Company, and Harold Ober Associates, Inc.

[29] Frank Tannenbaum, *Slave and Citizen: The Negro in the Americas* (New York:
Random House, Inc., 1946), p. 21.

[30] W. E. B. Du Bois, *The Negro* (New York: Holt, Rinehart & Winston, Inc., 1915),
pp. 155–56.

board ship for the next phase, which consisted of
le pasage." During this passage across the ocean,
in holds like cattle, with a minimum of room and
When they died, which was frequent, or became
s more frequent, they were cast overboard. The
consisted of the seasoning of the slaves on the plantations
of the West Indies, where they were taught the rudiments of New World
agriculture. They were also taught the rudiments of communication in
English so as to be able to carry out the instructions of the slave owners
and overseers on the plantations. The next stage consisted of the transportation of the slaves to the ports on the mainland, where they were sold
to local slave traders, who in turn auctioned them off to the highest
bidder, without special regard to their families or tribal connections. The
final stage consisted of their disbursal to the plantations in North and
South America. The whole process, from the time of a person's capture
in Africa until he was settled on a plantation in the New World, sometimes took six months to a year.

Slavery, then, was a massive disruption of the former cultural life of
the Africans, which at the same time, by its very nature, prevented the
adequate assimilation of the slaves into the New World culture. The
crass commercialism of the slave system dominated every phase of this
process.

In summary, the Africans came from a vastly different cultural and
social system than was known in Europe and the New World. They
came in chains under brutal conditions. Whatever their capacity for
adaptation, they were not permitted to adapt. They were often sold to
plantations and scattered without regard for their former tribal or family
connections. The difficulty of reestablishing and maintaining their cultural
systems was as apparent in this process as it was appalling. The small
number of slaves distributed on each plantation prevented their developing a reliable set of new cultural forms. And finally, the absence of powerful institutions for the protection of the slaves and their humanity
accounted for both the destruction of the previous cultural forms and the
prevention of the emergence of new ones as a free and open human
development. No other immigrant group can make these statements.

Dominant Patterns of Slavery

While slavery everywhere was cruel and inhuman, it did not everywhere take the same pattern. There were important variations and
degrees of cruelty, with differing consequences for the family life of the

slaves. Slavery was very different in the United States from what it was in the Latin American countries.

All the major historians who have treated slavery in the New World agree that it was a vastly different and much more oppressive institution in the United States than in Latin America. The essential distinction was that in Latin America slavery was an "open" institution, whereas in the United States it was "closed." These are relative rather than absolute distinctions, but the evidence supporting these general differences is striking.

If historians are agreed on the nature of slavery on the two New World continents, they are not completely agreed on the causes. The major distinction seemed to lie in the structure of the societies and economies of the United States and Brazil, with their different historical and cultural approaches to slavery. Stanley Elkins has pointed to the institutional nature of some of these social forces:

> In Latin America, the very tension and balance among three kinds of organizational concerns—the church, crown, and plantation agriculture—prevented slavery from being carried by its planting class to its ultimate logic. For the slave, this allowed for the development of men and women as moral beings, the result was an "open system"; a system of contacts with free society through which ultimate absorption into that society could and did occur with great frequency.[31]

Tannenbaum has laid heavy stress on the role of the church as an institution and on the Portuguese and Spanish slave laws, which helped to make the slave system in Brazil more humane. The legal system protecting the slaves in this area, and the strong intervention of the church on behalf of the slaves were absent in the United States, which accounts, in part, for the severity of the slave system here. The French slave-holding systems had the active interest of the Catholic church, but not the slave legal tradition.[32]

While not discounting completely the influence of the Catholic church and of the legal traditions protecting slaves, Marvin Harris lays much more stress on the third factor—the types of plantation agriculture involved.[33] In addition, he introduces a fourth factor, the demographic distribution of the population. The Negro slaves in Latin America significantly outnumbered the white settlers, in part because Spain, and probably also Portugal, had a permanent manpower shortage. Since England

[31] Stanley Elkins, *Slavery: A Problem in American Institutional and Intellectual Life* (New York: Grosset & Dunlap, Inc., 1963), p. 81.
[32] Tannenbaum, p. 65.
[33] Marvin Harris, *Patterns of Race in the Americas* (New York: Walker and Co., 1964), p. 81.

had a population surplus, the English colonies had many more white settlers. Still a fifth social factor which helps to explain the differences in the two systems of slavery is that the Spanish and the Portuguese both had a history of racial assimilation, while the English and other Northern European people had a history and tradition of racial homogeneity and exclusion of other peoples. A sixth factor is that the Spanish and Portuguese men came to the New World alone in large proportions, while the English brought their wives and families.

In our view, all these forces operated together in the Latin American countries to produce a kind of slave system which helped to generate the social, economic, and political climate for three basic conditions which were absent in the United States: (1) the protection of the physical and personal integrity of slaves; (2) the open, sanctioned, and actual encouragement of manumission; (3) the open, sanctioned, and actual encouragement of stable marriages among slaves and free Negroes.

Physical and Personal Integrity

Slavery in Latin America was a matter of a contract between the bondsman and his master, focused essentially on the master's ownership of the bondsman's labor under certain restricted conditions, with protections of the slave built into the law. In the United States, on the contrary, without such history of legal protections, slavery was allowed to reach its logical extreme of complete ownership of the slave by the master, who was free, depending on his needs, resources, and conscience, to do with his slave as he wished.

The Brazilian law provided for the physical protection and integrity of the slaves as it did for free citizens. For example, in Spanish and Portuguese colonies, it was illegal to kill a slave. In the United States, to kill or not to kill a slave was up to the conscience of the master, and he could beat, injure, or abuse a slave without just cause. In Brazil, if the owner did any of these things, the slave had access to the court, and the judge, if he found the owner guilty, required him to sell the slave to another and kinder owner, pay the original owner a fair price, and forbid the resale of the slave to that owner. This protection for the life and limb of the slave, so crucial to the maintenance and development of both physical and mental health, was completely absent from the legal system of the United States. In the United States, this legacy of the white man's prerogatives to mistreat the Negro man has myriad ramifications in the behavior and the personality structures of both white and Negro men today. For white men, even among liberals and radicals, there is a pervasive sense of condescension toward Negroes which is sometimes reflected in paternalism, sometimes in arrogant disregard, and often in both. Rarely does the sense of true fraternity exist. For the Negro, the chronic sense of inferiority, vulnerability, and submission is sometimes expressed in hostility and, at other times, in dependence. The dominance-submission pattern of white-Negro interrelationships, which often pervades interracial efforts, is a legacy of this slave tradition, in which the Negro slave in the United States was so completely at the mercy of the white man for his very life and physical safety. Elkins has likened the absolute authority of slavery to that of the Nazi concentration camps, in which Jews became dehumanized in a few years.

> The new adjustment, to absolute power in a closed system, involved infantilization, and the detachment was so complete that little trace of prior (and thus alternative) cultural sanctions for behavior and personality remained for the descendants of the first generation. . . . We do not know how generally a full adjustment was made by the first generation of fresh slaves from Africa. But we do know—from a modern experience —that such an adjustment is possible, not only within the same generation, but within two or three years. This proved possible for people in a full state of complex civilization, for men and women who were not black and not savages.[34]

Legal protections for slaves were not systematic; rather, they were sporadic and unevenly enforced. Every slave state had slave codes, but they differed according to time, place, and manner of enforcement.[35] A slave rebellion could set off a new pattern of enforcement. The essential feature of all the codes was, of course, the same. They were not designed to protect the slaves, but to protect the master in the exercise or use of his property.

The very essence of the slave codes was the requirement that slaves submit to their masters and other white men at all times.[36] They controlled his movements and communications with others and they forbade all persons, including the master, to teach a slave to read and write.

In the United States slaves accused of committing some act of misbehavior were dealt with, for the most part, directly and swiftly by the master or his overseers. If they were brought into court, it was most likely to be one of the informal slave courts with one Justice of the Peace or three to five slave owners sitting as judge and jury. Occasionally, for

[34] Elkins, pp. 88–89.
[35] Kenneth M. Stampp, *The Peculiar Institution: Slavery in the Ante-Bellum South* (New York: Vintage Books, 1956), p. 206.
[36] *Ibid.*, p. 207.

serious felonies, slaves might be tried in a regular court. The consequences for the slaves were pretty much the same whatever the form of adjudication. Only rarely, for example, did courts enforce laws against the killing of a slave.[37] Neither slaves nor free Negroes could testify against white people. White prosecutors, juries, and judges were not predisposed to provide justice for the slaves. This orientation, fortified by the legal system, was designed to protect the master and other white persons from the slaves and other Negroes.

In a chapter of his book entitled, "To Make Them Stand in Fear," Kenneth Stampp has described the six processes slavemasters used and recommended to each other in their common goal of reducing the slave to subhuman status and perpetuating that status.

> Here, then, was the way to produce a perfect slave: accustom him to rigid discipline, demand from him unconditional submission, impress upon him his innate inferiority, develop in him a paralyzing fear of white men, train him to adopt the master's code of good behavior, and instill in him a sense of complete dependence.[38]

All these efforts at suppression and submission of the slaves worked most of the time and exacted their heavy toll on the personality and behavior of the slaves and their descendants. It was not all smooth sailing for the masters, however. Numerous efforts on the part of the Negroes to fight back included runaways, fights with and murders of cruel masters, and actual insurrections. For all these acts of outrage, the penalties were as swift as they were harsh.

The most notable rebellion was led by Nat Turner on August 22 and 23, 1831. It lasted only forty-eight hours, killed only sixty whites, actively involved only seventy slaves. But it has been described as the most fateful of the slave revolts. It sent fear through the hearts of both whites and Negroes, and its multiple consequences were reflected in the loss of white lives, the retaliation of the whites, and the fear it engendered, in part, because Nat Turner had been such a model slave, deeply religious and obedient. He was sheltered by slaves for two months before he was caught, tried, and hanged.[39]

Manumission

A second respect in which the political, legal, religious, economic, and demographic forces combined to produce a different slave system in

[37] *Ibid.*, p. 222.
[38] *Ibid.*, p. 148.
[39] Meltzer, pp. 33–34.

Latin America involved manumission. Not only were slaves treated with certain limited, though specified, degrees of humanity, but the very system of slavery in Latin America encouraged the freeing of slaves. There were hundreds of ways in which slaves could earn their freedom, and slave owners were often rewarded for freeing their slaves.

Slaves could purchase their own freedom or the freedom of a wife or of a child at birth for money which they could earn from work performed on Sundays or any of the other numerous holidays in these Catholic countries. In Brazil, the Negroes had altogether 84 days a year in which they could work for themselves, save their money, and do with it as they wished. They could even purchase their own freedom on the installment plan. Each installment provided certain liberties. On paying the first installment, for example, a slave was free to move out of his master's house, provided that he continued working for him. The practice was so widespread that slaves often paid all but the final installment, so that they remained technically a slave while in most respects free, and thus avoided the taxes and military service imposed on citizens. Freedom societies sprang up; these were savings associations for the purchase of the freedom of their fellow members. A man would often purchase the freedom of his wife while he remained a slave, and thus their children would be free because their status followed their mother's. For the most part, the original purchasing price of the slave was the price a slave had to pay for himself, though he might actually be worth more on the open market.

In addition to purchasing his freedom, there were a myriad of other ways in which a slave in Latin America could become free. His master could simply free him of his own accord, provided that he did it in the church or before a judge or by some solemn and explicit procedure, such as making a statement to that effect in writing. If a slave was owned by two people—say husband and wife—and one wanted to free him, the other was bound to accept a just price fixed by a local judge and accede to the freedom. A slave could become free against his master's will for doing heroic deeds for the community, such as reporting disloyalty against the king, or by denouncing a forced rape or murder in the community. Under some circumstances, a slave could become free even against his master's will by becoming a minister. If a slave became heir to his master, or was appointed guardian of his master's children, he was automatically freed. A parent having ten children could automatically claim freedom. In addition, freeing of one's slaves became an honorable tradition. Masters often would free a slave or two on the occasion of their daughter's wedding or the birth of the first son in the family. Favorite house slaves were often freed on the occasion of their birthdays or weddings.

These measures, in which the law itself facilitated manumission, had far-reaching consequences in the whole social structure of Latin America, setting up social expectations and values favorable to the freeing of slaves, but totally absent in the system of laws, norms, and social values of the plantation South in the United States. A man wanting to free his slave in Latin America was encouraged by the system. A man wanting to free his slave in the United States had to go against prevailing norms. For the Negro slaves, slavery in Latin America was a burning caldron with a ladder and an open top. In the United States, there was no ladder, and though people sometimes found their way out by the aid of kindly masters, their own daring escapes, or the aid of abolitionists, including especially the underground railroad, the top of the caldron was not to any significant extent open. There merely were holes in it which served as "screens of opportunity," through which only a few were allowed to escape.

In Brazil, fully two-thirds of the Negroes had already been freed through various procedures by the time of general emancipation in 1888. In the United States, on the other hand, never more than 10 per cent of the Negroes were free. In Brazil, once the slave had been freed, he enjoyed all the ordinary civil rights of other citizens; in fact, if a Negro was not known to be a slave in Brazil, he was presumed to be a free man. A completely different culture existed in the United States. Freed Negroes had only limited and circumscribed privileges and almost no legal rights. And a Negro in the United States South, prior to emancipation, was presumed to be a slave unless he could prove his free status.

Among the most far-reaching consequences of the two different slave systems were the manner of their dissolution and the status of the masses of freed men after emancipation. Brazil managed to escape the bloody holocaust which ended slavery in this country and produced a crisis in the social order which has not yet been healed. Slavery was actually abolished gradually and in stages in Brazil. In 1871, the Portuguese government promulgated the "doctrine of the free womb." This doctrine held that since slavery in Brazil was ownership of a person's labor and not of his innermost parts, the womb of a slave woman was free, and consequently any issue from that womb was also free. In view of this practice of freeing all newborn babies, it was only a matter of time till slavery would have died a natural death in Brazil. In 1885, a law was passed declaring that all slaves should become free on reaching the age of sixty. And finally, on May 13, 1888, "The Golden Law" was passed, abolishing slavery and freeing all slaves in Brazil.[40]

There were, of course, exceptional men in the United States who violated the slave codes because of self-interest, paternalism, humanitarianism, or a combination of all three. Slaves were sometimes freed for such "meritorious" service as reporting a planned slave insurrection. Among the very rare instances of outright manumission for apparently humanitarian reasons, a man in the upper South who willed that his slaves be freed on his death gave four reasons for such unusual, if still cowardly behavior:

> Reason the first. Agreeably to the rights of man, every human being, be his or her color what it may, is entitled to freedom. . . . Reason the second. My conscience, the great criterion, condemns me for keeping them in slavery. Reason the third. The golden rule directs us to do unto every human creature as we would wish to be done unto. . . . Reason the fourth and last. I wish to die with a clear conscience.[41]

Another major distinction between the United States and Latin America is that while the emancipated Negroes in the United States were "freedmen," in Brazil they were for the most part simply "free men." They were accepted into the free society, not only of the other ex-slaves, but of the whites as well. The closed system of slavery in the United States had produced a caste-like set of relations between white and Negro unknown in Brazil, where a person was considered to be inferior only if he was a slave—a condition that could be remedied. In the United States, on the other hand, it was considered that a person was a slave because he was innately inferior, and both conditions were associated with his blackness. Consequently, it has proved, even after emancipation, much more difficult for our society to shake off the badge of inferiority associated with color and the caste-like qualities which confound the socioeconomic distinctions between the races. In Latin America, the distinction is primarily socioeconomic.

The Family

A third respect in which the Latin American legal system protected the slaves was by providing for the creation and preservation of the family.

[40] E. Bradford Burns, *A Documentary History of Brazil* (New York: Alfred A. Knopf, Inc., 1966), p. 278.
[41] Stampp, pp. 235–36.

In Latin America, the law and the Church provided certain protections for the family life of the Negro slaves. Slaves were free to marry, even against the will of their masters, provided only that they keep serving him as before. They were free to intermarry with free persons, provided only that their slave status not be concealed. Slaves who were married could not be sold apart from each other unless it was guaranteed that they could continue to live together as man and wife. None of these minimum protections of the family were built into the system of slavery in the United States, where slaves were often permitted to marry, but only at the discretion of the master. In the United States, the slave husband was not the head of his household; the white owner was the head. The family had no rights that the slave owner was bound to respect. The wholesale disregard for family integrity among the slaves may be suggested by the following quotation from an actual advertisement in a New Orleans newspaper: "A Negro woman, 24 years of age, and her two children, one eight and the other three years old. Said Negroes will be sold separately or together as desired." [42] Another, in South Carolina in 1838, offered 120 slaves for sale of both sexes and every description, including "several women with children, small girls suitable for nurses, and several small boys without their mothers." [43]

The official records of shipping companies also reflected this family disruption. "Of four cargoes, making a total of 646 slaves, 396 were apparently owned by Franklen and Armfield. Among these there were only two full families. . . . There were 20 husbandless mothers with 33 children." [44]

Perhaps the cruelest of all the forms of emasculation of the Negro family was the very widespread practice, perhaps in all the slave states, of breeding slaves for sale as if they were cattle. An enterprising slave master, then, could enjoy not only the emotional advantages accrued from sex relations with his female slaves, but also the economic advantage which accrued from selling his offspring in the open market. Such decadence was much too common to have been confined to a few undesirable or emotionally disturbed white citizens. It was widespread and normative, though of course not all planters engaged in such practices. More common, perhaps, was the practice of breeding slaves among each other. One advertisement of a shipment of slaves claimed that

they are not Negroes selected out of a larger gang for the purpose of a sale, but are prime. Their present owner, with great trouble and expense,

---

[42] Tannenbaum, p. 77.
[43] *Ibid.*, pp. 77-78.
[44] *Ibid.*, p. 78.

selected them out of many for several years past. They were purchased for stock and breeding Negroes and to any planter who particularly wants them for that purpose, they are a very choice and desirable gang.[45]

In the United States, then, contrary to Latin America, the legal system made no provision for, and took no special recognition of, marriage and family life among the Negro slaves. In addition, the slave owners and other whites took frequent sexual advantage of the slave women. Even if she were the wife of a slave, her husband could not protect her. The Attorney General of Maryland observed in one of his reports that "a slave never has maintained an action against the violator of his bed."[46] This statement apparently would apply in other states as well, regardless of whether the violator was slave or citizen. The powerlessness of the Negro man to protect his family for two and a half centuries under slavery has had crippling consequences for the relations of Negro men and women to this very day.

Slavery and Family Life in the United States

Marriage among slaves was not altogether absent in the United States, and was probably more common than has been generally recognized. It was, however, a far different institution with much less structural and institutional support in this country than in Latin America. The strong hand of the slave owner dominated the Negro family, which existed only at his mercy and often at his own personal instigation. An ex-slave has told of getting married on one plantation:

> When you married, you had to jump over a broom three times. Dat was de license. If master seen two slaves together too much he would tell 'em dey was married. Hit didn't make no difference if you wanted to or not; he would put you in de same cabin an' make you live together. . . . Marsa used to sometimes pick our wives fo' us. If he didn't have on his place enough women for the men, he would wait on de side of de road till a big wagon loaded with slaves come by. Den Marsa would stop de ole nigger-trader and buy you a woman. Wasn't no use tryin' to pick one, cause Marsa wasn't gonna pay but so much for her. All he wanted was a young healthy one who looked like she could have children, whether she was purty or ugly as sin.[47]

The difficulties Negro men had in establishing, protecting, and maintaining family ties, together with the strong values they placed on family

[45] *Ibid.*, p. 80.
[46] *Ibid.*, pp. 76–77.
[47] Meltzer, pp. 46–47.

life and responsibilities, are graphically depicted in the correspondence between ex-slaves and their ex-masters. It often happened that the slaves who escaped into freedom by the underground railroad were those who had been treated relatively well by their owners, and who even had been taught to read and write. Often they were the "favorite" slaves of the owners, highly trusted and considered dependable and grateful. Thus, it was not uncommon that when a slave holder found out the whereabouts of an ex-slave, he would write to him, imploring him to return. Three letters by ex-slaves written in response to such appeals will illustrate the damaging consequences slavery had for Negro family life. The first was written by Henry Bibb in 1844, after he had escaped into Canada by way of the underground railroad.

Dear Sir:—I am happy to inform you that you are not mistaken in the man whom you sold as property, and received pay for as such. But I thank God that I am not property now, but am regarded as a man like yourself, and although I live far north, I am enjoying a comfortable living by my own industry. If you should ever chance to be traveling this way, and will call on me, I will use you better than you did me while you held me as a slave. Think not that I have any malice against you, for the cruel treatment which you inflicted on me while I was in your power. As it was the custom of your country, to treat your fellow men as you did me and my little family, I can freely forgive you.

I wish to be remembered in love to my aged mother, and friends; please tell her that if we should never meet again in this life, my prayer shall be to God that we may meet in Heaven, where parting shall be no more.

You wish to be remembered to King and Jack. I am pleased, sir, to inform you that they are both here, well, and doing well. They are both living in Canada West. They are now the owners of better farms than the men are who once owned them.

You may perhaps think hard of us for running away from slavery, but as to myself, I have but one apology to make for it, which is this: I have only to regret that I did not start at an earlier period. I might have been free long before I was. But you had it in your power to have kept me there much longer than you did. I think it is very probable that I should have been a toiling slave on your property today, if you had treated me differently.

To be compelled to stand by and see you whip and slash my wife without mercy, when I could afford her no protection, not even by offering myself to suffer the lash in her place, was more than I felt it to be the duty of a slave husband to endure, while the way was open to Canada. My infant child was also frequently flogged by Mrs. Gatewood, for crying, until its skin was bruised literally purple. This kind of treatment was what drove me from home and family, to seek a better home for them. But I am willing to forget the past. I should be pleased to hear from you again, on the reception of this, and should also be very happy to correspond with you often, if it should be agreeable to yourself. I subscribe myself a friend to the oppressed, and Liberty forever.[48]

Another letter was written in 1860 by J. W. Loguen who escaped to New England:

Mrs. Sarah Logue: Yours of the 20th of February is duly received, and I thank you for it. It is a long time since I heard from my poor old mother, and I am glad to know that she is yet alive, and, as you say, "as well as common." What that means, I don't know. I wish you had said more about her.

You are a woman; but had you a woman's heart, you never could have insulted a brother by telling him you sold his only remaining brother and sister, because he put himself beyond your power to convert him into money.

You sold my brother and sister, Abe and Ann, and twelve acres of land, you say, because I ran away. Now you have the unutterable meanness to ask me to return and be your miserable chattel, or, in lieu thereof, send you $1000 to enable you to redeem the land, but not to redeem my poor brother and sister! If I were to send you the money, it would be to get my brother and sister, and not that you should get land. You say you are a cripple, and doubtless you say it to stir my pity, for you knew I was susceptible in that direction. I do pity you from the bottom of my heart. Nevertheless, I am indignant beyond the power of words to express, that you should be so sunken and cruel as to tear the hearts I love so much all to pieces; that you should be willing to impale and crucify us all, out of compassion for your foot or leg. Wretched woman! Be it known to you that I value my freedom, to say nothing of my mother, brothers and sisters, more than your whole body; more, indeed, than my own life; more than all the lives of all the slave-holders and tyrants under heaven.

You say you have offers to buy me, and that you shall sell me if I do not send you $1000, and in the same breath and almost in the same sentence, you say, "You know we raised you as we did our own children." Woman, did you raise your own children for the market? . . .

. . . But you say I am a thief, because I took the old mare along with me. Have you got to learn that I had a better right to the old mare, as you call her, than Manasseth Logue had to me? Is it a greater sin for me to steal his horse, than it was for him to rob my mother's cradle, and steal me? If he and you infer that I forfeit all my rights to you, shall not I infer that you forfeit all your rights to me? Have you got to learn that human rights are mutual and reciprocal, and if you take my liberty and

Ibid., pp. 100–101.

life, you forfeit your own liberty and life? Before God and high heaven, is there a law for one man which is not a law for every other man?

If you or any other speculator on my body and rights, wish to know how I regard my rights, they need but come here, and lay their hands on me to enslave me. Did you think to terrify me by presenting the alternative to give my money to you, or give my body to slavery? Then let me say to you, that I meet the proposition with unutterable scorn and contempt. The proposition is an outrage and an insult. I will not budge one hair's breadth. I will not breathe a shorter breath, even to save me from your persecutions. I stand among a free people, who, I thank God, sympathize with my rights, and the rights of mankind; and if your emissaries and venders come here to re-enslave me, and escape the unshrinking vigor of my own right arm, I trust my strong and brave friends, in this city and State, will be my rescuers and avengers.[49]

A third letter is from Jourdon Anderson, who was freed by the Union Army Forces during the Civil War.

Sir: I got your letter, and was glad to find that you had not forgotten Jourdon, and that you wanted me to come back and live with you again, promising to do better for me than anybody else can. . . .

. . . I want to know particularly what the good chance is you propose to give me. I am doing tolerably well here. I get twenty-five dollars a month, with victuals and clothing; have a comfortable home for Mandy, —the folks call her Mrs. Anderson—and the children—Milly, Jane, and Grundy—go to school and are learning well. The teacher says Grundy has a head for a preacher. They go to Sunday School, and Mandy and me attend church regularly. We are kindly treated. Sometimes we overhear others saying, "Them colored people were slaves" down in Tennessee. The children feel hurt when they hear such remarks; but I tell them it was no disgrace in Tennessee to belong to Colonel Anderson. Many darkeys would have been proud, as I used to be, to call you master. Now if you will write and say what wages you will give me, I will be better able to decide whether it would be to my advantage to move back again.

. . . Mandy says she would be afraid to go back without some proof that you were disposed to treat us justly and kindly; and we have concluded to test your sincerity by asking you to send us our wages for the time we served you. This will make us forget and forgive old scores, and rely on your justice and friendship in the future. I served you faithfully for thirty-two years, and Mandy twenty years. At twenty-five dollars a month for me, and two dollars a week for Mandy, our earnings would amount to eleven thousand six hundred and eighty dollars. Add to this the interest for the time our wages have been kept back, and deduct what

* *Ibid.*, pp. 120–22.

you paid for our clothing, and three doctor's visits to me, and pulling a tooth for Mandy, and the balance will show what we are in justice entitled to.

. . . In answering this letter, please state if there would be any safety for my Milly and Jane, who are now grown up, and both goodlooking girls. You know how it was with poor Matilda and Catherine. I would rather stay here and starve—and die, if it come to that—than have my girls brought to shame by the violence and wickedness of their young masters. You will also please state if there has been any schools opened for the colored children in your neighborhood. The great desire of my life is to give my children an education, and have them form virtuous habits.

Say howdy to George Carter, and thank him for taking the pistol from you when you were shooting at me.[50]

The Negro family existed during slavery in the United States, but it was a most precarious existence, dependent wholly on the economic and personal interests of the white man, and the grim determination and bravery of the black man.

Interracial Marriage

A fourth respect in which the slave system in the United States differed markedly from that in Latin America relative to family life was in the area of interracial marriage. Marriage between white persons and black persons, particularly between European men and African women, was common, sanctioned, and encouraged in Latin America even under slavery. It was forbidden by law in the United States, not only during slavery, but in modern times as well. Not until 1967 were the last legal supports for such bans were struck down by the U. S. Supreme Court. Even now, however, despite the lack of legal support for such bans on interracial marriage, the customs and norms of the white majority in the country, and to some extent the black minority, make interracial marriage a rare and deviant sort of behavior.

Marriage among peoples of different cultural backgrounds is considered, by many students of assimilation, to be the ultimate test of the process of integration, as well as of whether a caste system exists, separating two peoples into superior and inferior beings. In these respects, then, the question of interracial marriage is more than a matter of personal choice; it is an index of the view and place of different peoples in the national life.

[50] *Ibid.*, pp. 170–72.

It is not, of course, that miscegenation and other forms of interracial contact have been absent in the United States. In fact, they have been persistent. But they have been more or less illicit, unsanctioned by the wider society. Consequently, the white men who have been the chief exploiters of Negro women in such relationships have escaped the responsibilities associated with these relationships. The manner in which Negro women were exploited by white men during slavery, and the damage these relationships caused to the stability of Negro family life can be seen from two personal accounts provided us by two remarkable Negro women writers, Pauli Murray and Margaret Walker. Both accounts are taken from actual family histories.

Pauli Murray tells of her own great-grandmother, Harriet, who was born a slave in 1819. She was the product of miscegenation and described as mulatto. When she was fifteen, she was sold to a medical doctor in North Carolina who bought her as a housemaid for his own eighteen-year-old daughter. These two women, the slave and the mistress, grew into the most intricate of relationships filled with all the human drama of love, envy, and hate imaginable.[51]

When Harriet was twenty years old, she asked her owner for permission to marry a young mulatto man who was born free, and who lived and worked in the town. It is said that Dr. Smith, her owner, readily agreed. "It was good business. He had no obligation to the husband, and every child by the marriage would be his slave and worth several hundred dollars at birth." Harriet and her husband were not permitted to live together permanently, but he was permitted to visit her in the evenings after she had finished her work in the "big house." After three years, in about 1842, they had a child. Of course, this son became a slave like his mother, and was the property of Dr. Smith.

Sometime after this, Dr. Smith's two grown sons came home from college, and both took a special interest in Harriet. "Before long," Miss Murray tells us, "everybody in the house knew that a storm was brewing between the brothers, and that Harriet was the cause of it." The author then describes an encounter between Sydney, one of the Smith sons, and Reuben, Harriet's free Negro husband.

Sydney Smith informed Reuben that he could not be legally married to a slave, and that if he were ever caught visiting Harriet again he would be whipped and thrown in jail. The author continues: "Reuben had to leave without a word to Harriet. That was the last she ever saw of him."

[51] Pauli Murray, *Proud Shoes: The Story of an American Family* (New York: Harper & Row, Publishers, 1956), quotes from pp. 38–48.

It is not, however, that Reuben abandoned his wife, his child, and his rights so easily; he came back to see them one time, but the two Smith brothers saw him.

> The brothers beat Reuben with the butt end of a carriage whip and when they finally let him go, they told him if he ever came back on the Smith lot, they'd shoot him on sight. He disappeared from the county and nothing was heard of him again.

Shortly after Reuben was banished from his wife's cabin, Sydney Smith "had his way with her" in the presence of her little boy.

> He raped her again, again, and again in the weeks that followed. Night after night he would force open her cabin door and nail it up again on the inside so that she could not get out. Then he would beat her into submission.

Sydney's brother Frank was furious at the turn of events. One night he accosted Sydney on his way from Harriet's cabin.

> The brothers had it out once and for all, and there was a terrible fight. Early the next morning, one of the slaves found Sydney lying unconscious in the yard, his clothes soaked with blood and an ugly hole in his head. . . . He learned his lesson. He never touched Harriet again.

But already Harriet was pregnant with Sydney's child. This child, born on the Smith lot in February 1844, was Pauli Murray's grandmother.

After the baby was born, Sydney's brother Frank "had his way" with Harriet. This time she did not fight back.

This relationship was long and enduring. Over the course of five years, Harriet bore to Francis Smith three daughters. Harriet was now the mother of five children by three different fathers, all growing up on the same plantation but treated according to their father's positions. Julius, the oldest, was almost ignored by the Big House, and his mother was almost a stranger to him. When he was around thirteen, he got lost in the woods during a heavy snowstorm. They found him almost frozen to death. He was severely crippled for the rest of his life.

The girls lived lives of crippling ambivalence.

> The Smiths were as incapable of treating the little girls wholly as servants as they were of recognizing them openly as kin. At times the Smith's involuntary gestures of kinship were so pronounced, the children could not help thinking of themselves as Smith grandchildren. At other times, their innocent overtures of affection were rebuffed without explanation and they were driven away with cruel epithets.

In *Jubilee* Margaret Walker tells a similar story[52] of her own grand-mother Vyry, and her great-grandmother Hetta. Several generations before the Civil War, Hetta, a slave girl, had borne fifteen children by the time she was twenty-nine. She died in childbirth with the sixteenth. Many of them, including Vyry, were by the son of her owner. Vyry is the center of a most fascinating account of that pre-Civil War period in the life of the slaves, freedmen, and masters. Randall Ware, a young freed-man, who loved, courted, married, and lost her, is a most remarkable example of black manhood, who, despite the efforts of the system to crush him, managed to survive. There was a man, if only for one brief season! He insisted on exercising his freedom in the plantation South, which conspired to make slaves of all black people. He almost rescued his wife and family from slavery. He escaped to the North by way of the underground railroad and returned to fight in the Civil War. This is not, however, a story of essential triumph. It is a vivid illustration of the tragedy of slavery and the crippling consequences it had for Negro family life.

In summary, it may be said that the slave system had a crippling effect on the establishment, maintenance, and growth of normal patterns of family life among the Negro people. This impact was cruel in all the Americas. It was exceedingly vicious in the United States. There were several facets of this process of personal, family, and social emasculation. First, the family was broken up at the very beginning of the slave trade in the manner in which the slaves were gathered, the disregard the captors showed to family and kinship ties, the preference they showed for selecting young men in the prime of their life, and the consequent underrepresentation of females for hundreds of years, and the inhumane conditions under which the slaves were quartered, worked, and treated.

All these conditions were found everywhere in the slave system, al-though some evidence suggests that the living conditions were worse in the United States. The particular factors which characterize the im-pact of slavery on the Negro family in the United States include, in addition to the above, the absence of legal foundation, sanction, and protection of marriage as an institution among the slaves, the exploi-tation of slave women by white owners and overseers for both pleasure and profit; the systematic denial of a role for the man as husband and father; the willful separation of related men, women, and children and selling them to different plantations. In short, there was the absence, in the United States, of societal support and protection for the Negro family

[52] Margaret Walker, *Jubilee* (Boston: Houghton Mifflin Company, 1966).

as a physical, psychological, social, or economic unit. This crippled the development, not only of individual slaves, but of families, and hence of the whole society of Negro people. The consequences these conditions wrought for generations of Negroes under the slave system were direct and insidious. The consequences for succeeding and even modern generations of Negroes are, perhaps, less direct, but no less insidious. At no time in the history of this country have Negroes experienced, systematically and generally, the kind of social supports from the society which would even approach the intensity of the negative impact of slavery. Not only has the society not made any massive efforts to undo the damages of slavery and actively integrate the Negro people into the society on the basis of equality, but many of the explicit conditions of slavery still exist at the present time.

The Failures of Reconstruction After the Civil War

It is often said that slavery was a long time ago; that surely the freedom and opportunity granted to the Negro people by emancipation has been sufficient to overcome the ravages of slavery; and that, surely, contemporary white people and institutions bear no responsibility for slavery and reap no benefit from this dark chapter in human history.

But the historical facts are otherwise. The Negro people have never been indemnified, either economically, or politically, or socially, or psychologically for two centuries of bondage. And furthermore, the wider society has not reconstructed itself to any substantial degree in any of these areas of life.

The end of slavery with the Civil War in the United States brought a certain freedom to the slave and the free Negro alike, but it was also a crisis of major proportions. For tens of thousands of Negroes, emancipation meant the freedom to die of starvation and illness. In some communities, one out of every four Negroes died. The destitution and disease among the Negroes, who were now uncared for and had no facilities to care for themselves, was so great that the editor of a famous newspaper observed with considerable glee that "The child is already born who will behold the last Negro in the State of Mississippi." [53] And Mississippi had more Negro slaves than any other state. Nor were such dire straits and predictions confined to one state. The eminent southern scholar, Dr. C. K · Marchall, expressed a similar and more general hypothesis: "In all probability New Year's Day on the morning of the 1st

[53] Bennett, p. 188.

of January, 1920, the colored population in the South will scarcely be counted." [54]

The survival of the Negro people after such a holocaust can be attributed primarily to the resiliency of the human spirit. It most certainly cannot be attributed in large measure to the efforts of his society to help him survive. For the ingredient most absent to make freedom meaningful was the ingredient which has been most useful to other depressed people, namely opportunity.

There were no national, regional, or other large-scale plans for dealing with the ex-slaves. How could they be integrated into the life of the embattered republic as free men? Uncertainty abounded. There were enlightened voices who put forward suggestions. The most rational package suggested that the nation should give each ex-slave forty acres of land, a mule, the ballot, and leave him alone. Charles Sumner of Massachusetts plugged hard for the ballot, Thaddeus Stevens of Pennsylvania plugged even harder for the forty acres. And several generations before Justice Louis D. Brandeis was to expound his famous doctrine of the freedom to be let alone, Frederick Douglass, the ex-slave, echoed the same sentiment.

> The Negro should have been let alone in Africa. . . . If you see him plowing in the open field, leveling the forest, at work with a spade, a rake, a hoe, a pick-axe, or a bill, let him alone; . . . If he has a ballot in his hand, let him alone. [55]

But the nation's response was to be much more limited and temporary. The Freedman's Bureau, probably the first national social welfare administration, during six short years with severely limited funds, administrative imagination and courage, and in the face of apathy in the North and hostility in the South, strove to feed and clothe ex-slaves and poor whites, and to establish hospitals and schools. It did a commendable job under the circumstances, but much too little and over too short a time. President Andrew Johnson's heart was not in the efforts of the Freedman's Bureau, and despite certain efforts of Congress he crushed this program.

John Hope Franklin has summed up the period of reconstruction as follows:

> Counter reconstruction was everywhere an overwhelming success. In the face of violence the 14th and 15th Amendments provided no protection for the Negro citizen and his friends. The federal enforcement laws of 1870 and 1871 proved wholly inadequate, especially when en-

[54] *Ibid.*, p. 188.
[55] *Ibid.*, pp. 186–87.

forcement was left to the meager forces that remained in the South at the time of their enactment. Negroes could hardly be expected to continue to vote when it cost them not only their jobs but their lives. In one state after another, the Negro electorate declined steadily as the full force of the Klan came forward to supervise the elections that federal troops failed to supervise. . . . The federal government was, more and more, leaving the South to its own devices. Even more important was the enormous prestige that the former Confederates enjoyed. In time they were able to assume leadership in their communities without firing a shot or hanging a single Negro. What they lacked in political strength they made up in economic power. By discharging or threatening to discharge Negro employees who persisted in participating in politics, they could reduce the Negro electorate to a minimum. By refusing to pay taxes to support the expanded and inflated functions of the new governments, they could destroy Radical Reconstruction in a season. But the former Confederates relied on no one method. By political pressure, economic sanctions, *and* violence they brought Radical Reconstruction crashing down almost before it began.[56]

Of course, Emancipation had some advantages for the Negro family. Although family members could be whipped, run out of town, or murdered, they could not be sold away from their families. Marriages were legalized and recorded. The hard work of farming, even sharecropping, required all possible hands—husband, wife, and children.

Emancipation, then, was a catastrophic social crisis for the ex-slave, and Reconstruction was a colossal failure. At the same time, there were some "screens of opportunity" which did enable large numbers of families to survive, some to achieve amazingly stable and viable forms of family life, and a few to achieve a high degree of social distinction.

[56] John Hope Franklin, *Reconstruction After the Civil War* (Chicago: University of Chicago Press, 1961), pp. 172–73.

Chapter 3

Shadows of the Plantation: Contemporary Social Forces Affecting Negro Family Life

In this chapter we shall examine some of the current social forces which serve both as obstacles to the fuller development of Negro family life and as opportunity screens through which many families have been able to move toward social achievement. The general argument is that many of these social forces contain within them the legacy of slavery and are in that respect shadows of the plantation. These shadows, we suggest, are long and resilient, reaching into every aspect of Negro life, but having a particular impact on family organization, stability, and achievement.

These social forces must be seen in the dual context of industrialization and urbanization, for these are the principal phenomena which help to set the conditions for Negro family life that will be considered in this section. In this section, then, we will describe and discuss the forces of geographic mobility and social mobility, as representing two areas in which the Negro people have undergone majoi transitions from the end of slavery to the present time.

By geographic mobility we refer to the migration of the Negro people from the rural South to the urban North. Social mobility refers to the transition from an underclass to a more differentiated position in the socioeconomic structure. Each of these movements, we argue, provides basic ingredients for improvement in both the structure and the function of Negro family life.

GEOGRAPHIC MOBILITY[1]

A hundred years ago, more than 90 per cent of all Negro families lived in the rural South. Today, there are three major geographic centers of

[1] Unless otherwise specified, the data cited in this chapter are from the United States Census Reports for 1965.

this population: the rural South, where roughly 20 per cent of Negro families live; the urban South, where more than 30 per cent live; and the urban North and West, where nearly half of all Negro families reside. Furthermore, the rural Southern population is rapidly dwindling, and the Northern urban population is rapidly expanding.

This pattern of residence has been the result of far-reaching changes in the economic, demographic, and social structure of the country. Due largely to the migrations surrounding the years of World War I, the Negro population in the South had decreased to 85 per cent by 1920. Thereafter it decreased to 77 per cent by 1940 and to 60 per cent by 1960. By 1965, the proportion of Negroes still living in the states of the old Confederacy was 53.6 per cent. During the decade 1950 to 1960 alone, the Negro population of the North increased by over 50 per cent, while the Negro population in the South increased by only 10 per cent—this due largely to the increased birth rate among Negroes.

A most dramatic picture of the shift of the Negro population from the South to the North can be seen from the fact that every one of the Southern regions had a tremendous net outflow of Negro population for every decade between 1910 and 1960, while every one of the non-Southern regions had a tremendous net inflow. The trend has continued in the same direction through the 1960s.

The same social forces which moved large numbers of Negro families from the South to the North and West also moved even larger numbers from rural to urban areas. The Northern movement of Negroes has been almost wholly to the cities. At the same time, however, and even preceding that, there was considerable movement of Negroes from rural to urban areas within the South. Altogether, then, while 75 per cent of Negro families lived in the rural areas in 1910, today the pattern is just the reverse. Fully 73 per cent of Negroes lived in urban areas in 1960. The Negro population is, therefore, more urbanized than is the non-Negro population.

The urbanization of the Negro population, however, varies somewhat by region. In the South 58 per cent of the Negroes lived in cities in 1960, while in the North the percentage was 96 and in the West 93. Thus, while something better than half of all Negroes still live in the South, roughly six out of every ten Southern Negroes of those have moved to urban areas.

Furthermore, the urban Negro population is highly concentrated in the large metropolitan centers of the country. In 1910, while there were already a number of great cities in the country, none had a Negro population of as many as 100,000; in 1960, there were eighteen cities with a larger number of Negro residents than 100,000. In 1910, Negroes did not comprise as much as 10 per cent of the population in any of the large cities; today they comprise more than 10 per cent in the twenty-five leading cities in the country.

In twenty of these major cities, the Negro population exceeds one fifth of the population. In fifteen, it exceeds a fourth of the total; and in ten, the Negroes constitute at least a third of the population. In the seven where the Negro population now approaches or exceeds 40 per cent, Negroes will constitute an absolute majority by 1970 if present trends continue. This is already the case in Washington, D. C., and several smaller cities, including Newark, New Jersey, and Gary, Indiana.

A third and more recent pattern of geographic mobility has been the movement of Negro families from one urban area to another, resulting in increased concentration in the large metropolitan areas of the country. Among Negroes who moved to metropolitan areas between 1955 and 1960, fully half moved from another metropolitan area in a westward trend. This, however, varies by region. In the South, the rural areas still constitute the main source of Negroes moving to the cities. In the North, the main source is from Southern urban areas, and in the West, two main sources are the Northern urban areas and the western edge of the South. This urban migration picture shows, for example, that a majority of the Negroes who moved into South Los Angeles came from non-Southern states.

These new Negro emigrants not only are urbanized, in the sense that they have had considerable experience with urban living, but also are of higher education and occupational level than previous migrants from the rural South. Thus, nearly half of the Negroes moving into the twelve largest metropolitan areas between 1955 and 1960 came from other urban areas, and between 34 and 54 per cent, depending on the city (34 per cent in Atlanta, 54 per cent in Washington), had completed four years of high school or more. Between 22 (in Cleveland) and 40 per cent (in Washington) of the immigrants from other metropolitan areas were employed in white collar occupations. In five of these metropolitan areas, the white collar occupations of their Negro emigrants was about 30 per cent.

Within these metropolitan areas, white people are increasingly fleeing to the suburban fringes of the major cities, leaving the central cities to Negroes and other ethnic minorities. A tight white noose around the central cities has kept Negro families from being able to penetrate suburbia in any appreciable numbers. In 1960, only 20 per cent of Negroes, in all metropolitan areas combined, lived in the suburban fringes, as compared to over half of all white families. For white families, this suburbanization is moving at an ever-increasing pace.

The 20 per cent of urban Negroes who live in suburban areas does not in itself represent the opening of white suburbs to Negro families. More typically, it represents Negro families from the central cities moving into outlying areas which already contained small Negro enclaves. The situation in Chicago as described by Taeuber and Taeuber is an example:

> The Negro population outside Chicago city increased from 44,000 to 78,000 between 1950 and 1960. More than half of the 43,000 increase went to neighborhoods in such industrial suburbs as Evanston, Joliet, North Chicago and similar places. . . . These suburbs already had Negro communities in residentially segregated neighborhoods in 1950. . . . The addition of Negro population to these areas did not represent an opening up of suburbs in general to Negro residents. An additional one-fourth of the increased Negro population in Chicago's suburban ring is accounted for by the addition of Negro population to existing or newly created "Negro suburbs," entire communities or separate sections of communities developed expressly for the purpose of providing new suburban housing for Negroes. There are several such developments in Cook County just southwest of Chicago. The net gain of Negro population in all the rest of the suburban area surrounding Chicago was less than 6,000 in the entire decade.[2]

One of the striking features of the urbanization of the Negro population is that Negro residence in the suburbs is higher in the South than in the Northern cities. Thus, in 1900 Negro families constituted 2.5 per cent of the population of central cities and 2.1 per cent of the suburban ring in the North. In the South, they constituted 29.6 per cent of the central city populations and 13.7 per cent of the suburban ring. By 1960, Northern Negroes constituted 15.1 per cent of central cities and still only 2.8 per cent of the suburban ring. In the South, Negroes accounted for 25.8 per cent of the central city populations and 11.6 per cent of the suburban ring.

While Negro families do not move to white suburbs in any appreciable numbers, it is clear that when they do move within the city, they move for the same reasons and in the same directions as white families move. They move, as Frazer observed a long time ago, from the central, older parts of the city toward the edges of it. They move apparently to find

[2] Karl E. Taeuber and Alma F. Taeuber, "The Negro Population in the United States," in *The American Negro Reference Book*, ed., John P. Davis (Englewood Cliffs, N. J.: Prentice-Hall, Inc., 1966), pp. 133–34.

more space, less crowded schools, more trees and grass, and a better class of neighbors.

Causes of Geographic Mobility

The tremendous population shifts which have occurred in three centers of Negro population—the rural South, the urban South, and the urban North—have many causes and consequences which should be given some attention at this point. While Negro families have undoubtedly improved their conditions of life in every major respect by the movement from the rural South to the urban North, it would be a mistake to assign inordinate weight to the abject conditions in the South—both poverty and racial discrimination—as major causes of the movement to the urban North. Migration is much more complex than that and involves both "push" and "pull" forces. Thus, there were a variety of factors about life in the rural South which pushed the Negroes out at a faster rate than other Americans. The Negro proportion of the total population in the South dropped from 37 per cent to 21 per cent during the hundred years 1860 to 1960.[3] Of the two major factors in the South which helped to "push" the Negro people outward, the first was general oppression and blatant racism. The second and greater push was very similar to the push which sent other ethnic groups to the northern shores of the United States— economic disaster.

The absence of freedom in the rural South undoubtedly caused many men and families to leave. But this alone was not a major factor. The most striking evidence which helps to rule out a reaction to the lack of freedom is that during the worst periods of the early years of emancipation, when both the objective conditions of Negroes in the South and the suppression of their general liberty was worst—that is to say, during the first fifty years after emancipation—there was hardly any appreciable movement of Negroes from the slave-holding South to the abolitionist and freedom-loving North. To account for the massive movement of Negroes to the North half a century after Emancipation, we must search for additional, more basic changes in the structure of the larger society, and most especially changes in the economic subsystem of that society.

The first major out-migration of Negroes from the South started about 1915 and continued at a very high rate during most of the next ten years. We must, therefore, consider as a major push factor the tremendous failures in the agricultural crops in the South during that period, due in no small measure to the legendary boll weevil. "Conditions had often

[3] *Ibid.*, p. 111.

been depressed," say Taeuber and Taeuber, "but the devastation and depth of the agricultural depression in many counties were greater than ever before. Out-migration increased greatly from many of the hardest hit counties." [4]

But if people move from one place in massive numbers in part because there are factors which push them out, they move into another place because there are forces which pull them. The major single "pull" force during this period was World War I, its preparation, execution, and aftermath. We have already observed above that war is very good for the economic subsystem of our society. And each of our major wars, beginning with the Civil War, has been good for the Negro people, largely because it has been good for the economic sector of our society as a whole. The period surrounding World War I had three general effects in the industrial North which served as pulls for the Negro population in the South. First, the war "even before direct U. S. involvement, brought new demands upon Northern manufacturing industries." [5] Second, with the outbreak of the war in Europe, the sources of immigration from Europe, which had brought in more than a million persons a year to the Northern industrial cities, were cut off. Third, even though this European immigration was resumed briefly after the war, it never again reached its previous high proportions, in part because of the restrictive immigration legislation passed in the early 1920s, during that period of Americanization hysteria. Thus, many Northern industries sent agents into the South recruiting Negroes by the hundreds and thousands to come North for jobs. And while many elements in the society, including those in the North, had previously believed that Negroes were especially suited to plantation agriculture and unsuited to industrial occupations, they found—as they have always found during critical labor shortages—that Negroes were amazingly suited to and productive in this aspect of the economy.

Impact on Family and Community Life

These pushes from the South and pulls from the North combined to stimulate the most massive internal migration of recent history. Once Negroes gained a foothold in the Northern industrial sectors of the economy, they never lost it.

These population movements have had their impact not only on the quality of Negro community and family life in the Southern communities which they left, but on the Northern communities in which they settled

[4] *Ibid.*, p. 111.
[5] *Ibid.*, p. 111.

as well. One factor which makes such migration so disruptive to family life is that it is rather selective. Not all ages or family members—indeed, not always whole families—are necessarily caught up in the movement northward. Many men left their families behind, in part because it was expensive and somewhat uncertain to bring them along, and in part because the recruiters who paid the way of the men did not pay the fares of their families. The men were encouraged to go North, get settled, and send for their families later. While most of them did, in the meantime, the period of estrangement, both for the men in the cities of the North and for their families left behind, exerted definite strains on family solidarity and organization. Many men took longer than their families thought necessary to send for them; some families managed to arrive in the Northern communities without waiting to be sent for, sometimes to the surprise and embarrassment of the husband who was waiting to send for them. Some families never joined their husbands and fathers until years later. Some never did.

Moreover, there was an even more selective factor about the early stages of this migration. Like the slave trade two hundred years before, the industrial pull of the North greatly preferred young men. This also had a tremendous impact, both on the families and communities left behind and on the communities into which these large groups of young men, often without attachments, came to settle. The states hardest hit by these migratory patterns were Alabama, Georgia, and Mississippi at the Southern end, and Illinois, Michigan, and New York at the Northern end. Thus, in the decade from 1940 to 1950 alone, Alabama and Georgia lost nearly a third of their Negro men between the ages of fifteen and thirty-four, and Mississippi lost nearly half; while at the other end, the young Negro male population of Illinois increased by nearly 60 per cent, Michigan by over 80 per cent, and New York nearly 55 per cent.

But these figures understate the impact of these migratory trends. For the young men and other migrants came not from all over the whole state of Mississippi, for example, but from clusters of communities. Many Negro communities in these states lost all their young men. And in the Northern states, the clustering was also highly selective. Many Negro communities suddenly found the population of young men increased out of all proportions to what could be absorbed into the social fabric of those communities in an orderly fashion. There were, then, tremendous social upheavals at both ends of the transition from North to South. And, as always, these disruptions had their ramifications on the most basic of institutions in the black community, the Negro family.

SOCIAL MOBILITY

Accompanying the patterns of geographic mobility discussed above, has been a degree of social mobility which has enabled Negro families to survive and to move toward stability and achievement. Here we shall first describe some of the key elements in the social mobility of the Negro people, laying particular stress on education, occupation, income, and housing, and showing how these vary, particularly over time and from one region to another. Then we shall describe our conception of the Negro social class structure that has emerged as a consequence of the historical and contemporary social forces described above.

Education

There are three characteristics of education which make it a major key to the understanding of Negro family and community life. First, it is a most reliable index and a potent means of gaining social mobility and family stability in our society. The absence of systematic training and education during slavery and reconstruction depressed the social structure of the Negro people most, just as the presence of education in small and scattered doses proved such a powerful source of achievement. Secondly, education is a major tool which enables families to meet the responsibilities placed on them by society, helping them meet not only the instrumental functions of family life but the expressive ones as well. Third, education is a key medium for the interaction of family and society.

What, then, is the shape of educational achievement among Negro adults? in 1965, 3.5 per cent of all Negro adults twenty-five years and over had completed less than one full year of formal schooling. (See Figure 4.) At the other end of the range, 9.4 per cent had completed one

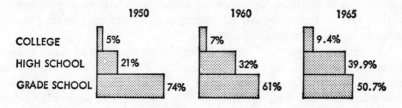

FIGURE 4
Range of Educational Achievement Among Negroes 25 Years Old and Over

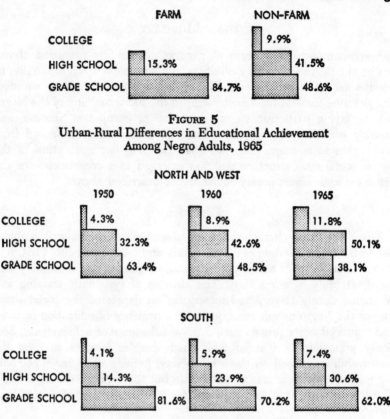

FIGURE 5
Urban-Rural Differences in Educational Achievement
Among Negro Adults, 1965

FIGURE 6
Regional Differences in Educational Achievement
of Negro Adults, 1950, 1960, and 1965

or more years of college and higher education. Between these two extremes, lies the bulk of Negro adults, with nearly half having completed eight years or less of formal education, and 40 per cent having one or more years of high school education.

The picture we get is of an adult population made up of three general levels of education, as in the pyramid in Figure 4. This educational pyramid has been undergoing small but steady changes over the past few years. In 1950, the proportion of Negro adults with some high school or more was about 26 per cent. By 1960 this had increased to about 39 per cent, and in 1965 nearly half of all Negro adults had completed at least one year of high school.

It is very important, however, to put this range of educational achievement in context by examining other factors which influence it. If we first consider urban-rural differences, it seems apparent that the transition of the Negro people from the farm to the city has strikingly increased their educational achievement. While the overwhelming majority (85 per cent) of Negro adults on farms have had no high school education, a slight majority (51.4 per cent) of nonfarm adults have at least some high school. (See Figure 5.)

When we consider differences between the North and South, the picture becomes even more revealing. Outside the South, the proportion of Negro adults with at least some high school was 62 per cent in 1965, an increase from 37 per cent in 1950; and the proportion with some college education was nearly 12 per cent, up from 4 per cent in 1950. In the South, on the other hand, the proportion with some high school was 38 per cent, up from 18 per cent in 1950, and the proportion with some college was 7 per cent, up from 4 per cent in 1950. (See Figure 6.) Regional differentiation is also reflected in the fact that the median level of education for Negroes in the North is nearly two grades higher than for Negroes in the South.

There are also sex differences in the educational achievement of Negro adults. (See Table 3.) But this sex difference is attenuated by geographic

TABLE 3

SEX DIFFERENCES IN THE EDUCATIONAL ACHIEVEMENT
OF THE NEGRO POPULATION OF THE UNITED STATES BY REGIONS
(1950, 1960, AND 1965)

| | North and West | | | | | |
| | 1950 | | 1960 | | 1965 | |
	Male	Female	Male	Female	Male	Female
College	6.3	6.4	8.9	8.8	12.9	10.7
Some High School	29.3	35.1	39.2	45.6	45.6	54.1
8th Grade or Less	64.4	58.5	52.0	45.6	41.5	35.2
	South					
College	3.5	4.7	5.3	6.5	6.9	7.7
Some High School	12.1	16.4	20.5	27.0	28.7	32.4
8th Grade or Less	84.4	79.1	74.2	66.6	64.4	59.9

region and the specific level of education under consideration. Thus while it is true that in the country as a whole Negro women have higher educational levels than Negro men (a median of 8.7 school years completed, compared to 7.7 for the men), in the North among adults with some college education or above, there was no appreciable difference between women and men in 1950. By 1965, the men had considerably outstripped the women, with 12.9 per cent, compared to 10.7 per cent of women with education at this level. In the South, on the other hand, college educated women somewhat outnumbered men—in 1950 by one per-centage point, and in 1965, though the difference had narrowed slightly, women were still more highly represented in this highly educated group —7.7 per cent, compared to 6.9 per cent for the men.

The more striking difference between women and men in educational performance is at the high school level. In both the North and South, and in both 1950 and 1965, a greater proportion of Negro women than Negro men had some high school education or had completed high school. But even this picture shows signs of being modified. While it was still true among the youngest adults in 1965, those between twenty and twenty-four, that a greater proportion of women than men had some high school, it was also apparent that once entering high school, men were more likely to remain in and finish than women. Thus, 33 per cent of the men in this age group who entered dropped out after three years or less while 41 per cent of the women did so. Once having finished high school, men and women in this group were about equally as likely to go to college. But once in college, the women were considerably more likely to finish than the men.

When we come, finally, to examine the impact of age on educational attainment, we find a number of anticipated patterns. (See Table 4.) It is particularly instructive to consider the education of the oldest and the youngest group of Negro adults in 1965.

Among adults sixty-five years old and over in 1965—that is, among persons born before the turn of the century—the overwhelming majority, or about 84 per cent, had not gone beyond the eighth grade, while among the youngest adults, those born just after World War II, between 1945 and 1949, the exact opposite pattern holds. About 85 per cent of these youths have gone beyond the eighth grade and into high school. While one would expect such a finding, it is perhaps of some significance in terms of social change that these youths are the first generation of Negroes of whom it can be said more finished high school than dropped out.

Occupation

The participation of Negroes in the occupational structure has closely paralleled the rise in educational level, though not exactly, and it has

TABLE 4

AGE DIFFERENCES IN THE RANGE OF EDUCATIONAL ACHIEVEMENT OF NEGRO ADULTS IN THE UNITED STATES 20 YEARS AND OVER, BY SEX, IN 1965

Age and Sex	No.	%	8th Grade or Less	1-3 Years High School	High School Graduates	1-3 Years College	4 or More Years College
20-24 years Male	674	100	17.9	32.5	32.5	12.2	1.9
Female	764		10.8	40.8	33.2	10.5	4.6
25-34 years Male	1,073		27.1	27.8	29.4	8.5	7.4
Female	1,302		21.6	32.6	31.5	7.8	6.4
35-44 years Male	1,120		40.8	26.8	20.1	6.9	5.4
Female	1,292		36.4	31.7	22.6	4.8	4.5
45-54 years Male	936		63.8	19.3	8.9	3.0	5.1
Female	1,053		54.7	19.9	17.2	3.3	4.9
55-64 years Male	691		75.8	13.9	6.8	1.2	2.3
Female	750		71.2	13.3	8.4	4.0	3.1
65-and over Male	578		84.3	5.7	6.2	1.4	2.4
Female	702		83.7	8.4	4.7	1.3	1.9

also followed even more closely the changes in geographic mobility. Changes in the occupational structure since 1910 are reflected in Table 5.

Negroes sometimes speak of jobs in several hierarchical categories, as follows: "just jobs" are at the bottom of the scale of income, security, and status. These are typically in the low income occupations of unskilled laborers and service workers. Higher up the ladder are "good steady jobs" of a semi-skilled nature. Higher still are "top jobs" requiring high level skills, typically in the unionized industrial sector. And at the zenith are white collar professional "positions." "Man, I don't want no job," a young man was heard to say recently, "I want me a position!" His meaning was clear, though his chances were not. If we apply this lexicon to the occupational categories reflected in Table 5, we may observe a slight, slow, but steady, change over the past half-century in the proportion of Negro workers occupying "just jobs" and those in the higher categories.

The most dramatic change has been the sharp decrease in the proportion of Negro workers on the farm. At the same time, there has been no striking change in the other "just jobs" category of laborers and service workers. If we combine all the good steady jobs of skilled and semi-skilled blue collar workers, a noticeable increase is discernible from a very small base of 7.9 per cent of the Negro work force in 1910 to an appreciable 40 per cent of all Negro workers in 1965. It will also be observed that the greatest percentage increase in good steady (industrial) jobs occurred in the decades of the 1940s and again in the 1960s. This undoubtedly reflects the heightened industrial activity surrounding World War II and the period of the Vietnam war. Finally, starting from an even smaller base, we may note an almost equally sharp increase in the proportion of Negroes in white collar "positions" between 1910 and 1965. Though the percentage of Negro workers in all jobs above the most menial category has increased from about 11 per cent in 1910 to nearly 55 per cent in 1965, it must still be remarked that only about half of Negro workers can count on the kind of job status that provides economic security for their families.

There are, of course, regional differences in the status of Negroes in the occupational structure as shown by Table 6. These differences are particularly striking in the higher status job categories. Thus, in the nation as a whole, 8.2 per cent of Negro men are in the categories of professional, technical, and managerial. In the North and West this rises to 10.3 per cent, and in the South falls to 6.4 per cent. The regional difference is confounded, however, by sex differences. In the United States as a whole, Negro women outnumber Negro men in the highest job categories, where 10.8 per cent of them compared to 8.2 per cent of

TABLE 5

PERCENTAGE OF NEGRO WORKERS IN MAJOR OCCUPATIONAL CATEGORIES (1910–1965)*

Occupational Categories	1910	1920	1930	1940 **	1950 **	1960 **	1965
White Collar	3.0	3.6	4.6	6.0	10.2	13.4	14.9
Skilled Blue Collar	2.5	3.0	3.2	3.0	5.5	6.1	10.7
Semi-skilled and Operatives	5.4	7.3	9.4	10.3	18.3	19.6	29.3
Laborers and Service Workers	38.7	39.5	46.7	47.3	45.5	44.5	37.6
Farm Workers	50.4	46.6	36.1	32.8	19.0	8.1	7.6

* Current Population Reports, Population Characteristics, Series P-20, #155, Sept. 27, 1966, U. S. Dept. of Commerce, Bureau of the Census. See also Eli Ginsberg and Dale L. Hiestand, "Employment Patterns of Negro Men and Women," in John P. Davis, ed., *The American Negro Reference Book*, op. cit., p. 220.

** Sum does not equal 100.0 because of those for whom no occupation was given.

TABLE 6

OCCUPATION OF THE EMPLOYED NEGRO POPULATION 18 YEARS AND OVER AND MEDIAN SCHOOL YEARS COMPLETED FOR THE UNITED STATES AND REGIONS, MARCH 1965 *

Sex and Occupation	United States		North and West		South	
	%	Median School Years	%	Median School Years	%	Median School Years
Male	100	9.9	100	11.1	100	8.6
Professional, Technical Managerial	8.2	16.5	10.3	15.6	6.4	B
Clerical, Sales, etc.	6.7	12.5	9.6	12.4	4.2	B
Craftsmen, Foremen, etc.	10.7	10.2	13.6	11.4	8.2	8.8
Operatives, etc.	29.3	10.0	33.6	10.7	25.5	8.9
Service workers, etc.	15.6	10.1	16.4	10.4	14.9	9.5
Farmers, etc.	7.6	4.8	0.7	B	13.5	5.2
Laborers, etc.	22.0	8.6	15.8	9.5	27.3	7.9
Female	100	11.1	100	12.0	100	9.9
Professional, Technical Managerial	10.8	16.2	9.8	B	11.9	16.4
Clerical, Sales, etc.	13.1	12.6	18.8	12.5	7.2	B
Craftsmen, Foremen, etc.	0.7	B	1.0	B	0.4	B
Operatives, etc.	14.8	10.7	21.4	11.2	8.1	B
Service workers, etc.	58.1	9.7	47.6	10.7	68.7	8.9
Farmers, etc.	1.5	B	0.1	B	3.0	B
Laborers, etc.	1.0	B	1.2	B	0.7	B

B = Base less than 150,000

* Current Population Reports, Population Characteristics, Series P-20, #155, Sept. 27, 1966, U. S. Dept. of Commerce, Bureau of the Census.

male workers are located. When we consider the North and West, men slightly outstrip women, but in the South, where schoolteaching has been traditionally open to Negro women, the 11.9 per cent of women in professional, technical, and managerial jobs considerably outstrips the 6.4 per cent of Negro men. A similar pattern is found in the area of clerical and sales jobs.

Labor Force Participation

The participation of Negroes in the occupational sphere cannot be fully appreciated without reference to those adults out of work. In 1966, fully 86.6 per cent of Negro married men were in the labor force. But at the same time, 5.1 per cent of them were officially unemployed, an unemployment rate over twice that for non-Negro workers.[6] This figure, however, understates the number of men out of work, for at least another 5 per cent of Negro men between the ages of eighteen and sixty-five were not in the labor force, which means essentially that they were out of work and had not been looking for work recently.

Among unmarried men who were heads of families, 75 per cent were in the labor force, and their official unemployment rate was 9.1 per cent. And among female heads of families, 51.4 per cent were in the labor force, with the unemployment rate among those actively seeking work 7.1 per cent.

In general, the participation of Negro adults in the occupational structure is mixed. It is depressed considerably by the combination of history and contemporary social forces, including the pervasive racial barrier which confronts black workers and potential workers at every stage of the occupational structure and in every part of the country. Occupational opportunities are greater for Negro workers in the North than in the South, and in the South, particularly, they are better for Negro women than for Negro men. They are better for Negro men between thirty-five and fifty-four and worse for men at the extreme of their adult years. Thus, Negro men are forced to enter the job market later than other men, and forced to leave it at early retirement on obviously inadequate pensions, if they have pensions at all.

At the same time, while the bulk of Negro workers are concentrated in the lower level jobs, there is a measure of occupational differentiation slowly emerging. The bulk of Negro workers is still confined to "just

[6] Special Labor Force Report No. 80, "Marital and Family Characteristics of Workers, March 1966," *Monthly Labor Review* Reprint from April 1967 issue, U. S. Dept. of Labor, Bureau of Labor Statistics, Washington, D. C., Table T, p. A–22.

jobs," but a small and ever so slowly emerging pyramid reflects the fact that many Negro workers are moving into "good steady jobs," "top jobs," and "positions" which provide a measure of economic security for their families. Surely one of the paradoxical consequences of this occupational differentiation is that "just jobs" are increasingly unavailable, and when they are available they are less able to satisfy the economic, social, and psychological needs of the ordinary black man.

Income

There are strong parallels among the levels of education, occupation, and income in Negro families. Just as about half of all Negro adults have less than high school education, and nearly half are located in the lowest levels of the occupational structure, so half of all Negro families had total family incomes of less than $4,000 in 1965. The relationship among these three factors, however, is not complete. Thus it would be a mistake to assume that Negroes are poor because they do not have good jobs, which is, in turn, because they are not highly educated. These factors are confounded by the color factor. For as poorly educated as the Negro population is, and as important as education is to achievement, we know full well that Negroes with similar education as whites do not have similar job opportunities, and that Negroes with similar jobs do not get similar pay, as a general rule. In 1960, Negro men between the ages of eighteen and sixty-four with less than eighth grade education could count on earning—over their working life—only about 61 per cent as much as white men of similar age and education.

In fact, Negro men must have between one and three years of college education in order to equal the earnings of white men with less than an eighth grade education. And after completing college and earning a one-year master's degree, the Negro man can count on earning only what a white man can earn who has only graduated from high school. There is, of course, some disparity in the quality of education offered Negroes and whites. But that is surely not the whole explanation. For how much education does a truck driver need? There are contemporary social forces at work independently of the ability of Negro workers which help to suppress their earning potential. And family income has a most powerful effect on the structure and function of Negro family life.

It is in part because of this discrimination in the opportunity structure, both historical and contemporary, that studies of Negro life which seek intimate comparisons of Negro and white behavior, even when they "control for social class," are not comparing comparable experiences. There are other reasons too, but money alone, we are now arguing, makes such comparisons misleading. Consider, for example, the lower class. In 1960, Negro families in the bottom 20 per cent of the income scale had average family incomes 43.2 per cent of the average income of the poorest 20 per cent of white families—a drop in relative position from 47.4 per cent in 1947.[7] Negro families in the highest 20 per cent of the income scale do a bit better. Their average earnings in 1960 were 63.5 per cent of white earnings in the same category, showing slight improvement over the 58.3 per cent in 1947.

The shadows of the plantation which linger in both the opportunity structure of the wider society and the capabilities of the Negro people are most glaringly reflected in family income. Yet despite this situation, Negro families show a variety of income patterns. It is no longer accurate to refer to the overwhelming majority of Negro families as poor. A number have managed to rise out of poverty—indeed, a few never knew poverty—and large numbers have moved into the marginal, middle, and upper income categories. The diversity of Negro family income is represented in Table 6.

The data also shows that Negro families who made the transition from the South to the North and West have appreciably enhanced their economic security. Thus in the country as a whole, 38.6 per cent of Negro families were in the poverty category earning less than $3,000 in 1965. Another 14.9 per cent of families hovered in the deprivation zone just above the poverty level, earning between $3,000 and $4,000, making a total of 53.5 per cent of all Negro families in the distinctly low income range.

In the Southern part of the country, these combined low income families accounted for more than two thirds of all Negro families, while in the North and West they accounted for only about a third.

A fifth of all Negro families were located in that vast marginal area where family incomes range from $4,000 to just under $6,000. Another fifth of Negro families had earnings in the solid middle income range between $6,000 and just under $10,000. And 6.6 per cent of Negro families count on the incomes in the comfortable to affluent range of $10,000 and above. It should be added that in this high income group, 90 per cent of the families could only remain there by having two or more wage earners, including typically both husband and wife.

Thus, at the time when the Labor Department estimated that a family of four required an annual income of $6,000 in order to maintain a modest

[7] Andrew Brimmer, "The Negro in the National Economy," in *The American Negro Reference Book*, p. 270.

but adequate standard of living, about a quarter of all Negro families could exceed that standard. In the North and West, nearly 40 per cent of Negro families could beat this standard, but in the South only about 15 per cent.

Housing

A fourth respect in which Northern urbanization has had an impact on Negro family life is in the area of housing. Here again the picture is mixed. Thus, despite the economic power of Negro families in the North, home ownership, an important index of social status, is greater among Negro families in the South than in the North. And within the South, home ownership is greater among Negroes who live outside the large, metropolitan areas than among the urbanites. This is, in large measure, due to the increased cost of housing in the urban and Northern communities, accompanied by more rigid standards of adequacy. It does not necessarily suggest that Southern Negro families are better housed than their Northern counterparts, although it may suggest a greater investment and a sense of belonging on the part of Southern home-owning Negro families.

In other respects, the housing picture is less ambiguous. While 10 per cent of Negro families in Northern metropolitan areas occupy substandard dwellings, this may be said of 30 per cent of Southern Negro families in similar metropolitan areas. Among Southern Negro families living outside metropolitan areas who own their own homes, fully 72 per cent are considered substandard. If we turn to the renters, the disparity between North and South is further apparent. Among Northern Negro families who rent, 28 per cent live in substandard housing, while among Southerners in metropolitan areas, this figure rises to 47 per cent; and if we consider Southerners living outside these metropolitan areas, the proportion living in substandard housing increases to 89 per cent. Thus, while home ownership is greater among Negroes in the South, it is apparent that the quality of those homes is somewhat inferior to the quality of homes in the North.

Another respect in which housing has implications for Negro family life is in the age of the housing. Here among both owners and renters, Negro families in the South are more likely to occupy new dwellings, built since 1950, than Negro families in the North. The reason for this is in part because the mobility pattern for Negroes in the North is one of residential succession. They are likely to move into the older neighborhoods being vacated by whites, and are not as likely to move into newly developed neighborhoods and housing. In the South, there is more of a tendency for Negro neighborhoods to expand by the addition of new houses within or adjacent to the neighborhood, in part because of the availability of land. Consequently, among Negro families in the North who own their homes, only 11 per cent of their homes were built since 1950, while in the South this percentage is 28. But the mean value of homes owned by Negroes is higher in the North than in the South. In the metropolitan North the mean value was $9,400, whereas in the metropolitan South it was $6,900, and in the nonmetropolitan South $5,000 in 1960.

Further indication of the pattern of residential succession among Negro families in the North is drawn from the census data of 1960. In that year, nearly 41 per cent of the dwelling units occupied by Negro families in the North had been occupied by white families in 1950, and only 13 per cent of the units occupied by Negro families was new construction. In the South, the picture is different; there only 15 per cent of the dwellings occupied by Negro families in the cities had previously been occupied by whites, and nearly 20 per cent was new construction.[8]

Thus, on balance, while the conditions of the urban ghetto are oppressive indeed, Negro families seem to improve their housing condition by moving to the urban areas, particularly of the North and West. Yet it must be stressed that for the Negro families in the Northern urban areas, housing is perhaps their chief external badge of inferiority. The housing is not only worse than that of their white neighbors, it is in many respects worse than that of their fellow Negroes in the South. It is little wonder that family life in the urban ghetto is grossly circumscribed and filled with potential for social upheaval. They have not been able to escape to the suburbs to find the grass and trees and open space they left behind, for suburbia, the great white noose around the urban center cities, has not been opened to them in any part of the country to any appreciable extent.

Negro families are more highly concentrated in the urban ghettos of our country than any other major social group. There are a number of indications that this concentration is on the increase. This is true not only for the major cities but for scores of minor ones as well. A study of residential segregation by Karl E. and Alma F. Taeuber, using relatively objective measures of the exclusive concentration of Negroes and whites,

* Taeuber and Taeuber, p. 143.

has suggested that in every American city the general pattern is for
Negroes and whites to live separately.[9] It is also true that Negroes generally live in the poorer sections of these cities. Taeuber calculated the
segregation index of 207 American cities, using a scale which ranged
from zero, representing complete residential integration, to 100, representing complete separation. His findings ranged from a low segregation
index of 60.4 in San Jose, California, to a high of 98.1 in Fort Lauder-
dale, Florida. The median for all cities was 87.8. It seems highly unlikely
that the historic Federal open housing legislation passed after the death
of Dr. Martin Luther King in 1968 will affect this pattern of segregation
without more basic reforms in the housing system.

Preference, Poverty, and Prejudice

When we consider the specific reasons for the concentration of Negroes in the ghetto, some attention must be given to preference. Negroes
live in the ghetto in part, then, because they like living there. They have
certain sentimental attachments to the place and certain broader cultural
attachments to their fellow urban villagers. In this respect Negroes are
not unlike other ethnic minorities. The in-group feeling among Negroes
is not often given recognition, in part because it is most often considered
a negative value by both whites and Negroes. Nor is the preference for
living in the ghetto confined to low income Negroes. In a study of residential preferences and practices among middle income Negroes in Boston, Dr. Lewis Watts and his associates found a surprising attachment to
the ghetto among middle income Negro families who were required to
move because of urban renewal and for whom houses in neighborhoods
outside the ghetto were available.[10] The researchers concluded that:

> The family willing to support the Negro rights' organizations in striving
> for wider choice in housing may, perhaps, be personally committed to life
> in Washington Park, at the same time regarding it as a social responsi-
> bility to fight for the opportunity *not* to live there.[11]

The preference factor for Negro residence in the ghetto would seem
to deserve further research. Whatever the strength of this factor, how-

[9] *Ibid.*, p. 147.
[10] Lewis G. Watts, Howard E. Freeman, Helen M. Hughes, Robert Morris, and
Thomas F. Pettigrew, "The Middle Income Negro Family Faces Urban Renewal,"
Research Center of the Florence Heller Graduate School for Advanced Studies in
Social Welfare, Brandeis University, for the (Massachusetts) Department of Commerce and Development, 1964.
[11] *Ibid.*, p. 112.

ever, it is obviously outweighed by the factor of poverty. For even a cursory inspection of residential patterns will show that those Negroes who do move out of the ghettos are those in the middle and upper income groups who can afford to purchase homes and who have the necessary social contacts with whites to make this possible. But it is becoming increasingly clear to social scientists who study the phenomenon, as it has been clear to Negroes for a hundred years, that the relationship between poverty and ghetto living for Negroes is largely spurious. Far more relevant than the existence of poverty among Negroes is the existence of prejudice among whites as a factor causing the concentration of Negroes in the ghetto. The Taeubers found that residential segregation is rampant throughout the country "regardless of the relative economic status of the white and Negro residents." [12]

It would seem, then, that among the major causes of the concentration of Negro youth in the urban ghettos are those factors associated with preference, poverty, and prejudice, but that chief among these is prejudice. The confinement of Negroes to the ghetto is not an isolated phenomenon, for it is both a result and a key index to a general pattern of social exclusion of Negroes from the mainstream of American life.

[12] Karl E. Taeuber and Alma F. Taeuber, *Negroes in Cities* (Chicago: Aldine Publishing Co., 1965), p. 36.

Part 3

BLACK MOBILITY

Chapter 4

Screens of Opportunity:
Sources of Achievement in Negro Families

Let us now specify and illustrate our own conception of "opportunity screens" which have enabled some Negro families to survive, and to move beyond survival to stability and social achievement. We use the term "screens" rather than "doors" advisedly, for as we have shown above, the doors of opportunity available to other ethnic groups in our society have been historically and persistently denied the Negro people as a whole—first by slavery, then by the failures of reconstruction, and persistently by contemporary social forces which exclude the Negro people from an equitable place in the society. At the same time, however, while life has not been a "crystal stair," it has not been all bleak. From time to time opportunities have been opened up in various levels of society, even during slavery, which have enabled a most resilient people to survive and in a few cases to prosper.

Opportunity Screens

Consistent with our view of the Negro family as a social system, four levels of opportunity may be specified, corresponding to four levels of society—namely, the individual, the family, the community (or neighborhood), and the wider society.

Some individuals seem to be born with talents denied others, enabling them to take advantage of opportunities in ways others are not able to do. We speak, then, of the personality dimension, that still mysterious inner recess of the human spirit made up of mixed but unknown quantities of inheritance and social conditioning.

Prominent in the background of Negro men and women of achievement is a strong family life. Strong families are those which seem to be guided in their patterns of interaction among members and with the outside world by a definite set of values or philosophy, with an accompanying pattern of behavior consistent with those values, and a certain degree of independence and control of the forces affecting the lives of their members. Strong families are often highly influenced by the religious convictions and behavior, the education or educational aspirations of one or more members. They often have an economic footing more secure than the average Negro family in their community. They often have strong social and emotional ties. These factors—religion, education, money or property, jobs, family ties, and other community-centered activities—are the chief ingredients of strong family life. As we shall see shortly, it need not be a great deal of money or education to set the family apart and provide a head start for its young members and those of succeeding generations; Negro families have shown an amazing ability to survive in the face of impossible conditions. They have also shown remarkable ability to take the barest shreds of opportunity and turn them into the social capital of stability and achievement.

But strong family does not necessarily imply that every single member must be present or strong. Many a Negro man or woman can point to the almost single-handed efforts of one parent or the other, or of an older or younger sibling, or of some extended relative or some member of the augmented family (nonrelative) who make remarkable contributions to holding the family together or helping to pull or push it to new heights of achievement, or to stimulating the dreams of junior family members. But the rest of the family, or at least major segments of it, must be responsive to the efforts of the strong one, or the interaction effect is lost, the social force is dissipated, the family does not become an achieving unit. Thus, each of the twelve major types of family structures outlined in Chapter I and, in fact, each of the derivatives of these major forms can sustain strong and viable family life given a judicious combination of strong individuals and strong societal supports.

The Negro community represents a third level of social support for the Negro family. In a stream of historical development reaching back to centuries in Africa—broken partly by the slave system—Negro families have placed heavy emphasis and reliance on interactions with both relatives and nonrelatives outside the immediate nuclear family. Thus figures of importance in the community—the chief, or elders, the minister, teacher, or other responsible adults—have always been called upon to help the family socialize its children. Many a Negro man or woman can point to a member of the community who made the difference in his success or failure in life. There are several ways in which community members supplement the efforts of the family to socialize their children to conformity and achievement. First, and historically, community members have served almost as extensions of the family and parents. In every aspect of the child's life a trusted elder, neighbor, Sunday School teacher, schoolteacher, or other community member might instruct, discipline, assist, or otherwise guide the young of a given family. Second, as role models, community members show an example to and interest in the young people. Third, as advocates they actively intercede with major segments of society to help young members of particular families find opportunities which might otherwise be closed to them. Fourth, as supportive figures, they simply inquire about the progress of the young, take a special interest in them. Fifth, in the formal roles of teacher, leader, elder, they serve youth generally as part of the general role or occupation.

It has often happened that when parents or other relatives had no special attachments to institutions in the community, children have nevertheless been brought into the orbit of such institutions. We have already referred to the church as chief among the institutions in the Negro community which has played a positive role with regard to Negro family life. The school, in a more specialized and limited way, has served similar ends. In Northern urban communities, settlement houses have played a similar, though minor role in this respect. However, the more middle class character building institutions, such as YMCA, YWCA, Girl Scouts, Boy Scouts, Campfire Girls, have seldom had more than a marginal place in the life of lower class Negro communities. Less formal groups, such as baseball leagues, have been of considerably more importance.

But both formally and informally, the wider society—that is to say, the white society—has held the keys to the survival and prosperity of Negro families and the achievement of family members. Families cannot meet their responsibilities unless the necessary resources and supports are provided by that society, including particularly the economic, health, educational, political, and other subsystems of the society. In thousands of informal and individual ways, too, members of the white establishment have provided opportunity screens for the survival and achievement of Negro families and members. Richard Wright, for example, tells of his indebtedness to the white man who lent him his library card, and the other who advised him to leave the South "and the others whose offers of friendship he was too frightened to accept." [1]

These four levels of society, then, serve as the sources of the achievement of Negro men and women. Many of them are mediated through

[1] Ralph Ellison, "Richard Wright's Blues," in *Shadow and Act* (New York: Random House, Inc., 1953), p. 93.

the family as the core institution of society. Let us now see how these supportive forces are generated within the experience of particular families to provide the opportunities, particularly for the socialization of young members of Negro families. It will not be our purpose to exaggerate the importance of any particular one of these resources. We aim, instead, to show that progress for the Negro people and success for Negro families have historically depended on the most tenuous holds on privilege and opportunity, and to show that many families have been able to take advantage of the most minimal scraps of opportunity and convert them into outstanding achievement, and not incidentally, to suggest that the reasons for the success of outstanding Negroes is often not as mysterious as we are often led to believe. The sources of such achievement could be replicated for hundreds of thousands of other individuals and families if there was conscientious devotion to the task on the part of social planners and institutions at the highest and at the most immediate neighborhood levels. (This last matter will be the specific subject of our final chapter.)

Before proceeding, however, it might be well to consider briefly the question: Why focus on social achievement among selected Negro families? First, in the interest of an accurate picture of Negro family life, it is important to know something about this substantial proportion of Negro families. Current studies of Negro families ignore these families in their concentration on those at the other extreme who tend to cause society a great deal of concern. Secondly, by focusing on families of significant social achievement, we may learn some of the factors which helped produce this achievement, in the hope that they may be applicable to other Negro families. Our view is that an understanding of the paths to survival, stability, and achievement among some Negro families may be more appropriate to helping other Negro families achieve than reference to the pathways followed by non-Negro ethnic groups. Third, we focus on social supports rather than on the personality characteristics of the individuals who have succeeded, in part because the personality data are not as accessible to us, but mostly because the social factors that obstruct or facilitate the family in producing achieving members are factors that the society can do something about. This more hopeful method of analysis stems from the perspective of social change. And finally, this kind of analysis suggests to us that if these Negro families could achieve such outstanding success with such limited supports, such scraps of privilege and opportunities, then, if our society can bring itself to abolish the legacy of slavery, to "heal our history," as President

Lyndon Johnson says, and to provide a more complete and systematic
set of social supports to Negro families, the level of achievement among
them would be remarkable indeed. The whole society would stand to
benefit. The history of the Negro people, and their ability to survive and
to achieve in the face of such overwhelming odds, attests to the resiliency
of the human spirit. For whatever else the Negro people may be, they
are "complexly and compellingly human."

THE POINDEXTER FAMILY

In order to clarify the manner in which achievement is nurtured by
the Negro family as a social system, let us consider three family histories:
The Poindexter family, the Langston family, and the King family.

Dr. Hildrus Poindexter retired on May 25, 1965, at the age of sixty-four
from his position as medical director, U. S. Public Health Service, after
thirty years of service.[2] A specialist in tropical diseases, he served in
more than seventy-five countries as part of his professional mission until
retiring to his home in Clinton, Maryland, to devote himself to the
writing of scientific papers. His achievement has earned for him a secure
place in the black establishment and, indeed, in the wider world of
professional and social status. What are some of the factors in his family
background that help to account for his achievement? What were some
of the opportunity screens which allowed him to succeed where others
could not?

In a letter he wrote to Horace Mann Bond on February 7, 1958, while
serving as Chief Public Health Officer in Paramaribo, Surinam, he provides us with his views on this question:[3]

My mother had a fifth grade education. She was an excellent mother,
quite robust and healthy. Her parents were slaves until emancipation. I
never saw them. She was born shortly after emancipation. She lived as a
child, wife, and mother, on farms in Virginia, Kentucky, and Tennessee
all her life.

My father was a mulatto and took the family name of the slave owner.
My father's mother I have never seen. My father's father I remember see-
ing when I was a small child. He was a white man who rode in a surrey
drawn by two fine horses. My father inherited a strong body and rather
fiery temper. He never attended any formal school. He always worked

[2] *Atlanta World* (Thursday, May 27, 1965).
[3] We are indebted to Dr. Poindexter for written permission to use these materials.

on a farm, rarely clearing a hundred dollars per year for the whole family. He never owned a farm. He worked the year round, farming, hunting, trapping, etc.

His children were well fed, poorly clothed, and poorly housed. We children never had more than a nickel per week to spend on Saturday at the store, until we were old enough to go out for extra work, but we always had plenty to eat. Thus the children grew up physically healthy, but only one chose to continue education beyond the high school level.

I began primary school at age seven years. Because of the difficulty of regular attendance at school in the rural district (eight miles walk daily), eight years were required to complete seven years of primary school. The average attendance per year was four months.

There seemed to be no decent future for an ignorant Negro farmer in the Delta of West Tennessee. But I noticed as a small boy, that there were certain Negroes who were respected in the community. Among them were a Negro doctor, a Negro minister, and a Negro school principal. These intellectuals were my inspiration and stimulated my desire to "escape" from a life of ignorance and poverty.

With my life savings of $40.00, at the age of fourteen years, I left farm, bed, board, and security of family to enter a Presbyterian High School and normal school at Rogerville in East Tennessee. I have not been back except for vacations.

There were three people who supported this rupture with the family and the beginning of an "adventure," viz., my mother, the local Negro doctor (Dr. Byas), and the Presbyterian minister, who also was my primary school principal, Reverend H. L. Peterson. It was Rev. Peterson, a Johnson C. Smith graduate, who arranged for me to enter Swift Memorial High School in Rogerville, Tennessee, as a special student. I could not qualify for regular admission because of the poor rural elementary school background.

At Swift Memorial High School in Rogerville, I had three jobs as well as three extra subjects each semester than that required of other students. I had no money or social ties, so I mostly worked and studied. In order to pay for my board, tuition, and clothes, the three jobs were: (a) firing the boiler to keep the girls' dormitory warm at night, (b) cleaning up a bank building in the town of Rogerville, Tennessee, in the afternoon— after school hours, (c) milking a cow and making a fire in the kitchen stove and living room of a rich family in the city every morning. For this I received a good breakfast and a few dollars each week.

I left Rogerville three months before the close of school in 1920, because I had finished all the required high school subjects. I left in order to work in Detroit to make money to come to Lincoln [University]. Even though my marks qualified me for valedictorian of my high school class, as you know, my diploma was held up because I left before Commencement. You may recall that I had to take an entrance examination to enter Lincoln. The record shows that I finished the four years required high school courses and most of the Normal School courses within three years. From the time I entered Lincoln to date, Dr. Bond, you know the story.

It is quite a story. Dr. Poindexter earned an A.B., cum laude, from Lincoln University, did further study at Dartmouth, earned his M.D. at Harvard, earned an A.M., Ph.D., and M.P.H. (Masters Degree in Public Health) at Columbia, and did postdoctoral studies in tropical diseases at the University of Puerto Rico. He holds certifications in preventive medicine, microbiology, epidemiology, and has been variously a university professor, medical practitioner, and government official.

When viewing such singular achievement in the face of such overwhelming odds, we are justifiably awed, puzzled, and proud. We are particularly impressed with the two elements which stand out immediately in the history of such a man. These are the tremendous psychological resilience of the man, which helps to account for his achievement, and on the other hand, the overwhelming obstacles which his society placed before him in the rural South just after the turn of the century. We are just as likely, then, to overlook or minimize two other very important social facts. The first is that he did not make it alone, and the second is that he was not alone in making it.

Sources of Support

Dr. Poindexter and others like him did not succeed solely and exclusively on the basis of their individual capacities and abilities. They succeeded where most Negroes did not, in large measure because of social supports available to them, however fragmentary and incomplete. These are what we consider the screens of opportunity. On the basis of Dr. Poindexter's letter, we can identify four major areas of these supports—namely (1) in his immediate family, (2) in the Negro community around him, (3) in the subsociety of his boarding school experience, and (4) in the wider world beyond Tennessee.

Let us consider first some of the social supports provided in his immediate family. We may conclude that he had a strong and supportive family. First, he had two parents. In that respect, we may say, as did a child in a California ghetto, that he was born "with a silver spoon in his mouth." [4] Second, both his parents were healthy. He had, in fact, two

---

[4] Red Stephenson in Charles E. Silberman, *Crisis in Black and White* (New York: Random House, Inc., 1964), p. 226.

strong parents, in both the physical and the social sense. Third, his
mother was literate. To say that she had only fifth grade education is
to place her at about the median level of education for Negroes of her
generation. But it is apparent from his letter that she was imbued with
the values of learning and imparted them to her children. Fourth, his
father was not only healthy, but industrious and able to work the year
round, even after the harvest had been reaped. The mulatto complexion
of his father was also a distinct asset to this family. Being the son of a
white man of means gave his family a certain social status, and even more
important, certain protections and opportunities not available to less
fortunate Negro families. Fifth, he had other siblings. He was able to
pursue his studies and to leave home, in part no doubt because there
were others left behind to help. Whatever the limitations and disad-
vantages of large families today, it is apparent that they were an economic and social asset in rural Tennessee in Poindexter's youth. The
sixth kind of family support is that he was always well fed. Many Negroes in the rural south of his generation and later, and even today,
would not be able to make that statement. Seventh, he and all the children were, like their parents, healthy. Finally, this family context provided him with spending money and the values and habits which go
along with that. Having only a nickel a week to spend is indeed little,
but only by comparison with those who have more. It was a fortunate
parent who could impart such wealth to his children during the period
of Poindexter's youth. When that provision and set of habits are combined
with the fact that as he and the children grew older, opportunities were
available to earn, to keep, and to spend larger sums, including his $40.00
savings at age fourteen, we are able to view this in the context of social
supports which provided an important background for his early childhood socialization. These conditions, however minimal they seem, were
not available to the vast majority of Negro youth of his generation.

Dr. Poindexter's social supports were not limited to his immediate
family. In the Negro community, which helped to define and to sustain
his family, he found two powerful sources of his head start. Most important of these were the Negro role models available to him who took
a special interest in him. Many a Negro boy has been encouraged in his
social achievement by the kind and sometimes forceful hand of members
of the black establishment. Thus the Negro minister, schoolteacher, doctor, and occasionally the undertaker have provided a kind of support
often absent in urban ghettos today. In addition, the community provided a school for young Poindexter. To enter school at age seven and
to take eight years to do seven grades of work may be viewed solely

as handicaps, but in the context of the time and place, they were privileges not universally available to Negro boys. He was able to go in part because he wanted to, in part because the school was there, in part because his parents and family let him, and in part because these role models encouraged him. It was not an inevitable development. Compulsory school attendance for Negro boys in the rural south is indeed a relatively recent development, whose enforcement followed only after the decline of the agricultural economy.

A third major source of support for young Poindexter came from the subsociety generated by his matriculation at boarding school. It is significant that this was a private, religious, boarding high school for Negro boys and girls in East Tennessee about the time of World War I. Here he came in contact with a variety of scholars. He was, for the first time, enmeshed in a total subculture which emphasized learning. The separation from home and peers, even for well-motivated adolescents, is often indispensable for achievement. "I had no money or social ties," he tells us, "so I mostly worked and studied." In addition, the very jobs he held provided important secondary socialization into upward mobility. His firing the furnace in the girls' dorm was a responsible job in which people depended heavily on him, and, indeed, a choice job at the school. His work at the bank brought him into the heart of the prestigious economic institution where he had a position of trust in very close contact with the world of middle class objects. His work for the rich white family gave him similar exposure. Thus, what may be conceived of as menial jobs, when placed in the perspective of steps toward the achievement of a very bright and ambitious boy from the rural south, can also be seen as the screens of opportunity which were available to him, and denied scores of other boys, and which helped him along his way.

Finally, we look to the fourth category of social supports from the wider world beyond Tennessee. Two social forces were paramount. First was the opportunity to go north to Detroit and find work. He does not tell us much about this in his letter, but we are very aware of the timing of this trip in 1920. He must have become aware of opportunities in Detroit in the years of World War I, and he must have known scores of young men and their families who went north on the crest of this great migration. Secondly, the Negro college again looms large in his career. It first became apparent in the background of the minister who urged him to go on to the private high school. Another such college, Lincoln University in Pennsylvania, provided for Dr. Poindexter a flexible entrance procedure and the intellectual environment for an outstanding academic career.

Thus, what at first sight may seem a very underprivileged and deprived background, when compared with the opportunity structure available to the majority of Negro lads, may be viewed as a background of selected and strategic opportunity screens, which, though grossly inadequate, were nevertheless instrumental in enabling a very able young man to pursue the highest calling our society has to offer. These opportunity screens were located in his family, his neighborhood, the subcommunity of boarding school, and the world beyond.

Furthermore, the social supports from all these sources were interlaced with each other. Thus the person, the family, and the community, with periodic healthy assists from unanticipated sources, combined to provide an environment for the remarkable achievements of this remarkable man.

THE LANGSTON FAMILY

Let us consider another achieving family, the Langston family, whose history has been made available to us.[5] The family tree is outlined in Figure 7. The earliest ancestor we have information about is Lucy Langston, who was of mixed Negro and American Indian ancestry. She was the slave of the white planter, Ralph Quarrels, in the years immediately prior to 1800. Quarrels looked upon her with favor, as they say, and took her as his wife. It was apparently an honorable and stable relationship, though without benefit of clergy or the state. Ralph granted Lucy her freedom, and together they had four children between 1800 and 1829 who were recognized as his offspring.

The manner in which this heritage redounded to the benefit of this family is quite impressive. Their son Charles got married, had a daughter Caroline, who got married to a man named Hughes, and in turn had a son, the famous American Negro poet Langston Hughes.

Ralph and Lucy's son, John Mercer, got married, had a daughter Nettie, who married James C. Napier. Napier was educated before the Civil War in a secret school for slaves, until the police discovered it, arrested the teachers, and dismissed all the pupils. He was later sent North to be educated.

While all the children were recognized as the offspring of Quarrels and benefitted thereby, Maria, the first-born, was favored. She inherited lands and slaves from her father. She could receive such inheritance by the

[5] Luther P. Jackson, in *Negro History Bulletin*, XI, No. 3 (December 1947), 51. This material also was made available to us by Dr. Horace Mann Bond.

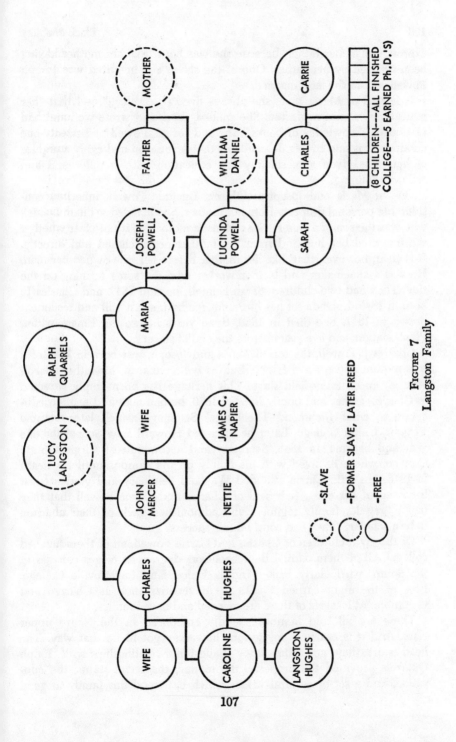

FIGURE 7
Langston Family

(8 CHILDREN---ALL FINISHED
COLLEGE---5 EARNED Ph.D.'S)

- SLAVE
- FORMER SLAVE, LATER FREED
- FREE

107

express will of her father, because she was born free, her mother having been set free by her father. One of the slaves she inherited was Joseph Powell, whom she later married.

It is said of Maria that "she always lived in comfort," and that "her education was not neglected. She spelled, read, and wrote well and had an unusual knowledge of books." She and Joseph Powell had twenty-one children. It is said by her descendants that "every son and every daughter of hers was given a reasonably fair education with sound moral and religious training."

One of Maria and Joseph's children, Lucinda Powell, inherited considerable personal property from her mother. She married William Daniel, who was the son of a free father and slave mother. It is not clear whether she inherited her husband from her mother or purchased him directly. It is clear, however, that, like her mother before her, she owned her man. He was a shoemaker and leather worker who did some farming on the side. They had two children, Sarah Daniels, born in 1842, and Charles J., born in 1845. Lucinda set her husband free by her last will and testament drawn in 1847. She died in 1860, three years before the Emancipation Proclamation, and five years before the end of slavery.

Charles J. Powell, the son of Maria and Joseph, was born in 1845 of a free mother and a slave father. But, as we have seen, his father Joseph was not an ordinary field slave. This heritage has been amply reflected in Charles' career and family life. By 1870, he had acquired enough education to enter Richmond Theological Seminary, which later became Virginia Union College. Later he attended Howard Law School for one year and became, in 1888, Secretary and accountant of Virginia State College, where he lived with his family on the campus until his death in 1916. His wife Carrie attended Wayland Seminary and graduated at the head of her class. It is said of Charles and Carrie Powell that they had a "regular family regimen, and admonished each of their children to be a scholar." They had considerable success.

Of the eight children of Charles and Carrie Powell, all of them finished college! All of them earned their bachelors degrees at Negro colleges in the South, particularly Fisk, Virginia Union, and Fayetteville College. Five of the eight earned Ph.D.s at universities such as Chicago and Columbia. At least six of them are married and have families.

These are all "old families," solidly ensconced in the Negro upper class. And it is not very mysterious how they got to be that way. The head start they got from Lucy Langston's relationship with Ralph Quarrels provided the property, the money, the social status, the education, and a set of cultural values which has stood this family in good stead unto the fifth generation. The history of freedom, property, literacy, mulatto status, and family stability in the early generations, and the influence of the Negro college in later generations are seen as cornerstones to the opportunity screens for this extended family.

This is not to minimize the personal abilities, ambitions, and attributes of the individual members of this illustrious family who continue to distinguish themselves today. It is, rather, to suggest that these personal attributes are the result, in major part at least, of the kind of head start and the kind of social supports they have received from their family and society. It is to suggest, furthermore, that by-products of these kinds of social support have benefitted not only these individuals and their families, but the Negro community as a whole and the wider society. For many of these individuals have made remarkable contributions to education, and thus to both the primary and secondary socialization of countless thousands of American youth, most especially black youth. Finally, this analysis suggests some clues to what the society may need to provide for all Negro families, if a significant number of them are to move beyond survival and stability to the kind of achievement this family represents.

Each generation builds on the assets provided it by the previous generation. For Negro families, these legacies often amount only to scraps of opportunity. They have, nevertheless, been indispensable to an explanation of why some families have been able to survive, conform, and achieve in a manner that meets both the needs of their members and the demands of society. These resources have come from strong individuals, strong families, supportive communities, and elements in the wider society which have often grudgingly and sometimes willingly allowed a few Negro families of each generation to survive and prosper.

THE KING FAMILY

When Dr. Martin Luther King, Jr. was felled by an assassin's bullet on April 4th, 1968, in Memphis at the age of 39, he was clearly among the outstanding leaders of the twentieth century. Among the many inappropriate responses white Americans made to his death and its aftermath, two stand out because they are consistent with the responses white Americans made to the life and work of this remarkable man. One of the responses was to ignore the central message of the man—namely, that racism is an evil which should be overturned—and to concentrate on the strategies he advocated for overturning racism, namely non-violent direct action and confrontation. It was a typical exercise engaged in by Americans of high and low status and of liberal and conservative persuasion.

At the same time even his strategies were widely misinterpreted. It was widely proclaimed by white persons and even a few Negro leaders that Martin Luther King's central message was for Negroes to be non-violent. Nothing could be further from the truth. For Dr. King was better able and more willing than most leaders to see and point up the essential violence in white society and institutions. He thought that Negroes could play a prophetic role in helping to overturn racism and violence practiced by white people and that among the strategies for doing that, non-violent direct action and confrontation should be given the highest priority.

A second major inappropriate response to Dr. King's death on the part of white Americans was to begin an intellectual search for his "successor." They took the man out of social context and tried to find another single Negro whom they could anoint as "leader of the Negro people," refusing at the same time to accept the mechanism which Dr. King had himself anointed.

It was convenient to ignore the fact that the best way to memorialize Dr. King would be to attend to his central message and work toward changing the institutional fabric of society.

Dr. King was surely a remarkable individual. And yet, much of the basis for his remarkable achievements lay within the context of his family, the Negro community which nurtured and sustained it, and the wider society which provided screens of opportunities not available to the vast majority of Negro families.

The King family illustrates the manner in which opportunity screens from the four levels of society are intertwined with hardships at each of these levels, to provide the background for a remarkable degree of achievement in a family spanning five generations. Life has been "no crystal stair," even for such an achieving family. Because of the candor and fullness with which members of this family have spoken with their biographers, and the richness with which these data illustrate our central thesis—about the Negro family as a social system, and the screens of opportunity which help to sustain it—this history of the King family will be considered in detail.[6]

* The data on the King family has been gathered from a variety of sources. A principal source has been Lawrence Dunbar Reddick's *Crusader without Violence*, copyright © 1959 by Lawrence Dunbar Reddick (New York: Harper & Row, Publishers, 1959). Used by permission of Harper & Row, Publishers.

In the first two generations of this family about which we have data, four factors stand out which are almost classical in the background of Negro families. These are (1) the legacy of slavery in which white men exploited Negro women, (2) the grinding poverty which almost all Negro families knew in the years after the Civil War, (3) a weak father who, nevertheless, did not desert his family, and (4) above all else, a strong, competent, and dominant mother who held the family together in the face of overwhelming odds. Both the causes and the positive functions of matriarchy are graphically illustrated in this family.

The earliest recorded member of the King family was James Albert King, whose own father had been white and of Irish descent. Albert's mother was a full-blooded Negro. Albert grew up in the years after the Civil War in Stockbridge, Georgia, where he was, at first, a landowner and independent farmer. But in addition to being a hard worker, he was also a hard drinker, and drink gradually got the upper hand. He lost his land and became a sharecropper. His wife Delia was a strong woman, physically and spiritually. They had ten children. It is said of them and their times, that "Life was hard, work and children plentiful, and material rewards slight." [7] Of the ten children, one boy died in infancy and a girl died at age fifteen. The others, Woodie Clara, Martin Luther, Leonora, Cleo, Lucille, James Albert, Jr., Henry Lincoln, and Joel Lawrence, all lived to maturity. The children grew up strong and healthy, but largely uneducated. There were about three months of school each year, and teachers were not always competent and devoted. Martin Luther, the second-born, was the illustrious father of the famous Martin Luther King, Jr.

Martin Luther was the second child of Albert and Delia King. He was born December 19, 1899. It is said that he was both physically and psychologically mature beyond his years. There was disagreement between Albert and Delia about the first name of their second child; she wanted him named Michael Luther and Albert preferred Martin Luther. The father won and the boy was officially named Martin, but he was called Michael by all who knew him until long after his mother's death. We shall refer to him as Michael for the sake of clarity.

The strong and dominant hand of a Negro mother in the face of a weak husband slightly suggested by this naming episode is more fully illustrated in its positive dimensions by the following incident. When Michael was about seven or eight years old, his mother sent him on an errand to a neighbor's house a short distance down the road. While walking along, he was accosted by a white man and commanded to take

[7] Reddick, p. 42.

a bucket and bring back some water from a nearby spring. He refused and kept walking on his mother's errand. The white man slapped him. Michael returned home and told his mother, who returned to the scene with her son in tow and confronted the white man: "Did you slap my child?" she inquired. When the white man admitted to the deed, she "struck him several sharp blows, threw him down to the ground and tore most of his clothes off him." [8] Afterward she made her son promise never to mention this to his father or anyone else. She was afraid the father would have wanted to speak to the white man about it, and there would have been trouble. She expected that the white man would be ashamed to face the fact that he had been beaten by a woman, and would not mention the incident on his own initiative. But for a white man to be challenged or assaulted by a Negro man would be a different matter. Thus the mother was able to protect her son in ways the father could not.

Another episode in the stormy life of this family illustrates the close mother-son relationship and the protective nature of it. When Albert got drunk on weekends, he often took out his frustrations on his family by abusing his wife and children. One Saturday night when Michael was about fifteen, Albert came home and began to abuse and beat his wife. Michael came to his mother's defense. He grabbed his father, picked him up, slammed him against the floor, then jumped down and began choking him. The father was rescued by the mother and the other children, and then reached for his shotgun as the son ran out the door. He did not come home that night. Later, when the father was sober, he apologized to his son and commended him for defending his mother. He never beat his wife again. A year later Michael left home, against the wishes of his father but with the support of his mother, who thought it was "for the best." [9]

He arrived in Atlanta in the midst of World War I at the age of sixteen. By putting up his age a few years, he was given an opportunity to try out for a job as locomotive fireman by a kindly white engineer. He did such a good job on his trial run that he was offered the job. He wrote to his mother about his job. Alarmed by the potential dangers, Delia King promptly took the next train to Atlanta and reported his correct age to the authorities. That was the end of one budding career.

But Michael had no difficulty earning money, for World War I served as an opportunity screen. However, the really good jobs always seemed to require a bit more education than he had, so he pursued his studies, and by 1925 was ready to enter Morehouse College. He had, meanwhile,

[8] *Ibid.*, p. 44.
[9] *Ibid.*, p. 45.

turned to preaching and was the pastor of two small churches which he served on alternate Sundays. This enabled him to help support his older sister, Woodie Clara, who had preceded him to Atlanta and who was studying there, and also to help support his family back home.

Meanwhile, his mother died in 1924. Michael was twenty-five years old. Most of his siblings left the South and joined the exodus northward to Detroit. His father moved to Atlanta and took a job at the railroad terminal. Father and son were reconciled.

Thus, in these two generations of the King family, there were a number of sources of achievement. Outstanding in the midst of this mixture of supports and obstacles was the strong, supporting hand of the mother and the robust and ambitious character of the son. His was a strong family despite the weakness of his father. The Negro church and the Negro college are preeminent in the achievement of this family. In the wider society, the transition from an agricultural to an urban society, the war, and the movement from South to North are already evident sources of support.

Martin Luther, Junior

The next generation in the life of this family we observe a shift from the matriarchy to a series of grand patriarchies. At the same time, the Negro school and the Negro church take an increased importance. While attending night school in the city, Michael's older sister Clara had boarded with "a good family," the family of Reverend A. D. Williams, a prominent Baptist minister. The Williamses had a daughter, Alberta, who became good friends with Clara. Clara introduced her brother to Alberta and the Williams family. It was a most fruitful encounter. Alberta was a student in the high school at Spelman College. She later studied at Hampton Institute in Virginia. On Thanksgiving Day 1926, Michael King, a struggling student at Morehouse College and an up-and-coming young minister, was married to Alberta Williams. It was the highlight of the social season. The wedding took place in Reverend Williams' huge Ebenezer Baptist Church, with Reverend Williams "giving the bride away." The wedding ceremonies were conducted by three of the city's most prominent ministers, Reverend James M. Nabrit, Sr., Reverend P. Q. Bryant, and Reverend R. A. Carter.

As a temporary measure, the young Reverend King moved with his bride into the home of her parents. This temporary arrangement was so successful that it was continued for many years. Thus the house on

Auburn Avenue became the permanent home for one of Atlanta's most celebrated extended families.

For the young Reverend King, the opportunity screens began to widen rapidly. He was now doing well as a student in a most prestigious college. He had a successful career in a very responsible and rewarding profession. He had an attractive, young, educated, working wife, and he had the guiding hand of a most prominent and devoted father-in-law. In due course, young Michael finished his studies at Morehouse and succeeded his father-in-law as minister at Ebenezer.

On January 15, 1929, Martin Luther King, Jr., was born. The long arm of the matriarchy hovered over his christening to cast a shadow over his name. Reverend King told the doctor the boy was to be named Junior, whereupon the doctor promptly listed the newest King as Michael Luther King, Jr. It was not until five years later, when the senior Mr. King needed a passport, that the legal ambiguities of their names were cleared away.[10]

If a Negro family at one point in history is matriarchal, time and circumstances can change that. The households of Reverend Williams and the Reverend King were distinct patriarchies. Their status in the community was reflected in the home.

When Reverend Williams died in 1931 at the age of sixty-eight, young Reverend King became the head of the patriarchy. It is said of him that "He was glad to assume the responsibilities of providing for and protecting his wife and children; and in the household, his word, considerate and benevolent as he tried to make it, was final." [11]

But to say that the house on Auburn Street contained one grand patriarchy, peopled by an extended family with shifting heads down through the years, is not to degenerate the role of the mothers and wives. For each of these women was outstanding in her own right. Mama Williams, a woman of robust health, competence, and cheer, took a special interest in her grandchild, Martin Luther, Jr., and exerted strong influence over him. It was a most intimate and protective relationship.

If the King household was a black patriarchy, it was also peopled by "Black Puritans."

The children were taught to love and respect their parents and elders. The old-fashioned verities of hard work, honesty, thrift, order, and courtesy were adhered to faithfully. Education was looked upon as the path

[10] *Ibid.*, p. 61.
[11] *Ibid.*, p. 51.

to competence and culture. The church was the path to morality and immortality.[12]

Order, routine, and ritual were highly respected. "There was a time to play, a time to work, a time to talk and a time to be quiet—for study or prayer, or out of consideration for others." [13]

The senior Martin Luther King had three children: Martin Luther, named for his father, Alfred Daniel, named for his grandfather, and Willie Christine. As they grew up in the big house on Auburn Street, they had a distinctly upper middle class upbringing. They had economic security, a strong father and mother, a protective network of extended kin, and a home atmosphere in which education, morality, and all the middle class virtues were consciously enforced. In addition, the church was an extension of the family.

Each of the three children attended private schools for some part of their lower school education—expected behavior for both the "best families" and the "families on the make," as private schools provided far better education than the public schools in the city. Each child received a good education and has made important contributions to his family, the Negro community, and the wider society. It was Martin Luther, Jr., however, who was most prominent in this generation.

In due course, Martin Luther, Jr., was to follow in his father's footsteps, and eventually to stand on his father's shoulders. He went to Morehouse and beyond. He entered the ministry and eventually became co-pastor at Ebenezer. No ordinary Baptist preacher, he was the foremost Negro leader since Booker T. Washington and the winner of the Nobel Peace Prize, who preached not only to Ebenezer as did his brother, his father, and his mother's father, but to the whole world.

Lawrence Reddick has summed up the first fifteen years of Martin Luther King, Jr.'s life:

. . . The first fifteen formative years of Martin's life had been fortunate. Diverse influences had helped shape and integrate his personality. One of his grandfathers had been a sharecropper; the other a college bred minister. One grandmother he never knew, the other he loved dearly. His own mother was gentle; his father was fearless and protective. He and his brother and sister were bound together by a thousand common experiences. He had pals of his own and was recognized and accepted by countless friends of the family.

Physically, Martin was healthy. Intellectually, he was slightly ahead of

[12] *Ibid.*, p. 51.
[13] *Ibid.*, p. 52.

his age group. Socially, he was enjoying the threshold years of self discovery and the companionship of the opposite sex. He wore good clothes,
had a little money in the bank—and was willing to work for more. Martin
was aware of mean policemen and curt clerks but there were friendly
white teachers at the Lab School. He was happy in his family, his neighborhood, his school and most of the time, his Atlanta. The church was
almost a part of the home.[14]

These are the essential elements of a varied family background and
the articulation of family and community life, which provided the framework for the early childhood socialization of Martin Luther King, Jr.,
as for his father before him. It is a framework of ups and downs, filled
with barriers and opportunities. It contained greater opportunities than
those the vast majority of Negro boys his age have today. This is due
to the remarkable influence of rising social status as reflected in economic security, education, residential pattern, the church, and the
attendant strong and viable family life. Even these, were not sufficient
to obliterate the effects of growing up black in the South. They did,
however, provide the opportunity screens through which this family
escaped the more crippling consequences of inferior status, and fulfilled to a remarkable degree the functions required of it by its members, the Negro community, and the wider society.

The many screens of opportunity available to the King family are
striking throughout five generations. They are reflected at one level
in strong individuals. Here we see the positive influence of the matriarchy as it operated throughout the first two generations and the
strong hand of the patriarchy which came with changing conditions. At
the second level, we observe strong, closely knit families often held
together by the dominant personality of a strong individual. In the
Negro community itself, the peer group, the Church, and the Negro
college are the dominating institutions. In addition, the wider white
society made opportunities available to the various King families not
available to ordinary Negro families in the South or the North.

The sources of stability and achievement in this family are, therefore, varied, long, and deep. They reflect the resiliency of the human
spirit, and the survival and adaptive capacities of Negro family life in
America. Yet the story is incomplete.

Martin Luther King III has an honorable tradition and heritage associated with his name. He was born into one of the world's leading
families. Yet the caste-like qualities of racism are resilient indeed, and

[14] *Ibid.*, p. 51.

the youngest Martin Luther has already felt the stigma of being part of a black family in white America.

FAMILY BACKGROUNDS OF NEGRO PROFESSIONALS

Other Negro men and women of this era have also succeeded in important social roles with the aid of similar opportunity screens. In 1965 there were still alive over 100,000 Negro men and women of the same generation as Dr. Poindexter and the Senior Reverend King who had completed high school at a time when the median education of Negroes throughout the nation was about fifth grade, the median education of Negroes in the South, where most of them were educated, was much lower, and the median education of southern whites was not much higher. They are, therefore, highly educated people. Altogether 30,000 of these men and women went beyond high school into some form of higher education.[16] These men and women are undoubtedly the backbone today of the old families of the Negro upper class. They are a most fascinating and strategic group of people. We need to know more about them and how they made it. We need to know more about the patterns of Negro family and community life about which many of them will have first-hand knowledge spanning as much as five generations. Such a comprehensive study is waiting to be done. Dr. Horace Mann Bond is in the midst of a most important study of the sources of the achievement of Negro professionals, and is finding that the family plays an inordinately large role, as do strategic and limited opportunities from the community and society.

In a letter to Dr. Sadie Daniel, dated January 15, 1963, Dr. Bond spoke of his research and some of his preliminary findings as follows:

> Indeed, prematurely, I would now project my guess to say that the majority of all Negro doctorates, physicians, and Negro college teachers is derived from perhaps less than 500 extended families in existence in 1860.
>
> I have also been astonished to discover how largely the 10 per cent of Negroes who were free in 1860 have dominated the production of Negro professionals (and intellectuals) up to the present day. . . .
>
> Meanwhile, I am quite sure that my final report will be a flop. The title of my research is "A Study of Factors Involved in the Identification and Encouragement of Unusual Academic Talent among Underprivileged Populations."

[16] U. S. Bureau of the Census, U. S. Census of Population, 1960, *The Negro Population* (Washington, D. C.: U. S. Government Printing Office, 1965).

First, I shall have to report that my Negro academic doctorates were not in fact from an "underprivileged" population. Indeed, they are from one of the most "privileged" populations in America.

Second, the factors are very simple. They are (1) a history—preferably long—of family literacy; (2) a father with a determination of iron, an ambition for his children that is illimitable, and a disciplined mind that will exemplify and induce and foster good habits in children; (3) a mother who shares these qualities with her husband, and like him, has boundless love and aspirations for her children; and (4) a good school.

In another letter to Mrs. Charles H. Johnson, dated January 11, 1963, Dr. Bond spells out his views on how a few extended families have produced such remarkable achievement:

> Saying it in another way: there were about 550,000 free Negroes in the United States in 1860. Let us suppose that they represented about 5,000 of the "extended" families I am talking about. I would then say that at least 75 per cent of the "leading" Negroes have come out of about 400 of these families and about 100 slave families that began on the basis of individuals of exceptional ability and status: house servants, etc.
>
> I do not believe this was because these people had a great deal of "white" blood or ancestry as compared to other Negroes. I believe it is an eloquent testimonial to what advantages accrue from somebody in the early history of the family getting a break, in terms of money and education.[16]

From this work of Dr. Bond's, and from my discussion with him, there emerged considerable verification, both for the importance of the family in the background of men of distinction and for some of the specific historical forces which helped to make for strong family life. These include (1) a history of literacy, (2) free status during slavery, (3) lineal descendants from slave masters, (4) special status during slavery—e.g., house servants or artisans instead of field slaves, (5) money and property, (6) a strong father, (7) a strong mother.

In addition, the work of Dr. Bond also illustrates the importance of the community as a source of support for the Negro family. Chief among the supports at this level are (1) a good school, (2) the church, and (3) an intellectual atmosphere in the community.[17] These community forces are, of course, all intertwined. The manner in which they interact to support each other and Negro families can be illustrated by reference to the case of Marion, Alabama.

Because I was born in Marion, Alabama, and consider myself to have

[16] We are indebted to Dr. Bond for making these materials available to us.
[17] Personal communication.

escaped from there at the tender age of seven, it came as something of a bolt of enlightenment for me to learn from Dr. Bond about the positive contributions this community has made to Negro families, including my own, and quite possibly to my own personal career. In going through four or five hundred biographies of men and women in his study, Dr. Bond became struck by the geographic clustering of their origins. He discovered that a relatively large number of Negro professionals and holders of the Ph.D. degree had roots in Alabama. This is shown by the map in Figure 8. The map also shows his discovery that among the doctorates with roots in Alabama, a relatively large proportion had roots in Perry County, of which Marion is the county seat. He then sought to ascertain what it was about Marion, Alabama, which seemed productive of such achievement on the part of Negroes.

He found five factors. The first had to do with the general level of literacy and culture of the white population. Marion was the cultural capital of Alabama before the Civil War, with seven educational institutions located there. Second, there seems to have been a relatively high proportion of domestic slaves, as distinct from field hands, in and around the town of Marion. Third, there was a relatively high degree of literacy among slaves in Perry County even before emancipation, which did not come in Perry County until the collapse of Lee's army in April 1865. A fourth factor was the atmosphere created by the First Congregational Church of Marion, which for thirty years after the Civil War exerted a powerful New England puritan-like influence on the acculturation of the freedmen. The church was also highly integrated with the private school for Negroes. Finally, then, and of most importance in the background of Negro professionals, was the school, the Lincoln Normal School, which started in about 1868 when a group of literate Negroes in Marion got together to organize a School Board, with universal suffrage for all male Negroes in the community. They bought a lot and put up a building, then deeded it to the American Missionary Association.

Dr. Bond was alerted to the importance of this school in the background of his current respondents by an engineer, Dr. William Childs Curtis. "I explain my academic performance," he wrote Dr. Bond, "by the excellent American Missionary Association school that my parents attended. That school was the Lincoln Normal Institute School in Marion, Alabama." This led Dr. Bond to the discovery that "all those dots representing doctorates in Perry County . . . came either directly, or by second or third generation, indirectly from the Lincoln Normal School at Marion, Alabama."

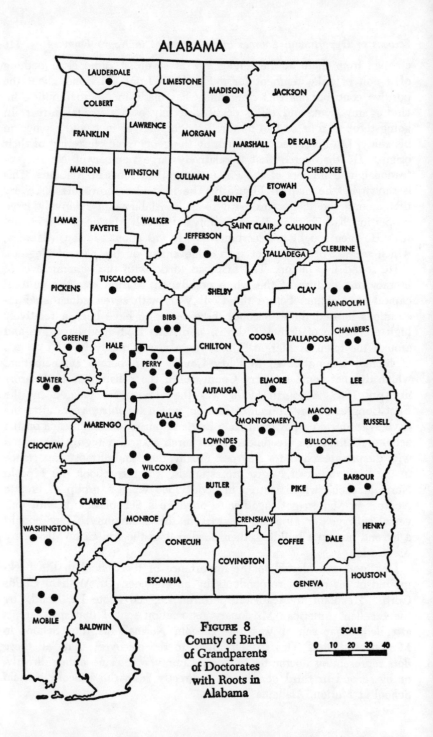

ALABAMA

FIGURE 8
County of Birth
of Grandparents
of Doctorates
with Roots in
Alabama

SCALE
0   10   20   30   40

Only then could I manage to confide to Dr. Bond that standing before him was further confirmation of his thesis. Not only was I, a freshly minted Ph.D. from Brandeis University, born in Perry County, Alabama, but my father was born there and received the only six years of education he ever had from the Lincoln Normal School in Marion. He was a very learned man.

Chapter 5

Social Status in the Black Community

The various social forces described above have converged to form a pattern of social classes among Negro families not altogether unlike that in the general community, but with its own features reflecting the history and struggle for survival of the Negro people.

There are no exact figures on the Negro social class structure. Despite all the references to the Negro lower class, no studies have been done which would estimate the proportion of Negro families in each of the social classes. It has not been done for some of the reasons we have cited in the Appendix. Still, more limited studies have been done, and the census reports have generated comprehensive data on the education, income, and occupation of Negroes. It is thus possible to make some approximations of the shape of the Negro class structure. In the early 1940s, Drake and Cayton, using a combination of education, rental payments, and occupation as criteria, estimated that about 5 per cent of Negro families in Chicago could be considered upper class, 30 per cent middle class, and 65 per cent lower class.[1] Today we would estimate that in the urban areas of the country, where nearly 75 per cent of Negro families live, roughly 10 per cent would be considered upper class, 40 per cent middle class, and 50 per cent lower class in the Negro community. This social class structure is illustrated in Figure 9.

The indices of social class which have been developed in social science research are relatively more reliable when used within white ethnic groups, where they were developed, than when used unmodified with Negro groups. For example, the family of a high school principal in a white community may be considered middle class. In a Negro community, however, in all probability, the Negro high school principal's family will be considered upper class. Not only do absolute levels

[1] St. Clair Drake and Horace Cayton (see footnote 9 and *op. cit.*).

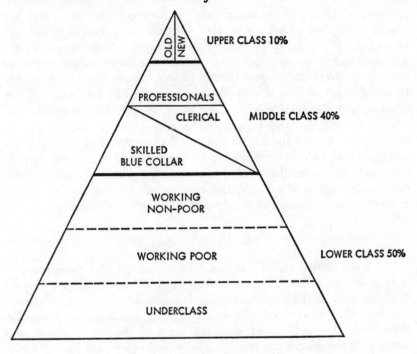

FIGURE 9
Social Classes in the Negro Community

of education, income, and occupation take on somewhat different meanings in the Negro community, but factors other than these, including respectability and community activity, loom large in the attribution of social status.

The problems associated with the description of Negro families in social class terms are so great, particularly at the lower social status levels, that a number of students of the Negro experience are beginning to question its utility. To refer to the masses of Negro families as lower class obscures rather than clarifies much of the variety of status and behavior in that group. And to combine two concepts and refer to this stratum as lower class culture, which is often done, further confounds the reality.

In our view, there is still considerable utility in the concept of social class if it is used carefully. However, the current popularity of the term probably adds to its distortion. It is probably most usefully employed as an index of economic and social position, or of level in the community. In the Negro community, it does not provide a very accurate description of who associates with whom, although it still has relevance for who looks up to or down to whom. It is completely inadequate and inappropriate for describing behavior or values or preferences or styles of life or child rearing patterns in the Negro community. Its chief value is as a description of the basic life conditions of the subjects, and these, of course, have some, though not complete, correlation to attitudes and behavior. The importance of social class for our purposes is that the higher the social class status of a family, the greater access its members have to the resources of the wider community, and the greater the level of supports they receive from the wider community, and consequently, the greater will be the family's ability to meet the requirements of society and the needs of its members.

The Upper Classes

The more differentiated the social class concept, the more accurate it is as a description of social status. It therefore seems very useful to divide each of the three major social classes into further subdivisions. At the upper class level, for example, two subclasses may be distinguished: the "old" upper class families and the "new" upper class families in the Negro community. These distinctions are more parallel than hierarchical.

The old upper class includes those families headed by men and women whose parents before them were upper or middle class. The families of Negro judges, physicians, dentists, high government officials, educated ministers of large congregations, college presidents, and wealthy businessmen, particularly insurance company executives and bankers, are prominent among the old upper class. It often happens that they have built on the head start given them by their parents. Sometimes their grandparents were considerably more privileged than the mass of Negroes, and further back, their ancestors were often either free Negroes during slavery or privileged slaves (house slaves or artisans instead of field slaves), who often inherited money or property, or were given a modicum of education by their masters. Negro families in the old upper class, then, reach back several generations for the roots of their achievement and current status. They have added to this head start and acquitted themselves well in the world of affairs. They are our "Black Brahmins."

The new upper class may have as much or more money, education, and status, but they are likely to have reached the top in one generation, due in large measure to their own talent and good fortune. Prominent among the new upper class are celebrities such as entertainers and athletes, who may become wealthy, famous, influential, and highly prestigious in the community. Still another prominent group in the new upper class which got to the top by talent and good fortune is the "Shadies," those gamblers, racketeers, pimps, and other hustlers who often manage to become wealthy, to wield a considerable amount of influence, and to garner a great deal of prestige in the Negro community.

The old upper class is probably the predominant element in the highest Negro stratum, though the new upper class is growing fast. The hustlers are only a very small segment of the upper class.

Let us illustrate the distinction between old and new upper class families. The Negroes who are now at the very apex of the three branches of the federal government are all excellent representatives of "old families" among the Negro upper class. These are Secretary of Housing and Urban Development Robert Weaver, in the executive branch, Senator Edward W. Brooke in the legislative branch, and Justice Thurgood Marshall in the judiciary. Even before reaching his present government position, each had been at the top levels of his profession, and each could afford to support his family at a level of living distinctly superior to the overwhelming majority of American families. These men are distinctly upper class by any careful assessment of socioeconomic structure, though they are often mistakenly referred to as "middle class" by the general writing public. They are also sometimes referred to in romantic terms as men who "pulled themselves up by their own boot straps." They did nothing of the sort. They are truly remarkable men, but the point we are making is that they had a head start in life, the kind of head start rare in the experience of Negroes of their generation. They are members and products of the "old upper class." They reached the top in large measure because of their origins and upbringing in upper middle class families. They have been able to build upon the head start provided them by their own family of orientation and the concomitant opportunities made available to them.

Each of these men had a distinctly upper middle class or upper class family background. Each had at least one parent who was a college graduate. Each had parents with professional occupations. Each had a measure of economic security denied 90 per cent of the Negro youth of his generation. Each had two parents who were prominent members of the community. Each has meaningful associations with extended families. Each has a light complexion reflecting both the ex-

ploitation and the privilege of the past. Each was able to spend long
years in college and graduate school preparing himself for major
professions. Two took their first degrees at Negro colleges a characteristic source of achievement for Negro upper class families. Two
took their advanced degree at white universities, another characteristic
pattern. Let us consider the family background of each of the men
briefly.

Secretary Weaver's father was a postal clerk, a distinctly middle
class occupation for Negroes even to this day. His mother was a
schoolteacher, a distinctly upper middle class occupation among Negroes. It should be observed that status in Negro families derives as
much from the mother's occupation and education as from the father's,
unlike the situation among white families. Furthermore, Weaver's
maternal grandfather was a graduate of Harvard and a dentist. Weaver
grew up in the Brookland section of Washington, D.C., where his
was one of nine Negro families among more than 3,000 white families.
His distinctly upper middle class background is also reflected in the
particular educational aspirations his parents held for the children.
"Their one ambition," he has said, "was to send us to New England
schools." They were eminently successful. Both Robert Weaver and his
older brother graduated from Harvard with honors. Both Weaver
and his wife are holders of the Ph.D. degree. Mrs. Robert Weaver is
the only wife of a presidential cabinet member to attain such high
academic achievement.

Senator Brooke is also the product of an upper class Negro family
in Washington, D.C. His father was a U.S. government attorney and
his family was among the prominent Negro families of the city. Despite
the Senator's oft repeated statement that he did not grow up in hard-
ship because of his race, there are indications that the racial barrier
constrained the level of achievement his father might have attained.
Referring to his father Brooke has said, "I thought of the frustrations he
must have had because he had the ability but not the opportunity to do
more." [2] It is also apparent that the Senator's grandmother played an
important role in his upbringing. "I thought of what my grandmother
used to say," he once observed, " 'stay in your place.' This advice was
given to protect me from injury because if you didn't follow this
advice, you knew what would happen. But this was a statement I
never could accept." [3]

[2] *Ebony Magazine,* April 1967, p. 153.
[3] *Ibid.,* pp. 153–54.

Such an economically secure, educated, and cultured family background provided not only a head start in social achievement for the future Senator, but also a set of values and preferences and a style of life. He has described himself as a natural conservative. He exhibits a kind of quiet elegance which makes him prominent among both white and black Brahmins. It is quite in keeping with his style of life, then, that he is president of the Boston Opera Society and not the Boston Jazz Society. But despite all his ability, achievement, and acculturation, he still is not simply an upper class American, but an upper class Negro American. This is in part imposed on him by society and in part a reflection of preference. He is a product of a Negro college and has characterized himself as a "soul brother." It is said that after his inauguration as the first Negro senator since reconstruction, he "retired to his hotel quarters and feasted on his favorite gourmet delight —hog maws and greens." [4]

Perhaps one of the more perceptive comments on the upper class morality of Senator Brooke was a comment by Thomas Pettigrew, a professor of social psychology at Harvard: "I really believe he will have an upgrading effect on the private lives of some senators." [5]

The final member of this illustrious triumvirate, Supreme Court Justice Thurgood Marshall, owes much of his development to his upper middle class family background and the opportunities this made available to him. His father held the highly prestigious position of country club steward. His mother was a school teacher. His brother, who is a physician, has described the Justice as very much like his father: "very argumentative and aggressive." [6] One indication of the father's influence on his son, as well as of the conditions of life they experienced, is reflected in the father's oft repeated admonition to his sons: "If anyone calls you nigger, you not only got my permission to fight him— you got my orders." [7] Again the Negro college played a key role in the achievement of this family.

Thus life in the upper reaches of Negro privilege and economic security provided the basis and the support for a progressively high level of achievement for these men and their families. Still, the racial barrier barred them from many opportunities, privileges, rights, and amenities which can be taken for granted by much less worthy white people.

[4] *Ibid.*, p. 150.
[5] *Ibid.*, p. 152.
[6] *Ebony Magazine*, November 1965, p. 69.
[7] *Ibid.*

New Negro Upper Class

Not all Negro families of outstanding achievement are products of these old established families with generations of privileges. Many whose achievement is equally great rose in one generation from poverty and obscurity to the top. These families comprise the membership of the new upper class.

Prominent among the new upper class are two men who are also government officials. These are Mayor Carl B. Stokes of Cleveland and Mayor Richard Hatcher of Gary, Indiana. Before their recent election, both were distinguished attorneys who reached the top levels of society in one generation. Both were born into lower class families. Stokes was born in the slums of Cleveland. His father, a laundry worker, died when he was one year old. His mother alternated between working as a maid and receiving public welfare assistance, making Stokes the only mayor of a large city who was supported as a child by AFDC. While his mother worked, he and his brother were cared for by their grandmother. Both he and his brother became distinguished attorneys. The strong commitment his mother had to education, plus the opportunities provided by World War II and big city politics are among the screens of opportunity which enabled these very able young men to move from the lower class into the upper class within the span of a few years. Stokes has told how he had to hide books under his clothes as he brought them from the library, because in his neighborhood reading books was "against the mores."

Mayor Hatcher is also a man of humble origins. Born in the slums of Michigan City, Indiana, he was one of thirteen children. His father was a factory worker, but was often out of work. Richard worked his way through college and law school. The sources of his achievement are many and varied. They are not as predictable as those of the old upper class. They are, nevertheless, firmly grounded in the Negro family and community institutions. After his election as Mayor, a reporter asked him how he accounted for his rise "from a very humble beginning to a position of national stature in only thirty-two years." Hatcher pointed to his father and the church as specific influences.

The one person who has had a steady and solid influence on me has been my father. He is seventy-six now. He was a laborer in a foundry for thirty-six years and retired from there six or seven years ago and became a custodian in a county building. He was absolutely honest about everything. He also paid his bills on time. Even if it meant going without meals, the bills were paid on time. I was impressed by those two things. He also put a lot of faith in God. I picked that up too.[8]

What the literature on Negro families needs is several systematic studies of the past, current, and future families of these remarkable men and the hundreds of others like them, not only as a chronicle of achievement on the part of selected families, but as an index of some of the fluidities and rigidities of our American society.

These two pathways to high social status, family stability, and achievement are also reflected in the lives and careers of thousands of less public figures than these high government figures. In a recent analysis of *Current Biographies* between the years 1945 and 1967 we found 120 entries of Negroes of outstanding achievement. These may be classified along several dimensions. This analysis shows that professional men and women are more likely to represent Negro families of the old upper class, while celebrities, including entertainers and athletes, are more likely to represent the new upper class. Among the forty-four professional men, for example, thirty-five (roughly 80 per cent of them) have family origins in the middle or upper classes. Among the twenty-one professional women, eighteen (roughly 86 per cent) may be so described. Among celebrities, on the other hand, only ten of the seventeen male entertainers (59 per cent) were from old upper class families, while just half of the female entertainers and only two of the sixteen male athletes had such privileged family backgrounds. Athletics, which offers an excellent opportunity for many Negro boys from humble origins, is nevertheless conspicuously oriented to social class origins. For example, while it is by no means clear that professional football, basketball, and tennis require more ability or hard work than baseball or boxing, it is obvious that the outstanding professionals in the first category tend to have middle class origins, while baseball players and boxers tend to have lower class origins. This is because the structure of athletics is such that recruitment to the professional ranks in the first category of sports takes place primarily through college teams, and Negro men are more likely to get to college and stay long enough to demonstrate their ability if they come from middle class backgrounds.

The data also shows that representatives of old upper class families are much more likely to be highly educated for the professions, are likely to have reached the peak of their fame at older ages than the new

[8] *Ebony Magazine*, January 1968, p. 35.

upper classmen, are more likely to be light in complexion, and to have grown up in nuclear families with strong fathers. Thus, getting to the top is a bit more assured and orderly for those with social origins in the middle class. Their families are the more likely to have the education, economic security and social connections to facilitate achievement. It is possible to make it without that particular kind of head start, but considerably more precarious and more heavily dependent on a great deal of talent, a great deal of luck, and the favorable operation of opportunity screens from the several levels of society where this potential lies. If these new families are at the top of the Negro social class pyramid, they are often precariously so, for they have not completely escaped the shadows of the plantation which stalk the Negro people whatever their status. The description of this upper class group advanced by Drake and Cayton is still appropriate. "It is," they found,

> an articulate social world of doctors, lawyers, school teachers, executives, successful business people, and the frugal and fortunate of other occupational groups, who have climbed with difficulty and now cling precariously to a social position consonant with what money, education, and power the city and the caste-like controls allow them. They are challenged at every point, however, by the same forces that condemn the vast majority of the people to poverty and restricted opportunities.[9]

The precariousness of upper class status is underscored by the facts that Negro professionals earn less in a lifetime than white professionals and that their wives often have to work to keep them in this status. Negro physicians, for example, who are at the top of the Negro upper class, can count on earning less than 60 per cent of what white physicians earn in their lifetimes. Of all Negro professionals, only engineers approach equity, with an income potential about 95 per cent of white engineers. Thus it is not surprising that engineers are prominent in the new upper class and are increasing much more rapidly than many other professional groups. Between 1950 and 1960, for example, there was a 400 per cent increase in the number of Negro engineers. Still, those 3,378 men represented only about four-tenths of 1 per cent of all engineers in the United States in 1960.[10]

The Negro upper class is an important and growing phenomenon. Andrew Brimmer has observed, for example, that "although the Negro

[9] St. Clair Drake and Horace Cayton, *Black Metropolis: A Study of Negro Life in a Northern City*, revised and enlarged ed. (New York: Harper & Row, Publishers, 1962), II, 522.

[10] We are indebted to Dr. Horace Mann Bond for this information.

community can claim only a handful of millionaires, it can boast of a fairly large number of prosperous families and individuals." He found that in 1963, 274,000 Negro families had incomes above $10,000 and over a quarter of these had incomes over $15,000. He also noted that "the $10,000 and over group rose by 50 per cent between 1959 and 1963."

> With incomes in this level, such families not only can afford comfortable housing (when they manage to purchase it in an essentially segregated market) but they can also provide a college education for their children. They can entertain graciously and participate in a variety of cultural activities. They can travel widely at home and abroad.[11]

These upper class families are much better able to meet the needs of their members and to fulfill the functions required of families by the wider society than are other Negro families. We shall see below some of the specific ways in which they are able to meet both instrumental and expressive functions of family much better than families with less resources and societal supports. At the same time, however, we shall also see some of the respects in which these families have not solved all the problems associated with being black in a white society, nor that myriad of other problems more generally associated with the human condition. Let us turn now, however, to an outline of some of the major dimensions of the middle classes.

The Middle Classes

Among the Negro middle classes there is a similar historical dimension of old families, with traditions of achievement. In addition, however, somewhat of an hierarchical differentiation is reflected in the three subgroups of the middle class. The first subgroup is the *upper middle class*, composed of families headed by persons in the minor professions which require college education but do not rank in prestige and status with the major old line professions. Prominent in the upper middle class are families of teachers, social workers, accountants, technicians. Many attorneys who have not yet established themselves, ministers of small congregations, and celebrities who have not yet reached the top or who are on the way down may also fall into this group. The line between the Negro upper class and the Negro upper

[11] Andrew Brimmer, "The Negro in the National Economy," in *The American Negro Reference Book*, ed. John P. Davis (Englewood Cliffs, N. J.: Prentice-Hall, Inc., 1966), p. 266.

middle class is a rather fluid one. For many purposes the two groups may be viewed as one. Since the majority of Negro families are considerably lower in social status than these two groups, one tends sometimes to lump both of them together. Indeed, it is difficult for any college graduate with any degree of visibility in the community to escape the attribution of status much higher than he could command in the white community.

Public school teachers with bachelor's degrees from college account for the major share of upper middle class Negro professionals. These teachers, in fact, make up more than half of all Negro professional, technical, and kindred workers. Elementary school teachers account for 43 per cent and secondary teachers account for 10 per cent. For men, 13 per cent of all professional, technical, and kindred workers were secondary teachers and 12 per cent were elementary teachers. Moreover, while there is a slight increase in the proportion of Negro teachers to the over-all teaching profession during the past few years, even this large group of professionals, the most highly developed in the Negro community, is underdeveloped. Negro public school teachers accounted for only 7 per cent of all public school teachers in 1960. (By 1966 this proportion had increased to 10 per cent.) Furthermore, these teachers are highly concentrated in the South, where they have been the outstanding representatives of Negro family achievement. The paucity of Negro teachers in the urban ghettos where most Northern Negroes live is approaching a national disgrace as the country becomes more aware of the important contributions these professionals can make, not only to black and white pupils and teachers in the school, but to community leadership as well.

Another relatively large group of upper middle class families is headed by ministers, who accounted for about 12 per cent of all Negro professionals in 1960. Other upper middle class occupations which received relatively high preference as goals for male college students were junior management level jobs in business and in government, preferred by 17 per cent of the men but less than 5 per cent of women. Social work was the choice of nearly 10 per cent of the women but only about 5 percent of the men. These are all respectable and responsible upper middle class occupations in the Negro community.

Families in this social class category often have incomes ranging between $6,000 and $10,000. Family income fluctuates widely, however, both above and below this range, depending on the part of the country and on whether one or two family members work. Incomes are higher in urban areas than in the country as a whole; they are higher in the North and West than in the South; and they are higher for the more highly educated families. Among Negro families in large urban areas where both husband and wife were college graduates, fully 76 per cent earned $6,000 or more in 1960.

It must be observed that being middle class for Negro families is not always as economically or socially secure as that status might seem to imply. It is often a precarious existence. Five case vignettes from families in a study of Negro families in a large Western city will illustrate this observation.[12]

1. By education, income, occupation, and residence, the Douglas family is distinctly upper middle class. Mr. Douglas is twenty-seven and his wife is twenty-five. They have been married for five years and have two children, Robert, Jr., who is four, and Sarah, who is 2½. Both parents are college graduates and both are schoolteachers. They have a combined income of $13,000 per year, an expensive house in a white neighborhood, and an expensive late model car. They hire "help" to take care of the children. Both have parents who were college graduates. It may be said that they have no money problems, except during those periods when Mrs. Douglas is on maternity leave and their income drops to $7,500 per year. Mr. Douglas has only one job. He is distinctly head of the house. Mrs. Douglas attends church on Sunday, but her husband stays home and reads the Sunday papers and does schoolwork. She is an avid tennis player but he prefers bowling. They take turns reading to the children and putting them to bed. He, however, is a bit more firm with discipline, while she leans toward permissiveness. He spanks a bit more than she thinks is necessary. It is essentially an equalitarian, upper middle class family with a slight tilt toward the patriarchal style. He would like it to be a bit more patriarchal and she would like it to be more equalitarian. It is not in danger of becoming matriarchal. And if he can ever manage to finish his master's degree, for which she nags him a bit, he can teach in a junior college and will, no doubt, fortify his status not only in the outside world but in the family structure as well.

2. The Baldwin family is also middle class. Mr. Baldwin is thirty-seven years old and Mrs. Baldwin is twenty-seven. They have been married for ten years and have two children, Larry, age ten, and Sonny, age six. The fact that Mrs. Baldwin was only seventeen and pregnant by another man was not a barrier to their marriage. They have had

[12] This study is being conducted by the author at the University of California under a grant from the Children's Bureau, U. S. Department of Health, Education and Welfare. All names are fictitious.

a successful family life for ten years, according to the social criteria of success. They are both high school graduates. He is a postal employee. She is a secretary-typist. Their combined annual income was $9,000 last year. Mr. Baldwin's sister lives with the family and helps care for the children in exchange for her room and board. They have a mortgage on a nice home in a Negro residential neighborhood. Mr. Baldwin is industrious. In order to help make ends meet, he drives a taxi after his regular job. Although the neighborhood they live in might be characterized as "poor," the house is "nice" and the furnishings are "expensive." The Baldwins are pillars of their community. They have surmounted many obstacles and achieved stability and success. Their status is heavily dependent, however, not only on the wife's working and the husband's having two jobs, but on the services of his sister. Between their jobs and community responsibilities, there is little time left for the "frills" of family life. It is not an uncommon predicament for the precarious Negro middle class.

3. Another striking example of the precariousness of Negro middle class life is the Adams family. They are in many respects a model middle class American family. Mr. Adams is thirty-four and his wife is thirty-two. They have been married for ten years and have three children, Michael, age six, Dennis, age four, and Denise, age two. An Army veteran with two years of college, Mr. Adams is a professional photographer with a steady income. Mrs. Adams also has two years of college. The family income was $10,600 last year. They have a heavy mortgage on their own home on the edge of a black ghetto.

They have planned their family to suit their economic abilities. They delayed having children for the first four years of their marriage, "in order to get on our feet financially." During those first years she worked as an office secretary while he worked at the Post Office.

In other ways, too, they are a model American couple. He is tall and slender, weighs about 185 pounds; he is good looking, dresses well and tastefully with a slight flair, and is in manner and bearing not exactly aggressive, but, as he would describe himself, "somewhat forward." He is industrious, works hard, likes spectator sports, drives a late model car, and drinks to be sociable. He does not go to church because he is tired on Sunday, likes to work around the house and watch television. Mrs. Adams is also an attractive, well groomed young woman, though perhaps a bit less sophisticated than her husband and not quite as forceful in manner. She pays the bills and takes the children to the Protestant church and Sunday School. She makes most of the decisions about the children. It is, on balance, an equalitarian family.

There are other aspects of their family life which support this middle class equalitarian mold. He gets out of bed first in the morning, for he is an "earlier riser." He dresses the three children and plays with them until she has breakfast ready. He kisses them all goodbye when he leaves the house. They even had a typical middle class family problem. She is often not ready for work on time, and he "cannot afford to be late." When they drive to work together in their one car, this causes friction.

But if this is in many respects a model American middle class, equalitarian family, it is only precariously so. Consider their education. While they are more highly educated than a majority of their fellow Americans, they do not have enough to fortify their middle class position. Their $10,600 last year put them in a distinctly upper middle income bracket but it was earned at a high price. As in 90 per cent of Negro middle income families, Mrs. Adams worked to help maintain that family income level. Besides, that income was for last year; this year, in keeping with their middle class style of life and their concern for the care and well-being of their children, particularly since the aunt who used to live there and care for them got married and moved to another city, Mrs. Adams decided to stop work and become a full-time housewife. She enjoys the role very much. But this year the family income from Mr. Adams' earnings alone will be $6,400. Now they will still be a middle class, educated, handsome American couple, but the precariousness of their status and the tenuous hold they have on their economic and social well-being are apparent. Mr. Adams has taken an extra job a few hours a night "so that the washing machine and dryer could be paid for without sacrificing the house payments."

Now Mr. Adams, though still keeping up a well dressed appearance in public, does not bathe quite as often as he used to. Now when he leaves his extra job at night he lingers a bit longer at the tavern than he used to. He even seems to drive his car faster and more recklessly than he did before.

4. Mr. and Mrs. Earley are both high school graduates. He is the owner and operator of his own janitorial service. Last year he earned $10,000. Mrs. Earley worked as a bookkeeper in a department store for three years, until the first baby was due. Now she stays home and cares for their four children, three girls, ages nine, three, and two, and a boy, age one. They have a spacious, attractive two bedroom apartment in a very nice, middle income Negro neighborhood in a fairly large city. Their apartment is attractively decorated with modern

furniture. These surroundings reflect the willingness of Mr. Earley to "provide a decent standard of living" for his family. They are even more reflective of the "good taste and ingenuity" of his wife. The couple is saving money for a down payment on a home.

The Earleys are middle class, upwardly mobile, hard working—a model American family. He is thirty years old and she is twenty-eight. They have been married for ten years. They grew up in the same city and went through school together. After high school he served two years in the Army. Upon his discharge they got married. He took a job as a janitor by day and completed high school by night. He saved enough money to get a loan and open his own business. Now he works for himself. Like a typical small businessman, he works long hours, six days a week. He rests on Sunday. His habits are exemplary. He neither smokes nor drinks nor runs around with women. In spite of his long working hours, he spends at least two hours a day helping Mrs. Earley with the children.

In a number of respects, life has been good to the Earleys. Their education, income, residence, and style of life put them distinctly ahead of their less privileged kinsmen and countrymen. But their middle class status is more than a bit precarious. Mrs. Earley has recently become pregnant with her fifth child. This will be a second unwanted baby, just as she was beginning to look forward to returning to work. Neither the family budget nor the family home is adequate to take in one more member. Should they force themselves to buy a house before they have sufficient down payment and before Mr. Earley has paid off the mortgage on his business, or should they try to rent a larger place? Renting a larger place on their present budget means returning to the ghetto. But the problems presented by the new baby are not all financial and social. Some are intensely personal. Mr. Earley is inclined to tighten his belt and make a place for the new one, but Mrs. Earley is not at all sure that she has "enough energy, strength, or desire to love and care for another baby."

5. Mr. and Mrs. Franklyn had a family income of $10,400 last year. They have one child, a ten-month-old girl. He has a high school education and works as a janitor. She has finished junior college and works as an office clerk. Both her parents are college graduates; his never went to high school. Her parents were distressed with her marriage, feeling that she was "selling herself short." Mr. Franklyn presently works at two jobs in order to earn $135 a week. Mrs. Franklyn wants him to find another job in "some kind of business or management." She also wants him to go back to school. He works at night, she works during the day. They have few mutual friends, partly because of their work schedules, but also and more

importantly because of their different social class orientations. Most of their contacts are with "his friends" because she is not sure her friends will accept him. Thus, even in the black middle class viable family life is ever threatened.

The Lower Classes

Most Negro families are composed of ordinary people. They do not get their names in the paper as outstanding representatives of the Negro race and they do not show up on the welfare rolls or in the crime statistics. They are headed by men and women who work and support their families, manage to keep their families together and out of trouble most of the time. They are not what might be generally conceived of as "achieving families." They are likely to be overlooked when the white community goes looking for a Negro to sit on an interracial committee, or take a job where Negroes have not been hired before. For they have not gone to college and they are not part of that middle and upper class group most likely to come into intimate, daily contact with the white world. At the same time, they are likely to be overlooked by the poverty program and other efforts to uplift the poor and disadvantaged. They often do not qualify to take part in these programs because they are not on welfare. They are, in a word, just folks. They are the great unknowns, typically left out of the literature on Negro family life. Once in a while they appear in fiction, but even then generally as oversimplified stereotypes rather than in all their ordinary, human complexity. And yet, these ordinary Negro families are often the backbone of the Negro community. They are virtually unknown to white people, particularly white people who depend on books and other mass media for their knowledge of life in the most important ethnic subsociety in America today.

Dr. Charlotte Dunmore has done a study of 173 families in a Negro ghetto of Hartford, Connecticut, which provides considerable support for the above description. She has described for us the "average" family in her study, as the picture was developed by IBM computers from responses of all her study families.

The family is Negro and Protestant. The mother was born and reared in the rural or semi-rural southern United States. She came to live in Hartford sometime after her eighteenth birthday. The family has two legally married parents and contains 4.7 members. Father is the chief breadwinner earning $4,800 per year from his employment as a skilled craftsman, steward, or machinist.

Mother, who stays home to take care of the children, perceives them as growing, developing human beings amenable to her control, if only to a limited degree.

The parents want their children to have at least some college education. They hope that their children will become skilled technicians, specialized clerical workers, or go into one of the minor professions—library science, teaching, the arts. The children are involved in at least two organized community activities (Scouts, the "Y," settlement house, etc.). Previous to the summer school project, they had been actively involved in some other type of voluntary educational opportunity program.

Mother has achieved a rather high degree of integration into her neighborhood and is involved in a meaningful (to her) give-and-take relationship with her neighbors. At the present time, she is participating in at least two community activities. She is a registered voter and voted in the last election. She listens to the radio, watches television, and reads one of the two Hartford newspapers every day.

The family is geared to obtaining a better life for its children, including more education and more materially rewarding, status-giving employment. Hartford is perceived as a racially prejudiced community and education appears to be considered the primary method for circumventing this prejudice.[13]

Families like these, despite their stability, achievement, and contributions within the Negro community, are often ignored by the wider society because of the general tendency to lump all "lower class" Negro families in the ghetto into a single category and to focus on the most dysfunctional patterns of family life there.

Half of all Negro families may be considered distinctly lower class. They view themselves that way and are viewed by their fellows as such. It should be added, however, that this large group of people is highly differentiated and is by no means a uniform mass. Three distinct groupings within this lower class may be identified, including (1) the working nonpoor, (2) the working poor, and (3) the nonworking poor.

At the very top of the lower class is a group of families headed by men in the semi-skilled, highly paid, unionized, steady industrial jobs. These are members of the *industrial working class*. Families of Negro men holding good steady jobs as truck drivers (in the Teamsters Union), construction workers, and semi-skilled factory workers are in the upper reaches of the lower class. If it were not for the color of their skins and the housing discrimination they face, many of these men would be able to

[13] Charlotte Dunmore, "Social-Psychological Factors Affecting the Use of an Educational Opportunity Program by Families Living in a Poverty Area" (unpublished Ph.D. dissertation, Brandeis University, October 1967). Chap. 3. Reprinted by permission of Charlotte Dunmore.

join the ranks of the new majority of labor union members who, it is said, now drive from work to their homes in the suburbs, sit in the backyard drinking martinis, and complain about high taxes. But if this is an elite working class, it is indeed a small one. Less than 7 per cent of Negro working men are truck drivers, constituting about 12 per cent of all truck drivers. But not all of them are members of the Teamsters Union. About 3 per cent are lumbermen, but many of these are in the south where wages are low. Less than 2 per cent are auto mechanics and semi-skilled factory workers. Less than 1 per cent are longshoremen, though they account for a third of the workers in this class, often earning $12,000 to $15,000 a year. When to the secure occupational base of these men and their wives are added the style of life they can afford and a degree of community activity in the church, or lodge, or other specifically Negro institution, their status can be considerably higher than that suggested by the term lower class. Dr. Dunmore's "average" family in the Hartford ghetto is among the working nonpoor. She found, in fact, that between half and two thirds of the families with school age children in her study would meet none of the current official definitions of poverty.

A second category of lower class Negro families is the working poor. The fact is not generally appreciated in the wider society that the majority of poor Negros live in nuclear families headed by men who work hard every day, and are still unable to earn enough to pull their families out of poverty. Each point of this statement should be emphasized.

1. The majority of poor Negros live in nuclear families, and not in segmented families. Nearly 60 per cent of children in families with less than $2,000 annual income were living with both parents in 1959. If we consider families with earnings between $2,000 and $4,000, the proportion of children living with both parents rises to over 80 per cent. It increases, of course, as income does.[14]

2. The majority of poor Negroes live in nuclear families headed by men and not by women. Among families earning less than $3,000 in 1966, nearly 60 per cent were headed by husbands and fathers. Among those earning between $3,000 and $5,000, the proportion of male-headed families increased to nearly 75 per cent.[15] As income increases the proportion of male-headed families increases.

3. The majority of poor Negroes live in families which are self-supporting and are not supported by public welfare. While 41 per cent of all

[14] "Social and Economic Conditions of Negroes in the United States," Joint Report of Bureau of Census and Bureau of Labor Statistics, BLS Report No. 332, Current Population Reports, Series P-23, No. 24, October 1967, p. 76.
[15] *Ibid.*, p. 71.

Negroes were living in poverty in 1966, only 14 per cent were supported
by public welfare. Thus, nationally about a third of all poor Negroes
(3.2 million out of 9.6 million) were supported by welfare. This proportion varies by communities. In her Hartford neighborhood, Dr. Dunmore estimated that nearly 60 per cent of her poor families were self-
supporting. These are the working poor. It seems obvious, then, that the
guaranteed family allowance of $3,000 per year for a family of four, the
most generous figure being considered in discussions of proposed family
allowance systems, will in itself do little to alleviate the conditions faced
by the overwhelming majority of poor black people, to say nothing of
the social and economic hardships faced by that even larger number of
black people who do not now qualify as "poor." Most poor black people
live in poor black neighborhoods. The open housing provisions of the
Civil Rights Act of 1968 are not likely to change that fact.

The working poor families are often headed by unskilled laborers, service workers, and domestics. More Negro men work as janitors or porters
in this country than in any other specific occupation. In 1960, 7.3 per
cent of all Negro male workers were janitors and porters. These 235,000
men comprise 37.2 per cent of all men in this job category. But Negro
women, who are often heads of families in this group, are even more
highly concentrated in low level, unskilled jobs than men. More than a
third of all Negro women who were employed at all worked as private
household domestics. These men and women support families in that
dominant segment of the lower class which outnumbers every other class
stratum and includes probably a third of all Negro families. It should be
noted that these men and women work and support their families on
very low wages. They are the *working poor*. They are an unorganized
mass of workers, in whom labor unions are only now beginning to express an interest, as among the hospital workers of New York, and the
hotel and restaurant workers in a number of large cities. They are engaged in a struggle for economic existence, and the vast majority of
them is self-supporting. Even among female-headed families, the majority of the mothers work and support the family.

So far we have described in socioeconomic terms 80 to 85 per cent of
Negro families. We come, finally, to that group on the bottom of the
economic ladder who occupy the lowest status in both the general community and the Negro community. These are the *nonworking poor,* that
15 or 20 per cent of Negro families headed by members with less than
eighth grade education, who are intermittently if at all employed, and
who have very low levels of job skills. These are families often supported by relatives and by public welfare. In many respects, though we

describe them as part of the lower class, they may be more appropriately referred to as the *under class*,[16] for like the majority of Negro families a hundred years earlier, they are outside and below the formal class structure. In this sector, the basic conditions of life are most abject. Many of these family heads have not gone beyond sixth grade, and their incomes are often below $2,000 per year, and sometimes below $1,000. Among them are families living in dilapidated housing or, if they are very fortunate, in public housing projects.

Even in the under class, however, there are some variations in life conditions. For example, there are geographic variations. Families in the under class are in the most dire straits if they live in the rural South, where nearly a quarter of Negro families still live, and especially if they live in one of the 135 counties in the South where Negroes constitute a majority, and more especially still, if they live in the black belt counties of Alabama, Mississippi, or Louisiana. The nation learned dramatically in the summer of 1967 that literally hundreds of families in these areas were not able to prevent their children from starving, while local and state authorities looked the other way. And even the federal government seemed helpless to prevent it, although it has several programs specifically designed to combat starvation in communities where authorities permit these programs to operate and among families with sufficient money income and foresight to purchase food stamps. But hundreds of families have no money income whatever.

Families in the under class are somewhat better off if they live in the urban South, where welfare payments, though pitifully low, are nevertheless available to a few Negro families provided they meet the standards of morality decreed by the local establishment. And still better off are those under class families living in the urban ghettos of the North, where the economic opportunity structure, including welfare policies, is likely to be more supportive. Even here, it should be observed, in most states it is not possible for families to qualify for federally supported welfare payments if there is a husband and father in the home. Opportunities for jobs that pay a minimum wage are better for men between the ages of thirty-five and forty-five than for youth or older men. Opportunities for just any job, including domestic work, are better for women than for men. Opportunities for welfare payments are similarly better for female-headed families than for male-headed families. But more important, regardless of whether these very poor families are a little better off in one community or another, because of the color barrier

[16] Joan Gordon, *The Poor of Harlem: Social Functioning in the Underclass,* (New York: Office of the Mayor, 1965).

they are all considerably worse off than white families in similar circumstances. Both the treatment they receive when in this status, and the pathways out of it are conditioned by the long, resilient shadows of the plantation.

Living Poor and Black

What does it mean, then, to be living poor and black in America more than a hundred years after emancipation? The meaning varies. But in many respects the conditions of life for Negro families in the ghetto are getting worse rather than better relative to the conditions of middle class white Americans.

As a society, we have not made an appreciable dent in the wall of discrimination which separates Negro people from other Americans. At the same time we have made no appreciable dent in the twin problem of poverty. Thus, the abolition of racial discrimination and poverty remain the nation's and the Negroes' chief cross and chief hope for viability. Low income Negro families in urban slums and rural conclaves are the chief victims of this double jeopardy. These are the most conspicuous residents of that other America which has been described so vividly by Michael Harrington.[17]

Thus, to be living poor and black in 1968 means severe restrictions in the most basic conditions, particularly focused in the areas of family income, education of parents, occupations of family heads, family housing, and health care. And, if the conditions of life in these five crucial areas are not met, the Negro family can not be expected to assume the same structure as other, more achieving and affluent families. And, if they do not have the basic supports for their society in these areas and do not develop the most effective structures of family life, they cannot be expected to meet the functions of family life required of them by their members and their society. And yet, they are expected to do these things. And many are able to perform in a remarkably functional manner. Just as there is variety and range in the basic life conditions and societal supports available to Negro families, there is variety and range in both the structure and function of Negro family life. There is no single uniform style of Negro family life, not even in the most depressed sections of urban ghettos. But if there is not complete uniformity, there also is not random variety. There are patterns, and modalities of life which are

[17] Michael Harrington, *The Other America: Poverty in the United States* (Baltimore, Md.: Penguin Books, Inc., 1963).

eminently tied in to the basic conditions of life, both contemporary and historical.

There are several bases for the patterning of life among low income Negro families. First, there is geographic patterning. Some families live in the rural South, others in the urban South, and still others in the urban North and West. In the latter category some families live in the heart of the ghetto, others live on the fringes, and still others live outside the central cities. The conditions of life for low income Negro families are most abject in the rural South, less so in the urban South and less so still in the urban North and West. The ability of Negro families to meet the requirements of society, particularly for achievement, is highly associated with this geographic patterning.

A second basis for patterning is socioeconomic. Even among the lower class, there are at least three major groupings, the *working nonpoor*, the *working poor*, and the *nonworking poor*. Both family stability and family achievement, and thus viability, follow very closely variations in socioeconomic status.

Thirdly, there are patterns in the structure of Negro family life, based on household composition. Thus some families are *basic families* with only the two married adults present. Others are *nuclear families* with two married adults and children. Still others are *attenuated nuclear families* with one adult missing. And each of these three types of primary family groups may be further elaborated into *extended families, sub families,* or *augmented families* with non relatives functioning as intimate members of the household.

Still a fourth type of patterning is related to size. There are small, medium, and large sized families in the lower class. Size may serve as both an obstacle, and a facilitator of achievement depending on the age, sex, relationship, character, and contribution of the various family members.

A fifth type of patterning is associated with authority and decision making in the family. Here there are three distinct groups. There are the vanishing *patriarchies*, where men make most of the decisions in crucial areas of family life. They form a minority among low income Negro families, but they still exist to some extent. Then there are the resilient *matriarchies* in which the wife and mother exerts an inordinate amount of authority at the expense of or in the absence of the husband and father. This is the second most common authority pattern among low income Negro families, and not the most common as is often assumed. Then, finally, there are the expanding *equalitarians*. These are families in which both husband and wife participate actively and jointly in decision making in the major areas of family life. Their tribes are increasing at the expense of both the patriarchy and the matriarchy. This is the most common pattern of authority among lower class Negro families today.

A sixth type of patterning has to do with family division of labor. Some families have a more or less strict, traditional division of labor based on sex. The man earns the livelihood, and does little else of the household and family chores. The wife and mother has her work which she performs largely unaided. These are role segmented families. In still other families, however, there is role flexibility and mutual cooperation between husband and wife in meeting the instrumental needs of the family in both the external world and within the family. Still other families have children or other relatives able and willing to participate jointly with husband and wife in these major functions of family life. Among low income Negro families, the segmented role relationships are probably most common, although, as the above discussion has shown, collaboration is probably more common than is generally thought. Also, when there are older children in the family, they are drafted into service with household tasks, including child rearing tasks at a much earlier age in these families, than among other ethnic subsocieties.

Seventh, and finally, there are patterns of Negro family life reflected in their attitudes and behavior toward the socialization of children. Some low income Negro families take very good care of their children and inspire and aid them on toward conformity and achievement in the major areas and institutions of life. These are families that are considered to function adequately. They are able to understand, intervene actively and manipulate to some extent the plethora of institutions on which they depend and which, often, in themselves, function most inadequately. A second category of families function less adequately. They function better in some areas of life than others; and better at some times than others, and always they function better under some (favorable) conditions than under others. These families may be on and off welfare. Their children may be in and out of trouble. They are engaged in a struggle for respectability, conformity and achievement. Then, at the bottom of life's resources, is a relatively large group of low income Negro families who have been most deserted by their society. They receive the least supports from the major institutions of society. They are the most victimized by discrimination and poverty and general lack of opportunity. They are, consequently, the most chronically unstable, dependent and deviant. Their children are most likely to get into trouble or to be neglected.

These are the problem families and the long term welfare recipients. But it cannot be stressed too strongly that not all lower class Negro families are poor. Not all poor families are broken. Not all single parent families are on welfare. And not all welfare families are chronic problems. A more adequate income structure would remove many of them from the arena of social concern.

These are the major dimensions along which Negro family life is patterned in the other America. They interact with and overlap each other. Families move from one category to another as time and circumstances change. They do this in response to life conditions and in an effort to survive, to conform, and to achieve in a society which expects these ends, but often provides them with inadequate means to their attainment.

Summary

While this discussion of socioeconomic status and mobility has been confined to the social forces defining the basic conditions of life, particularly jobs, housing, education, and income, it is easy to anticipate the relationship between these basic conditions and the behavior of family members. The ability of the Negro family to meet the needs of its members and the functional requirements of society is intimately associated with its position on the socioeconomic pyramid.

We have observed that while a hundred years ago more than 90 per cent of Negro families subsisted in abject poverty, and as late as 1900 the overwhelming majority was still confined to the lower reaches of the lower class, there has been a transition, paralleling the rise in geographic mobility, which has resulted in a highly differentiated socioeconomic structure of Negro family life. A tenth of Negro families may be considered upper class, and another 40 per cent may be considered middle class, but half are still clustered in the lower classes. Each of these major class levels is further subdivided, however, into substrata of meaningful proportions. There are two upper classes, the old upper class of families whose status is built upon that of previous generations of privilege, and the new upper class built in one generation on the basis of talent and good fortune. The middle class is stratified into a comfortable upper middle class of educated professionals and businessmen, a middle middle class of white-collar clerks and salesmen, and a lower middle class of skilled artisans and small businessmen. The lower class is stratified into three components, including an upper lower class of steadily employed, relatively high earning tradesmen, a middle lower class of unskilled laborers, service workers, and domestics, and an under class composed of families headed by intermittently employed and unemployed persons largely assisted by other relatives and by a grossly inadequate welfare system. We are faced with a highly differentiated group of families, reflecting the differential availability of the basic perquisites of life which enable them to meet the needs of their members and the requirements of society. At every level, however, Negro families and their members are faced by obstacles associated with the color bar which restrict their resources, opportunities, and choices—and consequently their ability to survive, to conform, and to reach the level of social achievement of which they are capable.

Part 4

BLACK
RECONSTRUCTION

Chapter 6

The Agony and the Promise
of Social Change

Toward the end of 1967, Daniel Collins, a Negro dentist, educator, and outgoing member of the California State Board of Education, rose, looked around at his largely white audience of California School Board officials, and spoke to the heart of the foremost issue facing the country in this period: "If the Judeo-Christian ethic, and the democratic way of life are going to survive, it will be because a way was found to meet the needs of the Negro people." [1]

The issue is precisely the same as it was a hundred years earlier—namely, to translate into meaningful reality the emancipation of the Negro people. The broad outlines along which this problem must be resolved are also essentially the same. The difference is that now the stakes are higher, for both the cost to the society of continued failure to resolve this problem and the pressure on the part of the Negro people to have it resolved are considerably higher and considerably more interrelated than they were a hundred years ago, when the first efforts at reconstruction failed so miserably.

The need is so urgent, so pervasive, and so interlocked with other aspects of the national life that extraordinary special efforts are called for. Negro family and community life cannot be assured of viability by ordinary means which have been followed by the ordinary institutions of society administered in ordinary ways by ordinary white men and women who attained their positions of power by ordinary means. These ordinary institutions, men, and means have proved chronically insensitive to the Negro experience.

The Negro people must be viewed, not as carbon copies of white people, but as a people with a distinctive history, a distinctive place in American society, a distinctive set of life chances, and a distinctive set of contributions to make to the wider society. The Negro people can-

[1] *Chronicle* (San Francisco), December 9, 1967, Sec. 1, p. 2.

149

not be expected to melt or blend into the white society, except psychologically, and at great personal expense to the few individuals who manage to do so, and at some loss to the general welfare of the Negro people and the society.

We have urged that the Negro family be viewed as a social system, deeply imbedded within and highly interdependent with a variety of other systems, both smaller than and larger than itself. According to this theoretical and philosophical perspective, the Negro family is a creature of the Negro community, which surrounds it, defines it, and gives it its identity and mission. Both the family and the community are creatures of the wider society, which provides or withholds the resources for its creation, survival, and development. The Negro family cannot be understood, appreciated, or enhanced in isolation, but only in relation to its place in the Negro community and the wider society. In this regard, we have taken exception to students of the family who view the Negro family as an independent unit which serves as the causal nexus for the difficulties Negroes often have in the wider society. We have argued that while the family and the society are interdependent, the greater force for defining, enhancing, or obstructing, comes from the wider society to the family, and not the other way round. The far-reaching implications of this point of view suggest not only where one might look in an effort to get a comprehensive understanding of the Negro family, but also at what levels of society one might intervene in order to enhance the functioning of Negro family life.

The second point we have made is that Negro families can best be understood by putting them into historical perspective. We have, then, examined some of the major historical transitions or crises in the life of the Negro people moving from their African origins to contemporary social forces, including a kind of caste system which has plagued the Negro people from their first introduction to America in 1619 until the present time. It is within the context of these historical experiences, both negative and positive, that the Negro people have nurtured a sense of historical identification, which we have labeled black peoplehood.

Third, we have argued that the Negro people have developed over the years a highly differentiated set of social structures which help to define certain ethnic subsocieties. Thus, being Negro is not a uniform experience, but is conditioned by such factors as geographic residence and social class. Again, it is not possible, in our view, to understand or enhance Negro family functioning without regard to these important types of differentiation.

Fourth, we have urged that Negro family structure be viewed in its complexity as adaptation to conditions in the wider social environment of the family. In addition, we have argued that the relationship between the structure and the function of Negro family life is not a simple straightforward one, similar in all respects to the relationship which exists in the white subsociety. The variety of structures are often means of trying to meet the demands of society and the needs of family members. We have sought to distinguish instrumental functions—those required for physical survival—from expressive functions—those associated with the social and psychological requirements of life. Both are highly interrelated and highly dependent on the resources available to the family from the wider society. We have used the concept "screens of opportunity" to describe the limited opportunities available to some Negro families which have enabled them to survive and prosper. In addition, we have described several levels of achievement among Negro families. We have argued against the overwhelming concentration, in the literature and in social reform circles, on the lowest income, most troubled and troubling Negro families as an index of Negro family life, or as the exclusive point of entry for efforts to enhance Negro family life. Throughout, we have laid as much stress on the phenomenon of social caste as on social class, and we have sought to depict the Negro community as a mixture of strengths and weaknesses, conformity and deviance, achievement and failure, with the more positive virtues predominating despite historical oppression.

In this chapter, then, we set forth some general strategies which are consistent with the foregoing perspective, and which seem to offer considerable promise as parts of a general effort of the society to enhance the functioning of Negro families. The central line of our reasoning in this chapter is that the development of ever more viable forms of Negro family life depend on the development of more viable institutions within the Negro community, and of more open and responsive institutions in the wider society, so as to incorporate the Negro experience and the Negro people, thereby reversing the ancient and contemporary practices of exclusion and negative valuation.

Two broad strategies are required for the reconstruction of Negro family and community life today. The first must take place at the level of the wider society. The second must take place at the level of the Negro community. In short, all the major subsystems of the larger society, and particularly those that impinge directly on the Negro community, must be reconstructed in order to incorporate within their framework a greater measure of the Negro experience in this country and the world. At the level of the Negro community itself, the major institutions there, including traditional ones, new ones, and those which have not yet been created, must be strengthened in order to create, nurture, enhance, reflect, and project the Negro experience into the mainstream of the wider society.

From the perspective of the Negro community, these two general strategies may be referred to as "external development" and "internal development," or as the "white strategy" and the "black strategy," suggesting which segment of the community needs to take the initiatives in each case. For example, if we think about the problem of racism, the most pervasive obstacle to viability in Negro communities and Negro families, it is clear that white people must take the initiative. Similarly, the white power structure must take the initiative to solve the problem of economic insecurity. Negro leaders do not have it within their power to deliver full employment in the Negro community.

Racism is deeply imbedded within the institutional fabric of American society. All the major institutions including the political, economic, educational, social, and others have systematically excluded the Negro people in varying degrees from equal participation in the rewards of these institutions. None of them works as effectively in meeting the needs of Negro families as they do white families. The keys to the enhancement of Negro family and community life are therefore institutional keys. These major institutions of the wider society must be changed so as to more adequately reflect the existence, the needs and the contributions of the Negro people. External strategies of reform are aimed at this kind of institutional change. Several elements are necessary. First, the very conception of the purpose of all these institutions must be expanded to include specific recognition of the Negro people as a substantial element in our pluralistic society. Second, the very structures of these institutions should be changed to incorporate Negroes at every level including policy making, executive, administrative, and operational levels, as customers, clients, and constituents on equal footing with white people. The responsibility for this massive inclusion must rest with the institutions themselves, and not with the Negro people. But to say that white people of power, influence, and privilege must take the initiatives in these areas is by no means to call for unilateral action. We argue instead that these white institutions must make the initial move toward incorporating the Negro people into themselves, if Negro efforts to overcome racism and establish economic viability are to be more successful.

One crucial function that Negroes must serve in the external strategy is to interpret the nature of the Negro experience to the white power structure. And since the Negro experience is not a uniform whole, but a complex thing, it should not be surprising that different interpreters will seize on different aspects. It would be distressing, in fact, if there was such uniformity of interpretations. And yet it must be said that on the basic issues facing the Negro people, there is an amazing unanimity among artists, scholars, and protest leaders. Each in his own way carries the same central message: The Negro people have been subjugated by the white people, both historically and at the present time; they are determined that it shall cease; the white establishment should proceed immediately and massively to redress these historical and contemporary wrongs; if this is not done, the whole society will suffer. It is necessary that black people continue to serve in the wider community, so that the white society may take the initiatives which it must take on the basis of the realities and complexities of the Negro experience, in order to fully realize the positive contributions the Negro people have made and can make to the total society. Thus, while Martin Luther King spoke with more moral urgency, while Stokely Carmichael speaks in more strident tones, Whitney Young in more eloquent tones, and Roy Wilkins in a more modulated voice, they all have three things in common in their interpretation of the Negro experience to the white world. (1) They all speak with great passion, urgency, and commitment. (2) They all point to the problem of racism. (3) They are all substantially ignored by the white power structure which refuses to reform itself.

If there are areas and strategies in which the initiative and responsibility rests so clearly with white people of power and influence, there are others in which the initiatives must be taken by Negro people themselves. Internal community strategies are in this category. Negro people must take the initiatives in building up the Negro community as a viable entity. They must begin to define themselves and not accept the negative definitions which have been handed down by white people. They must exercise power and control over the institutions and services which operate in their community. This does not mean, however, that there is no place for white people in this black strategy. On the contrary, our view of the community as a social system suggests that efforts to build up Negro institutions, power, and control cannot succeed without the understanding, acceptance, and support of major segments of the white society. It does mean, however, that the role of white people in the black community must be redefined, and that black people must take the initiative in such redefinition. It also suggests that leadership in this effort must come from within rather than from outside the Negro community. Finally it suggests that institutions and agents from the wider society which operate in the Negro community, for whatever purpose, must do so on terms acceptable to and formulated by the responsible elements of these communities.

If the larger society is to set the conditions for the enhancement of Negro family life, a number of changes must be made in the way the general society views, evaluates, describes, and defines the Negro experience in America. How can this be done? At a minimum, it requires a program of reconstruction involving: (1) changes in American values, (2) changes in the economic structure, (3) changes in the political structure, (4) changes in the educational system, (5) changes in the health system, (6) changes in the system of social services, and (7) changes in mass communications. In fact, every major institution in the wider community has an important role to play in such monumental social changes.

The reformation of these major institutions is long overdue. There are, of course, a lot of things wrong with the way they work, but for our limited purpose in this discussion, two specific problems are paramount. (1) They must be made to reflect to a much greater extent the nature of the Negro experience in this country and in the world. (2) They must incorporate the Negro people into themselves bodily and personally at every level of policy formulation, administration, operation, and evaluation. These measures of reform are necessary and inseparable. White people must begin to learn more about the Negro experience. We need more books and more courses, and a greater incorporation of Negro experience into the regular courses, so that both white and black people develop as sensitive and positive an appreciation of the black experience as has been accorded the values of the white experience.

But it is not enough for white people to read about the Negro experience, particularly as this is interpreted by white experts on the Negro people. It is very common now for white institutions, whether universities, businesses, social agencies, or churches, to get some white person to come and talk with their staffs about Negroes. Sometimes, though much less often and with greater trepidation and self-congratulation, they invite a Negro to come and tell them what it is like to grow up black—and occasionally, how their institutional policies should take this experience into account. Another common approach is to get a grant from a foundation or the government, with which to hire white persons to do studies of Negroes. The most popular mechanism for this now is to set up an urban affairs institute, where white people study and make recommendations on what should be done about Negro ghettos. Such practices certainly move a step beyond simply reading books, and perhaps they are necessary if these institutions and institutional leaders are to begin reorienting themselves. But they are also made necessary because white people in general, including white liberals, are not yet ready in large numbers to embrace the black experience as anything more than a token part of these institutions. It is clear, then, in this context, that the second approach to reconstruction, the building up of specifically Negro institutions, not their destruction or neglect, is a high priority item. It is not whether one or the other of these approaches to reconstruction is advisable, necessary, nay, urgent—they both are. Both approaches are indispensable if Negro families are to survive, and move beyond survival to stability, and beyond stability to viability, and beyond viability to the highest levels of achievement required by a complex and ever more pluralistic democratic society. Let us consider, then, in more detail, some of the inherent strategies involved in and consistent with these two approaches to the reconstruction of Negro family and community life.

Racism: The Illusion of White Superiority

Racism, the oppression, exclusion, and discrimination of Negro people on the part of white people and white institutions, infests our whole society and operates as a barrier against the freedom, opportunity, and manhood of all the Negro people, whatever their level of achievement or socioeconomic status. It is the most important obstacle to the progress of the Negro people and the aspect of the American value system which needs most to be changed.

We have argued that the psychological, social, economic and political exclusion of the Negro people is an outgrowth of the Anglo-conformity doctrine based on a number of illusions glorifying European-oriented ways.

Racism limits the viability of Negro families in hundreds of ways. It prevents the newborn child from having an equal chance of being born in a healthy condition, and it severely restricts his opportunities of getting a first-rate education. Even if the child surmounts these obstacles, racism prevents him from having equal access to jobs that maximize his abilities. Even if he gets a good job, it limits his opportunity of getting equal pay with white workers. It increases his chance of dying early, and prevents him from being buried in the cemetery of his choice. Thus, literally from the cradle to the grave, the Negro family is threatened by the specter of racism. It is true, of course, that many families escape the worst features of oppression. It is also true that many families have shown an amazing ability to survive, conform, and achieve in the face of impossible obstacles. Still, when compared with white families, Negro families are systematically assigned inferior status, position, and opportunities.

We need to know more about the dynamics of racism. In order to trace its dynamics and learn how it is transmitted, we need studies of the white family. We need to study all the major institutions, both historical and in current operation, to analyze their operation. And we need also to study the processes by which racism is absorbed, deflected, denied, combatted, succumbed to, and overcome by particular Negro families. But more important than studies, we need strategies of action to combat, deflect, and overcome this insidious limitation on the ability of Negro families to care for their children and teach them to be human, American, black, and beautiful all at the same time.

Racism is not always blatant, gross, and straightforward. It often lies hidden in some of the grand illusions which infest the American value system. There is deeply ingrained in the American collective unconscious a number of illusions, particularly as they bear on and affect the Negro people. Many of these are outgrowths of what we describe in the Appendix as the Anglo-conformity doctrine; they are at the head of a modern type of racism which infects the wider society. They include the illusions of stability, of excellence, of wisdom, of morality, of normality, of beauty, and of power.

The Illusion of Stability

There is in the American culture a strong valuation placed on stability. This is perhaps understandable for a mature, economic, and political democracy, but it carries over into almost every aspect of social life. No field of study is more fixated on stability than the study of Negro family life. In reality, family stability is rapidly becoming an illusion. It is a vanishing phenomenon, even for white families in our society. For the only meaningful definition of family stability is that two people marry and stay married until one dies, and that the children, all conceived after marriage, live within the family household until their maturity. With rapid social changes and, indeed, social explosions all around us, the society still holds fast to the notion that Negro families should be stable, and that if they are, this supreme virtue produces a great many other desirable consequences. This is part of the illusion.

The major problem facing the Negro people is not stability, as such, but the ability to survive while being black in a white society. Many low income Negro families are often forced to choose between a father in the home and money in the home, and many make the pragmatic choice for money. This behavior is generally viewed as dysfunctional and a sign of the disorganization of Negro family life. It is, on the contrary, quite functional, indicative both of the ability of low income Negro families to survive and of their concern for the welfare of their children. Stability, then, sometimes may be a means toward viability, but sometimes it may be an obstacle. It is always a goal, highly to be desired, but, in the Negro experience particularly, it is never a substitute for survival or viability or social achievement.

The Illusion of Excellence

A second change needed in the value system is to abandon the illusion of excellence. All the major institutions of society should abandon the single standard of excellence based on white European cultural norms. In general, white people, culture-bound by their own European heritage, decide which values are to be honored and rewarded. They design tests to measure these values; they standardize these tests on other white people like themselves; then they administer them to Negroes without regard to cultural diversity and basic life conditions. Through interpretation of these tests, they make the major decisions affecting the lives of Negro people. Little wonder that on every single major kind of standardized test designed by white people, Negro people, whatever their social class status, do not generally do as well as whites. If Negroes were free to make the decisions about which values and life styles to reward, white people certainly would not demonstrate the consistent superiority on these test performances they currently do. Of course, white people would not show up as badly as Negroes now do—largely because Negroes, in general, are more sensitive to the needs of other people than white people have shown themselves to be. Three examples from our recent experience will illustrate the point we are making about the dysfunctions of the white standards of excellence. Two are negative and one is positive.

One example comes from the recent experience of the San Francisco Human Rights Commission, whose job it is to work with Negro and Mexican-Americans of the city toward minority group advancement. Of the eight professional staff members on the commission, only two are Negroes and one is Mexican-American. One Negro and the Mexican-American are temporary members, although they are considered by the commission to be two of its most experienced and effective civil rights peacemakers. Recently civil service examinations were held to fill the commission jobs permanently. Since these jobs pay between $10,000 and $15,000 per year, there were a number of applicants, both Negro and white. As might have been anticipated, all the persons who placed in the highest range on the examination were white. Now both temporary members face almost certain loss of their jobs, and the city faces the loss of their effective service. It is not as if incompetent persons were being replaced with more competent ones: the Negro being replaced holds a masters degree in social science, is a former president of the local NAACP, and an expert on work with Negro youth. A colleague said of him, "he has a tremendous capacity for working with angry young men. He knows so many things that examinations can't measure." [2] And what do San Francisco and other major cities of the country need more than people who have the capacity to work with angry young men in a responsible capacity?

The commission does not seem able to respond to that need. When the local NAACP president heard of this situation, he protested that the exams were not designed to reflect the unique responsibilities of the Human Rights Commission. "They were prepared," he observed, "for persons of white, middle-class experiences." The manager of the Civil Service Department giving these exams was blandly defensive. As far as he was concerned, he was color blind and concerned only about excellence. His tests had shown that the best people had qualified for the jobs. "We cannot set up special considerations for minorities or anyone else," he was quoted as saying. "The examinations are structured for the jobs involved, and the people who qualified are well educated and experienced." It is enough to make sensitive young persons despair that the establishment can ever reform sufficiently to save itself and the society from destruction.

Another example of the dysfunctions of imposing white values on situations involving Negroes comes from the U. S. Post Office Department. As I look out the window of my study, I often see the postman delivering the mail. Two years ago my postman was a very handsome, very friendly, middle-aged Negro man dressed in a smart blue uniform with white shirt and tie who wore a cheerful disposition with his mail pouch. Today as I looked out the window, I observed my new postman. She is a very young, very attractive, white female with very long hair and a very short dress, who wears a very somber disposition as she pushes her mail cart along the sidewalk. It's the new thing for the Post Office. White hippie girls who have dropped out of college or graduate school for a few months make very high scores on the civil service exams used for judging

[2] *Chronicle* (San Francisco), December 8, 1967, p. 4.

the competence of people to be postmen. And the Negro men, high school graduates with families to support, who have traditionally found a friend in the Post Office Department, are now being bested by a new enemy. Far from implementing Moynihan's idea of having the Post Office Department hire more Negro men, thereby enhancing Negro family life, the reverse seems to be happening. Nationally, there is a 2 per cent drop in the number of Negro postmen.

A third example comes from academia. There is, perhaps, no segment of our society which is more enamored of standardized tests as a measure of excellence than the educational system. About four years ago, the graduate school of social welfare at the University of California in which I teach decided to "set up special considerations for minorities," and do something special to recruit and educate larger numbers of Negro professionals. Our major innovation was to relax the rigidities of our procedures for measuring competence to do graduate work and to perform in the profession. We de-Europeanized the tests and made them more relevant to the experience of prospective Negro students, and to the realities of life in the ghettos, into which many of our white middle class graduates are still reluctant to tread. Someone said in the course of our considerations that any Negro who manages to graduate from college in our society, considering all the obstacles to that achievement, has already, by that fact alone, demonstrated outstanding ability whether or not his grades placed him in the top of his class. Moreover, we convinced ourselves that the Negro experience itself had something special to offer our profession.

With our new convictions and new procedures, we saw the Negro enrollment in our school increase from one or two to about thirty-three, an increase from less than 1 per cent of the total enrollment of the school to more than 10 per cent. We have found, much to our delight and sometimes to our surprise, that these students do very well in our graduate school. And what is of even more importance, after they leave our school, they perform very well in the ordinary roles social workers are expected to perform, and even better in the extraordinary roles. Thus we are particularly proud of the community leadership our Negro graduate social workers are providing in the ghettos of Watts, as well as in those of Oakland, San Francisco, Richmond, and other communities. We are proud of the more relevant approaches they are able to bring to family counseling, youth work, and other duties.

The two negative examples can be found, multiplied a thousand times, in every major institution or subsystem of our society, with the partial exception of athletics These techniques, based on the standardized tests, have had the effect of barring Negroes from equal participation in our society, robbing the society of the leadership and other contributions this participation would contribute. A reversal of this preoccupation with standardized evaluations of Negroes is a major prerequisite for the reconstruction of Negro family and community life. What must be substituted are tests that Negroes participate in designing, administering, and interpreting, based on values which Negroes play an important part in defining.

Specifically, then, every major institution and subsystem of society must have the active participation of Negroes in meaningful roles and meaningful numbers at every level of the system. If Negroes cannot be found who are qualified, we must change our definition of qualifications. If after vigorous and sustained efforts, they still cannot be found in sufficient numbers, they should be hired and then trained by the institutions themselves, with Negroes taking a major part in the development and execution of the training programs. In short, the society must make a serious and sustained effort to include Negroes in the mainstream; in the process, the nature of the mainstream will change and reflect more adequately the nature of our pluralistic society.

The Illusion of Wisdom

Thirdly, we must abandon the illusion that a major share of wisdom lies with white people, especially white liberals and professionals, when it comes to designing programs to benefit the Negro people. The circumstances surrounding the Moynihan report are a good example of this illusion.[8] The President of the United States would have been served much better in his efforts to develop a government policy toward Negro family life if he had consulted with and followed the advice of a number of Negroes, including some of his own appointees, rather than relying so heavily on the advice of those persons he did consult. Such illusions of wisdom are commonly supported by considerable arrogance on the part of white men of power and intellect.

In a symposium with James Baldwin and several white liberals, Kenneth Clark described an episode which helps to illustrate the point we are making.

In this very room, about 24 hours ago, a group of social scientists, liberal social scientists, met to talk about how they could be more effective in the study of race relations. The chairman of the department of

[8] Lee Rainwater and William Yancey, *op. cit.*

social psychology at a major university in America said that he had got some money to do something in the area of race relations. So what did he do? He and his department decided that they would not hire anybody who had done any research in race relations; they would hire somebody who had done extremely good experimental work in the psychology of visual perception. When I heard that, I suspected, as a Negro—bitter, distorted—that maybe one reason they did not invite anyone who had done work in race relations was that they might have had to think of a Negro.[4]

During 1968 the Ford Foundation made a grant of over ten million dollars to Harvard, M.I.T., Columbia, and the University of Chicago to support institutes for the study of problems in Negro ghettos. My first reaction was to applaud this grant and to regret only that the University of California had not been included. On more sober and skeptical reflection, however, I began to wonder if this was not merely another effort on the part of great universities to support their regular programs with new funds. When I read further in *Time* magazine that these universities intend to establish fourteen major professorships, and to provide fellowships for the training of sixty-five Ph.D. students, 390 other graduate students, and 390 undergraduates in urban studies, I could not help wondering how many of the professorships, doctoral fellowships, and other supports would go to Negroes. I concluded, on the basis of past and present experience—that these funds would be used to support more white professors who would train more white students to become experts on Negroes, according to what these professors already know. I was not entirely correct. Columbia, on receiving its grant promptly appointed the honorable Franklyn Williams, distinguished Negro attorney, civil rights leader, and U. S. Ambassador to Ghana as director of its Urban Affairs Institute. Then after the assassination of Dr. Martin Luther King, Jr., and the subsequent demands of Negro and white students for more Negro students and faculty members, a number of these universities began to search earnestly, intensively, and deliberately for Negro faculty members. But these universities must move beyond token appointments to substantial representation of Negroes at every level of their structure and operations. The view that Negroes are not qualified for such participation is highly ironic when it is expressed by universities whose major commitment is qualifying people for the most exacting roles in society. Furthermore, the student unrest in the spring of 1968 emphasizes the urgency that Columbia and other white institutions located in the Negro

⁴ Kenneth Clark in "Liberalism and the Negro: A Roundtable Discussion," ed. N. Podhoretz, *Commentary*, XXXVII (March 1964), 39.

community recognize their responsibilities toward those communities and deal with responsible leadership in those communities as equals, not as subjects whose interests, needs, and peaceful protests may be ignored.

It is not, of course, our contention that only Negroes can accurately study and make effective recommendations about the Negro experience and the urban condition. We need both Negro and white scholars to undertake these studies. The point is, however, that Negroes have been systematically barred from the opportunity structures which produce such experts. And the white people who make most of the decisions about who are experts and who can be trained to be experts generally decide that the wisest and most competent people to study and make recommendations about Negroes are other white people of European heritage, who have made high scores on certain standardized tests. The illusion of wisdom, like the illusion of excellence and the illusion of stability, dies hard.

The Illusion of Morality

Fourth, there is the illusion of morality. Negro families in the lower classes suffer no greater public approbation than the accusation that they are heavily invested with immoral behavior. Americans are very easily convinced that they are right and good, and that anyone who differs from them is wrong and bad. And since middle and upper class white people do most of the defining of right conduct, it is little wonder that lower class Negro families are viewed in our society as hotbeds of immorality.

Certain national and state government leaders who defend the killing of thousands of innocent persons in Vietnam condemn the Negroes who revolt in the ghettos with the most passionate appeals to morality. The same government officials who bend every effort to pay extravagant prices for goods purchased from private industries for governmental use condemn in the loudest tones the Negro mother who collects a few hundred dollars in public assistance while her unemployed husband returns home for visits with his family.

One of the most highly regarded aspects of social welfare in our society is adoptions. When a white middle class housewife, who is infertile, adopts the illegitimate child of another white woman, society bends every effort to make sure that both women are protected from condemnation, for they both have "done the right thing." This contrasts sharply with the general efforts to expose to ridicule the Negro woman who has an illegitimate child and chooses to keep her own child, or must do so because of the policies of adoption agencies.

The Illusion of Normality

Fifth, there is an illusion of normality. Stemming again from the Anglo-conformity doctrine which still dominates the essential values of this society is the deeply held view that patterns of responses generated, practiced, or sanctioned in the white community are normal, and that any deviations from those norms which might be relevant or common in the black community are abnormal, deviant, and to be highly disvalued. One of the most common approaches social scientists make to the study of the Negro experience in this country is to draw up a questionnaire based on the white experience. Then they ask white and black people the same questions, in the same way, on a variety of matters. When they find that the response patterns of the Negroes differ significantly from those of the whites, they conclude that the Negro responses are deviant and need to be explained. This habit of mind is perpetuated even to the present time, largely because the American value system has not made room for the Negro experience as a part of the normal values of the society.

The Illusion of Beauty

Sixth, there is an illusion of beauty, the assumption that physical characteristics associated with white people are more beautiful than those associated with black people. This assumption is too common, widespread, and pervasive to require elaboration. The Negro people are beginning to say, in a variety of ways, that black is beautiful—a most human response, which is especially revealing about the Negro people's transition from self-hate to self-appreciation. One of the reasons this bothers white people so much is that it casts doubts on the illusion that white is beautiful and, therefore, black is ugly.

The Illusion of Power

Finally, there is deeply ingrained in the American belief system an illusion of power—the belief that physical force, economic force, and military force are more powerful than the human spirit, love, will, or determination. As Americans we easily convince ourselves that we have the most powerful army, navy, and air force in the world. And yet, all this might does not seem able to subdue the Vietnamese people. There is little doubt, we are told, that the American economic system is the most powerful weapon for the proliferation of wealth, and yet it seems hopelessly unable to secure economic viability for the majority of Negro families. The political system, we are convinced, is the strongest type of governing mechanism imaginable. Yet the President, the Congress, and to some extent the courts themselves, are often unable to provide justice for the Negro people. It is not without significance that while white Americans have won a number of world prizes for their physical power, and indeed for other virtues as well, the only American persons to be awarded the Nobel Peace Prize in recent years have been black— Ralph J. Bunche and Martin Luther King, Jr. And if we consider the other recent American winner of the Peace Prize, the American Friends Service Committee (Quakers), we must observe that this religious group also departs strikingly from the basic American illusion of power. In this same connection, when we think of the ghetto uprisings that began to take place during the summer of 1964, we must be impressed anew with the American faith in the power of the police and the military to crush those rebellions. No doubt, military force will succeed to a degree and for a time. Yet the overwhelming faith the American people place on that approach to a most complex human problem must be considered, in the long run, one of the greatest illusions of our time, and most symptomatic of the value crisis in American society—perhaps even surpassing the crisis which brings on the uprisings themselves.

Thus, in one major area of life after another, strongly held values in our society assume that white is right and black is wrong. It is not enough that white people in positions of power who are able to establish the norms of our society attribute greater virtue to themselves. Many people honestly believe that white people in general are more stable, more able, wiser, and more virtuous than Negroes. But what is even more devastating and crippling to the advancement of the Negro people is that many Negroes have fallen victims to these same illusions. How else could it be? It is a most human characteristic to define one's self and one's behavior in terms sanctioned by the most powerful and relevant persons in one's larger social environment. And that is why these illusions, and others too, are so insidious. The Negro people have to stop believing them. That is one of the most agonizing aspects of the American dilemma. Destroying these illusions, and others like them, is a most urgent prerequisite to the reconstruction of American society and the enhancement of Negro family and community life. For while it is difficult for black people to recognize their worth, dignity, and beauty in a society committed to denying them, it is unthinkable that the white world will change until it is made to do so by black people. The hope is that activity in other areas of American life not bearing directly on these values at all, including activity in the Negro ghettos on the part of Negroes and whites of various statuses, will help force a reevaluation of these cultural configurations. Perhaps another ray of hope is reflected in the fact that many middle and upper class Negroes are returning to the ghettos in spirit and in action. This is, no doubt, in large measure because it has become apparent that the white devaluation of the Negro experience limits the freedom and opportunity of the privileged Negroes as well as the underprivileged. The Northern Negro upper class, for example, is vulnerable in hundreds of ways to the ebb and flow of the civil rights revolt. No particular group of Negroes is immune to the castelike barriers that separate black and white in our society.

If these values are to be modified substantially, all the major institutions in both the white and the black community must begin more vigorous efforts to question them and present alternatives to them. It is most distressing, for example, to walk into a Negro church and observe the pictures on the walls and in books depicting good people who are all white. Or to consider the matter of children's literature in general, which we know, from the pioneering work of David McClelland,[5] both reflects and generates the dominant values of a society. Negroes are almost completely absent from this literature; and when they do appear, the situation is so distorted that one wishes they had been ignored altogether. My wife spends an agonizing period between September and December 24 each year and before birthdays and special occasions trying to find children's literature and toys which reflect the Negro experience in a positive light. It is a most frustrating undertaking. She has not yet been able to find a black Santa Claus. Or consider television and other mass media. They seem to have a special fascination for violence, whether in war, crime, or ghetto uprisings, but ignore completely the ordinary aspects of Negro family life. Each major network and publication should carry regular and sustained news, features, and dramatic programs—including soap operas—on some aspects of the variety and complexity of Negro family life.

In our view, then, the society would help Negro families meet their functions much better if it placed more emphasis on the values of freedom—including freedom of choice in family form—and equality—in-

[5] David C. McClelland, *The Achieving Society* (Princeton: D. Van Nostrand Co., Inc., 1961).

cluding equality of opportunity to survive and prosper—with much less emphasis on the illusions of stability, excellence, wisdom, morality, normality, beauty, and power. These grand illusions are the handmaidens of a subtle, persistent kind of racism which stifles the development of the Negro people and of the Negro family, and thus also of a pluralistic and democratic society.

Chapter 7

Strategies
of Social Reform

Toward Economic Viability

If the first prerequisite for reformation of the wider society is a change in some of the basic values to make room for the Negro experience, a second, equal, and related imperative is for changes in the economic system of the society in order to enhance the economic viability of Negro families. The evidence is clear that economic viability is one of the major factors which enables families to meet the functions required of them by society as well as both the instrumental and expressive needs of their members.

There is considerable evidence that economic viability is now receiving increasingly high priority in the country. A number of very imaginative plans are being advanced and a number of halting steps are being taken by government and industry. Three problems, however, inhibit the current planning with respect to providing economic security to all American families. One is the very restricted view of the nature of the problem. In our view, poverty is only the most conspicuous area of economic insecurity facing Negro families. We have indicated above that many families who do not qualify for aid from welfare or the Office of Economic Opportunity are, nevertheless, unable to provide economically for all the necessities of life. This has been recognized in the State of New York, where a family of four with an income of up to $6,000, distinctly beyond all the definitions of poverty, may be considered financially unable to provide adequate medical care for its members, and may consequently be eligible to take part in the government-supported medical care program.

A second conspicuous limitation of current national planning, and to a certain extent, of national thinking about economic security for Negro families, is that tremendous faith is placed in single and simple solutions to very complex problems. There is a tendency to suggest that the government should give low income Negro families economic security through jobs and income supports, thereby making opportunities for Negroes substantially equal to those of children from white families, and ushering in family stability, conforming behavior, and school achievement. It is not often explicitly recognized that a tremendous time lag will be necessary for these particular solutions to show their particular effects. It was the Negro sociologist, G. Franklin Edwards, who pointed out that in education, the area in which Negroes are making the most progress relative to whites, it will still take more than fifty years for the Negro population as a whole to catch up to the educational levels of the white population, at the current rate of progress.[1]

In specific economic areas other than education, the process will apparently take longer. Herman J. Blake, a young Negro sociologist, has reflected on the agony associated with such a realization. Commenting on his experience as a student in a white university, he observed:

> You learn—in your objective search for truth—that white America accrues gains from racism and discrimination. Although people use you as an example of what the Negro can do, you acquire objective evidence that the overwhelming majority of Negroes see little change in their life conditions. For example: the sociologist from the University of Texas who analyzed the rates at which Negroes were overtaking whites in their struggle for equal treatment, and then extrapolated these rates to see how long from 1960 it would take the Negro to reach full equality.
>
> The answer: at the 1950–60 rates of change it would take 60 years in education, 93 years in occupation, 219 years in income of persons, and 805 years in family income. And you get angry.[2]

At a hearing in late 1967 of the Senate Subcommittee on Urban Problems, a number of white liberal senators, including Jacob Javits and Abraham Ribicoff, and social scientists, including Daniel P. Moynihan, Lee Rainwater, and Herbert Gans, seemed to coalesce around three economic programs essential for establishing viability among low income families who live in ghettos.[3] These included (1) full employment, (2) massive training and retraining programs, and (3) a guaranteed minimum family income of about $3,000. Only Professor Kenneth B. Clark, a Negro psychologist, commented substantially on the limitations

---

[1] G. Franklin Edwards, speech at Conference on the Negro Family, Plan of Action for Challenging Time (PACT) and University of California Extension, October 1964.

[2] Herman J. Blake, "The Agony and the Rage," *Negro Digest*, March 1967, pp. 9–15.

[3] Special Report: "Sick Cities—and the Search for a Cure," *Transaction*, IV, No. 10 (October 1967), 34–54.

of this economic approach unless it was coupled with some other efforts to solve the problems of self-respect and self-worth as well as problems involving the respect other persons have for ghetto people. "These," he concluded,

> are as important for the human spirit as merely providing the material economic basis for living. . . . I think if you were to give every poor family $5,000 now, the way welfare is administered, it is my personal opinion that this would not affect one iota the observable pathologies of our slums. I think the way welfare is administered, it seems to be calculated to dehumanize people, to make them see themselves as not worthy; and when human beings see themselves as not worthy, they tend to act in ways which create the reason for hearings such as this. . . . [4]

He need not have confined his indictment to the welfare system. All the major subsystems of society, as we have argued, have failed in the same way.

But the white, liberal senators on this committee were not very sympathetic to Professor Clark's point of view. They were much more interested in the program advanced by the white liberal professors. It had a ring of concreteness. It is easier to introduce legislation about a certain guaranteed annual income than to worry about the complexities of guaranteed annual dignity.

Clark's testimony caused Senator Javits to follow up the line of questioning which had been introduced by Senator Ribicoff: "I gather," Javits said, "that you are against the guaranteed annual income to the welfare family." Clark responded: "I did not say I was against it. I said I am dubious about it unless it is tied to certain guarantees of self-respect." Then Clark drew an analogy from the earlier testimony of Moynihan on the inadequacies of public housing.

> You remember that he said that merely to place human beings in new homes or housing units and have them bring with them their other problems unresolved did not really answer the question. I would like to use that same point in reference to the guaranteed annual income. Merely to assure an economic base without the society addressing itself to all of the other and related problems will not in itself be a solution. I just do not think there is any single gimmick-type solution to these problems. [5]

It should be clear in this presentation, as it was in the hearings, that Professor Clark was not opposed, but emphatically in favor of, economic

---

[4] *Ibid.*, p. 40.
[5] *Ibid.*, p. 40.

investment in the problems of the ghetto. He observed in his formal presentation:

> I think the budget is about as good an index of the priority society gives various problems as one can find. Our space program and our Vietnam war have budgetary supports which indicate tremendous seriousness. Our anti-poverty programs have budgetary indications of secondary, tertiary, peripheral priorities, and I don't think that we will solve the problems of our inner cities by relegating [them] to peripheral priorities. . . . We must use the same approach we use in other areas.[6]

Why, then, did Professor Clark feel called upon to demur from the program being advanced by the liberal senators and experts? In part, I believe, because he knows and is in close personal touch with the Negro experience. Having grown up in Harlem, he knows that money alone will not solve the problems of the Negro families there, any more than any other simple, single program will. But in addition, being in close personal contact with other Negro families who have middle and upper incomes, and even with those who have managed to move into white suburbs, he knows also that money has not given them the sense of mastery over the conditions of their life that is available to white families of similar economic status. If they do not protest as loudly or in the same manner as Negroes living in the ghettos, it is because their social class and style of life provide them with other less visible means of protesting, and with less motivation to protest, because they have been misled into believing that a rise in status and improvement in manners and conduct would carry with it the rewards of such status and behavior, and are only gradually becoming disillusioned with that promise.

In addition to being Negro, Dr. Clark is also a psychologist, and a clinician who has worked intimately with people under stress and who knows that money alone will not cure all their ills. The other liberals on the program spoke from a greater degree of detachment from these two experiences. Therefore, they run the danger of exhibiting a much more intelligent commitment to *programs* than to *people*, with all the complexities of their needs. This suggests that even the most informed, enlightened, and liberal members of the American establishment, whether in the government, in universities, or elsewhere, must pay more attention to the special nature of the Negro experience in this country when designing solutions to the problems Negroes face. And the solutions must be as comprehensive and complex and massive as the problems, or they

* *Ibid.*, p. 39.

will surely fail and perhaps cause even deeper levels of disillusionment and even greater expressions of discontent.

As important and indeed indispensable as are jobs, job training, and a minimum income floor for Negro families, nothing in any of these programs necessarily speaks to ownership, control, management, independence, high status, or power. Without other measures, they could fail to solve the essential problems of economic, social, and psychological dependence and the sense of alienation which accompany these phenomena. A massive job development program is an urgent necessity. But it must be designed to meet today's physical, economic, demographic, social, and psychological realities. It is no simple task to turn men who have had no jobs and little hope all their lives into productive workers, even when jobs are available. The Detroit industries, which made 23,000 jobs available to unskilled, unemployed Negroes after the Detroit riots of July 1967, have had mixed records of work commitment. The Employment Director of the Detroit Urban League estimates that the 23,000 jobs have been occupied by over 100,000 persons during the first five months of the program's operation because the dropout rate is so high. "They drift in and they drift out," he was quoted as saying.[7] The record has been particularly bad at Chrysler, which estimates that of the 12,000 men originally hired after the riots, only about 1,200 were still there six months later. But the record at General Motors Pontiac plant was exceptionally good. There, of the 230 men originally hired, 219 were still on the job six months later. What is it about the men, their histories, their family situations, or the job situations themselves that accounts for these very different patterns of performance? One factor seems to be a sense of belonging. A voluntary effort among the workingmen to develop and sustain this through mutual aid seems highly promising. But much more needs to be known and done. The Urban League undertook a program to help supply answers to these questions with half a million dollars contributed by Chrysler.

The experience in Detroit illustrates our own conviction that any massive job development program must be accompanied by a social program designed to support these men and their families so that they can take advantage of the programs, a great diversification of kinds of work, and a research program designed to document what kinds of programs work with what kinds of people with what social and psychological consequences.

Job development, as important as it is for the development of viability

[7] *Time Magazine* (December 8, 1967), p. 28.

in the Negro family and community, is not enough. It should be remembered that most of the Negroes arrested for taking part in ghetto uprisings of recent years have been employed. Job development must be interlaced with a program of economic development for the total community. This requires a massive program of financial investment in the Negro communities of all the large urban areas of our country. Government, voluntary associations, and private business interests can all play a role in this investment. The treasurer of Illinois, Adlai E. Stevenson III, recently announced that the funds invested by the state government in commercial banks would henceforth not be invested in financial institutions which discriminated in the hiring of Negroes and other minorities. This pioneering effort has not been followed by other political jurisdictions, but let us suppose every major industrial state with a large Negro population followed the Illinois example and took it one step further. Suppose funds of the state were invested in large degree in specifically Negro-owned banks and financial institutions, in the Negro community. If such institutions did not exist, with such a guaranteed source of investment, they could be created. In a similar manner, the State of New York has recently, after many years of delay and controversy, finally decided to construct a major state office building in Harlem, and is going to extra efforts to enable local contractors to bid on the construction of portions of the State Center. In other ways, too, the State is consciously bringing local people into partnership with the State and with white contractors.

Nonprofit voluntary associations, including churches, have recently announced small-scale investments in the urban ghettos. Labor unions and other groups with large funds for pension, welfare, and other purposes should consider investing these funds in Negro-owned institutions which do business in the Negro communities.

It may well be that the government will continue to sponsor only token approaches to the economic reconstruction of the ghetto channeled through "safe" political and economic structures. For neither liberal nor conservative political leaders on the national level seem capable of using the sound judgment of economists and others who have pointed up both the necessity and feasibility of massive governmental programs. They seem almost completely constipated by timidity, racial prejudice, or both in their approach to the economic development of the Negro communities. It may be, then, that private industry will have to take the lead in this massive undertaking.

In this respect, the recent announcement of the largest insurance

companies that they intend to invest a billion dollars in urban rehabilitation over the next few years is a welcome indication. It must be stated
in all candor, however, that a one billion dollar investment is pitifully
small, not only in terms of the need, but in terms of the amount of money
the insurance companies take *out* of the Negro ghettos. The large white
insurance companies are collecting considerably more from the Negro
communities than they reinvest in them. Their current investments in
the Negro community are primarily. in jobs for Negro sales people, and
a few scattered middle income housing developments. It has been estimated by Andrew Brimmer, Negro member of the Board of Governors
of the Federal Reserve Bank, that any one of the six largest white-owned
insurance companies takes more money out of the Negro neighborhoods
than all the Negro owned insurance companies combined.[8] Furthermore,
the one billion dollar investment projected over the next few years is a
pitifully small portion of the resources available to these large life insurance companies, resources which they invest in other segments of the
economy. Andrew Brimmer has estimated that in 1966 alone, these insurance companies put 37 billion dollars into *new* investments.[9] In comparison to this, the one billion dollars to be invested in urban ghettos
over several years is peanuts.

Yet, it is a step in the right direction, particularly if it is invested in
cooperation with Negro financial institutions which already operate in
the ghetto or which might be formed. Brimmer believes that such practices not only will help to build up the economic fabric of the black
communities, but also will be of enormous benefits to the insurance companies putting up the investment capital. It will make available to them
a kind of expertise in Negro community conditions, particularly ghetto
housing problems, not otherwise available to such large companies.

An example of what happened in Philadelphia in 1966 illustrates the
necessity of such collaboration. Four Philadelphia Savings Banks launched
a program to invest $20 million in homes in the Negro community to be
insured by the Federal Housing Administration. After eighteen months
they had been able to make firm commitments for only $1.5 million worth
of housing. Of the many obstacles they have faced, the major one involves working with the ghetto residents themselves. While relying mainly
on their own employees and previous (white) mortgage brokers active
in real estate, it has taken these companies an inordinate amount of time

---

[8] Andrew F. Brimmer, "Financial Institutions and Urban Rehabilitation," *Urban West*, I, No. 2 (November–December 1967), 20.
[9] *Ibid.*, p. 21.

to contact "ghetto residents and to instruct many of the potential buyers
about the process—and responsibility—of becoming homeowners." Brimmer concludes as follows:

> From the experience of the Philadelphia institutions, it seems clear that
> Negro bankers, insurance company officials, and others with a specialized
> knowledge acquired through lending funds against ghetto properties
> could make a major contribution in helping to translate the recently
> announced one billion dollar life insurance company program into a
> significant effort of urban reconstruction.[10]

A greatly expanded program of investment, running into the hundreds
of billions of dollars, could provide not only housing for ghetto residents,
but jobs as well.

It is very important, however, to emphasize that jobs in the Negro
community should not simply be "just jobs," or even "top jobs" with
good pay. For the advantage of the kind of mutual economic development which would join the large insurance companies with smaller Negro financial institutions in the reconstruction of Negro communities is
that it could also provide jobs for Negro professionals and business executives. The Negro community needs leadership and it needs responsible, secure, and independent leadership with a major stake in the community and a great deal of freedom. Again, Brimmer has pointed out that
the number of Negro professionals is not increasing rapidly enough to
keep up with the expanding population.

> The number of Negro lawyers is growing slowly, while the number of
> Negro physicians and dentists is actually declining in relation to total
> Negro employment. Even the number of schoolteachers is declining rela-
> tive to the Negro labor force.[11]

There has been, then, a relative standstill in these high level professional jobs for Negroes, while there has been an expansion in technical
and middle level, white-collar civil service jobs. The problem is that these
latter jobs do not provide positions of community leadership. Brimmer
has observed that "although a computer programmer may earn as much
as (or more than) a high school principal, he clearly has less weight in
the community's affairs." We have already commented on the social status
of the high school principal in the Negro community. Brimmer continues:

> A Negro reservations clerk in a leading downtown hotel is in the same
> business as the former Negro hotel owner, but here, also, his community

[10] *Ibid.*, p. 23.
[11] *Ibid.*, p. 20.

role is less significant. In my opinion, the expansion of opportunities for Negroes in the truly professional and managerial occupations should be a prime goal of the Negro business community.[12]

Indeed, it should be a prime goal of the federal, state, and local governments, and of the large industries and voluntary associations which wish to make a major impact on the reconstruction of Negro family and community life.

One would hope that the President of the United States would listen to the advice of his most distinguished appointee to the Federal Reserve Board. Brimmer is an outstanding example of the new Negro upper class, who uses both his professional expertise and his Negro experience to analyze the conditions and prescribe solutions to the problems which beset the Negro community and the nation.

Economic Strategies, not Programs

The economic viability of large numbers of Negro families depend, then, rather heavily on the economic viability of the Negro community in general, which in turn depends on changes in strategies and current behavior and on adoption of new strategies by major social systems outside the Negro community, including government, business, and nonprofit corporations. We need massive new economic inputs into the Negro community. These inputs must be appropriate in size, complexity, and flexibility to the needs they are designed to meet. A new book by General James Gavin supports this line of reasoning. One is always surprised and impressed when a man who has devoted so much of his career to military affairs shows so much insight into the social problems of our day. His vision is much broader than that of some of our most outstanding social reformers. "To attack our decaying environment," he has observed,

> we need to undertake simultaneously a series of actions, each one of which is staggering in itself. . . . We must build 5,000,000 new homes. We must end discrimination. We must redirect our use of farm land. We must construct 100,000 new schools and provide a philosophy, atmosphere and teachers for these schools so that rapid learning can take place for all. We must provide a decent standard of living for those not able to work. We must create new social services, provide new hospitals, find more doctors, build new libraries responsive to electronic data processing, and halt the pollution of our environment.

[13] *Ibid.,* p. 20.

According to Gavin: "we need to find jobs for roughly 20,000,000 people." [13] The jobs take their place in a massive program of economic and social development.

General Gavin also calls attention to the need to harness human energy in the solution of human problems. "The key group whose energies must be involved in the solutions of their own problems is the ghetto dwellers. They do not want to be handed out solutions to their problems without any say, any more than anybody else." He has found a new social mechanism, operative on a small scale in some communities, which conform to our own view of how the Negro community might organize to play a major part in its own economic development. He calls this the Neighborhood Development Corporation.

> Though designed primarily to liberate energies in the ghetto, the Neighborhood Development Corporation indicates a process that could be of benefit to all of us. With the Neighborhood Development Corporation providing the means, local residents can now take part in the process of changing their environment. If a business wants to construct a plant in the neighborhood, its officers would deal with members of the Neighborhood Development Corporation. The corporation would make certain that local (i.e., black) officials had some say in the plant's policies, that local (black) contractors were used in construction, that local (black) businessmen supplied the plant with goods and services, that local (black) banks handled the plant's business—in short, that the plant conform to neighborhood standards. [14]

This is precisely the kind of economic development of the black community we have in mind. General Gavin's Neighborhood Development Corporation in the economic sphere is remarkably similar in structure and function to our own conception of a Neighborhood Multipurpose Service Center, which we later describe, in the social welfare sphere.

For now, however, we must observe that General Gavin's ideas help us make the point that a complex, massive, and highly interrelated series of strategies—not set, predetermined, and prepackaged programs—must be available in the Negro community, with community residents given maximum control over the operations of these programs and thus maximum benefits of the programs plowed back into the community to build it up. The goal of economic development in the Negro community should be not only to raise the level of income of low income families but to

[13] General James Gavin, "Crisis of the Cities: the Battle We Can Win," *Saturday Review*, L (February 24, 1968), 30ff.
[14] *Ibid.*, p. 33.

build up Negro institutions, Negro leadership, and an expanded Negro middle class.

THE POLITICAL SUBSYSTEM

Among the subsystems of the wider society with power for setting the conditions which affect Negro family life, the political subsystem ranks second only to the economic. It may even rank higher. No subsystem has been more oppressive of the Negro people or holds greater promise for their development. It is, therefore, a major target for reform.

We think of the political subsystem of society as involving the executive, legislative, and judicial branches of government which operate at the national, state, and local levels. In our view, a new level of government which should be given increased responsibility, autonomy, and power is the neighborhood. One of the more obvious facts of our time is that nowhere in the country at either of these levels of government, or in any of the three branches of government, is the black perspective adequately reflected—and nowhere are the Negro people adequately represented. For example, the six Negroes in Congress in 1968 comprise only about 1 per cent of that body, while Negroes comprise 12 per cent of the national population. Let us consider the implications of this disparity. If it is true, as we have argued, that we live in an essentially, though subtly, racist society, then for the Negro people to be so completely governed by white people makes it impossible for them ever to receive justice, to say nothing of equality or fraternity.

It is true that for a brief two years after the assassination of President Kennedy in 1963 and the ascendancy of President Johnson, all three branches of the national government seemed oriented for the first time to the problems of poor people, and to a lesser extent, to the problems of black people. Even this passing commitment was limited in vision and scope, in part because the national government got very bad advice from the white liberal intellectual community about the nature of the problems facing poor people and black people. The government was convinced by these experts that the problems facing these two groups of people were essentially the same and could be attacked effectively with the same strategies. The problems facing the Negro people, it was commonly heard, are not those of race, but of class. Thus, instead of launching a program to abolish racism, the government launched a program to abolish poverty, and assumed that poverty among white and black people would respond to the same programs. The notion that these two problems could be resolved with one strategy was no more successful than the proverbial notion that one can kill two birds with one stone. After two brief years of concerted activity, the national government withdrew from the struggle, disappointed that the problems had not been solved and that the Negro community had not been pacified. With rare exceptions, the state and local governments never really joined in the fight. And after fleeting efforts to establish neighborhood governments for limited aspects of the poverty war, this effort too was abandoned. However, the national judiciary, particularly as represented by the Supreme Court, has had a clearer vision recently about the nature of the problems facing poor people and black people, and also a clearer commitment to the democratic values of our heritage—no doubt, because the judiciary is somewhat more protected from the passions of racism than the other two branches.

If the Negro people cannot trust the white-dominated political system to look after their best interests, then two interrelated strategies are required in the wider society: first, relentless efforts to interpret the Negro experience to the powerful centers of government and the people generally; second, at least equal representation and, ideally, overrepresentation of Negro people in all the key levels and branches of government. But not just any Negroes will do. *Almost* any Negro will do better than the white liberals and white bigots who now represent Negro communities in the government, but often an elected Negro official is forced to be so beholden to the white power structure that he becomes more responsive to them than to the Negro people he represents. What the government needs in this period of national crises is "maximum" Negroes—those who are able, willing, and in fact commanded to reflect as accurately as they can the interests, values, and perspectives of major segments of the Negro community.

If Negro members of the government are genuinely free to do this, and not bound by the white establishment, they will reflect a variety and range of commitment, ability, and philosophy. They will not all be radicals, any more than they will all be conservative. But they will be *authentic.* One of the problems with tokenism in any field, but especially government, is that unless the wider community is exposed to the variety and range of interests and conditions in the Negro community, it will be reinforced in its stereotypes of the Negro experience. This is not to suggest that such variety and range obviate the common interests of the Negro people. On the contrary, they reflect and express it more accurately. Thus, instead of the six Negro elected congressmen we have in

1968, there should be a minimum of sixty. The responsibility for this political equality rests squarely on the established political institutions. Again, however, they seem unable to change and reform themselves of their own accord.

An even greater thrust of Negro participation in government will, undoubtedly, be felt at the state, local, and neighborhood levels in the large urban areas where the Negro population is increasingly more heavily concentrated. Scores of large cities, following the lead of Cleveland and Gary, should have governments in which Negroes play the majority role. A few state houses should also reflect this new equality. The lowest level of government which needs to be formalized, namely neighborhood government, should have Negroes in complete control of governing their own communities. Nowhere in the country was this the case in 1968. If this suggested level of political participation seems excessive to some—for after all, Negroes are only 12 per cent of the population—three factors should be kept in mind. First, that a number of other ethnic groups, who constitute considerably less than 12 per cent of the population, already participate in the government of their own communities *and* of Negro communities, and are much more adequately represented in city, state, and national governments than Negroes are. Second, it should be observed that Negroes are highly concentrated in large urban areas, and that such concentration will continue to accelerate. But more important than any of these facts is the new determination on the part of the Negro people to control the conditions which affect their own lives, to organize in order to express their will, and to use their ethnicity as a positive force in this direction, as is done by other ethnic groups. Such political reorganization, however, is dependent not alone on the nature of the Negro community, but on the response of the white community as well.

In order to facilitate such political realignment, all branches of the government, at all levels, must make a maximum commitment to political democracy. It is asking a lot. As a first step in this direction, all white liberals who represent Negro communities should resign and campaign for their black replacements, selected by the black community. As a second step, all Southern whites who represent Negro communities should be expelled by the Congress or by the Courts, for they are clearly in violation of the constitution. Thirdly, the doctrine of one man, one vote should be extended to all levels of government and enforced with open and explicit, rather than devious, recognition given to ethnicity. Fourth, the voting age should be reduced to eighteen years, as two states have already done. Young people seem more reconciled to the twentieth century than their elders. Furthermore, eighteen-year-olds are adults with a great many of the abilities and responsibilities of citizenship. They should have the opportunity to participate in governing themselves.

None of these things is likely to happen. It would be asking too much of the white communities to make a voluntary commitment to democracy. Therefore, black strategies, internal to the Negro communities, seem to hold greater promise for political change. Here, too, the obstacles are great. That is why the development of strong institutions, independent leadership, and an expanded Negro middle class are indispensable, not only to the economic viability of Negro communities, but to their political viability as well. These communities should be aided in their efforts to organize and express their collective wills to a maximum degree by the government, foundations, political parties, and other citizen groups in the white community that are concerned about the survival of political democracy. These communities should be aided, of course, on their own terms—that is, on the terms expressed by their changing, evolving, and various leaderships. The implications for the Negro family are clear. These are the conditions which make it possible for families to survive and to prosper; to meet the demands of their society for conformity, commitment, and achievement; and to meet the needs of their members for physical, social, and psychological integrity.

Local Judiciary

While we have argued that at the national level the judicial arm has been the branch of the political system most sensitive to the state of affairs as it exists today, it cannot be said that the lower levels of the judicial system reflect this level of sensitivity and passion for remedy. The lower courts and juries are embodiments of racial separateness and inequality. Under the present system, it is difficult indeed for Negroes, particularly low income Negroes, accused of crimes to receive justice. Even when there are Negro judges, as there are in increasing numbers, and Negro lawyers, and an occasionally token number of Negroes on juries, the system of local justice is inherently reflective of the racism in our society. Even in jurisdictions where Negroes dominate, such as in the central cities of large urban areas, a Negro youth accused of a major crime has about the same opportunity of receiving a fair trial by a jury of his peers as he would have had during slavery. Both grand juries and trial juries are most likely to be white, middle class, elderly, and prejudiced.

There are indications that the judiciary might reform itself. In early

1968 there were two cases, one in New York and one in California, in which Negro youths, accused of crimes, were brought to justice by elderly, affluent, white citizens without the participation of the defendants' peers. These cases are being seriously challenged in higher courts, which are more responsive to the question of abridgment of constitutional guarantees. One hundred years after the end of the Civil War, the process is just beginning.

The police arm of the executive branch of local government epitomizes an even purer form of white domination over black people, with extremely high levels of insensitivity, unresponsiveness, and downright bigotry toward Negro people. Unfortunately, there are no indications that the large city police forces are yet ready to reform themselves. Here, where the ghetto rebellions of the past few years demonstrate that the need is greatest for reform, the white strategy of reform seems weakest. The white establishment, including the liberal establishment, seems resistive to change. Except in a few major cities, including New York, Atlanta, and Detroit, not the least token effort has been advanced to make the police responsive to the Negro experience and representative of the Negro people. Clearly, black strategies are called for. Since most major crimes against Negroes, both by other Negroes and by white people, are committed within the confines of the Negro communities, it is clear that the Negro people must have control of the police protection in these communities. It is not sufficient to have a token or generous number of Negro police patrolling these areas, subject to control of the traditional police system downtown. And if the process of gaining influence on the formal police system in their own communities seems to be moving at best slowly, then more informal methods of policing Negro neighborhoods must be invented by the Negro people. There are already some indications that such social inventions have exceedingly high promise. What must be recognized in the wider society is that Negro people both need and want police protection to a much greater extent than other ethnic communities. But what they don't want is what they now have— law and order without justice. The Community Alert Patrol in South Central Los Angeles is an excellent example of the creative potential of a neighborhood group. They have shown that it is possible to police their community and the downtown police at the same time.

EDUCATION AND HOUSING

Ask almost any Negro family head what he (or she) wishes most for his family, and the response would be "a decent house in a decent neighborhood." Ask that same parent what he wishes most for his children, and the response would be "a decent and effective education." The system of education and the system of housing people in this country have failed miserably to meet the needs of Negro families. They must be reformed. There is, fortunately, a high level of awareness, concern, and activity in these two areas. However, this has not yet moved out of the token and pilot phases.

The reformation of both these systems should follow, in our view, the same basic principles as in all the other major subsystems. Thus, the external strategies should be designed to make the white establishment more sensitive and responsive to the needs of the Negro people, and to engage in extraordinary efforts to include the Negro people in these systems at all levels. At the same time, the black strategies should be designed to enhance the control of Negro communities over the educational institutions and housing programs which operate in them.

Some of the educational reforms now under way seem to hold high promise for strengthening the fabric of Negro family and community life. We must begin at the lowest levels. Both my wife and I have served at different times as members of the California State Advisory Commission on Compensatory Education. We have been highly impressed with the promise inherent in the strategy of the Elementary and Secondary Act of 1965, which sponsors these compensating education programs. We have been particularly pleased with the manner in which programs have been launched and coordinated in California, under the most able leadership of Dr. Wilson Riles, State Director of the program. However, it is deeply distressing to see the vulnerability of this program in Congress and in state governments. It is even more distressing to see the token and pilot nature of these programs as they have been applied and administered across the country. Finally, many of the rigidities which affect the educational system have operated against the effective launching and imaginative execution of many of these programs. We do not expect such limited and circumscribed efforts, applied to a very few children over a very limited time with very inadequate resources, to solve the problems of learning these children have inherited. Rather than spend much money and effort trying to research infant programs, the government should plunge right in, expanding and applying them flexibly and imaginatively to all children who need them. They should then be evaluated after a number of years of operation, not so much to answer definitively whether they raise the absolute levels of achievement, as to determine what changes in focus will accomplish such results.

It should be clear by now without waiting for definitive research that every school in the Negro neighborhoods needs to be extended down to three-year-olds. But it is at the other end of the educational process, in education beyond the high school, that we wish to offer some brief observations.

It has become quite fashionable for white liberal intellectuals to suggest that the more than one hundred Negro colleges should be closed down. Our view throughout this book is that Negro institutions should be built up rather than closed down. We have also shown what a strategic place the Negro college has had in the history of achievement on the part of Negro families. The simple fact is that the Negro people would be grossly uneducated today, there would be no substantial middle class, and no substantial Negro leadership, were it not for the historic role of the Negro colleges. White institutions and professors have shown considerably more imagination in condemning Negro colleges than they have in educating Negro youth. It is still true that most Negroes with doctorates from major white universities received their first degrees at Negro colleges. Most Negro college graduates received their degrees from a Negro college. Half of all Negroes in college today are enrolled in Negro colleges.

Clearly the wider society needs to make a major commitment to the education of Negro youth in whatever kinds of institutions these youth seek to be educated. Part of this major commitment involves upgrading the faculties of the Negro colleges, not by importing large numbers of white teachers to them, but by educating larger numbers of Negro teachers, including those already in those colleges, others who will be attracted to them, and Negroes in other colleges and universities as well. In addition, the time has come for the wider society to guarantee to every Negro who completes high school the financial and legal support for him to pursue advanced training and education to the limit of his capacity. This should be one of the most important actual and symbolic acts the society can perform to indemnify the Negro people for centuries of exploitation, neglect, and tokenism.

Furthermore, it is now a most appropriate time in history for some of the large foundations, such as Ford or Carnegie or Rockefeller, and some of the large white universities, such as Harvard and Vanderbilt, to work in collaboration with a half-dozen of the Negro colleges and universities to make the latter institutions among the finest in the world. We do not suggest that they should be the biggest, or the whitest, but only the best. It could certainly be done with sufficient commitment, money, imagination, and time. They should, of course, remain distinctively Negro in administration, faculty, and student body.

At the same time, they should encourage the development of an inter-racial and international community of scholars. They should not only be among the world's finest institutions in all the basic areas of knowledge appropriate to a small university, but should make a special and distinct contribution to knowledge about black people, and perhaps other non-Western peoples in this country and abroad.

There are a number of links being established between large white universities and colleges and some of these Negro institutions. We have a very imaginative program at Berkeley, under the able and committed leadership of Professor Edward Barankin and supported by the Ford Foundation, involving intervisitation, faculty and student exchange, and graduate student recruitment. Other universities have similar programs. All of them, however, are small pilot projects which involve the part-time allegiance of a small number of scholars. Each of the major universities needs a black vice president in charge of a comprehensive system of internal and external programs for the development of Negro scholars, professionals, and community leaders.

Professor Lewis B. Mayhew of Stanford University recently expressed the need for such extraordinary efforts on the part of the educational establishment:

> The major universities must be willing to support Negro graduate students for a year or two years of pre-graduate work. The states must be prepared to offer massive scholarships of $2,000 to $3,000 for Negro youth, regardless of past academic achievement and regardless of whether or not they appreciate it. . . . If every predominantly white institution represented in this audience set as an immediate institutional policy the recruitment of 10 per cent of its total student body from the Negro community without respect to formal admission requirements, this might signify an interest in reform.[15]

Extraordinary efforts seem called for in the field of housing. All the reforms in public housing, rent supplements, and urban renewal now being advanced are inadequate. Despite the historic open housing legislation passed by the U. S. Congress in 1968 which offers some hope for middle and upper income Negro families, clearly the basic problem is financial insecurity. A government truly concerned for the stability, conformity, and achievement of Negro families could undertake no more effective action than to guarantee to every Negro family a stake in an apartment or house of its own. These two measures, a guaranteed education for Negro children, and a guaranteed equity in a home for every

---

[15] Lewis B. Mayhew, *Times* (Palo Alto), Wednesday, March 6, 1968.

family in the neighborhood of its choice, would be the modern equivalent
of the legendary forty acres and a mule which Negro families needed
but never received after more than two hundred years of working without pay. Surely there will be objections. Why should the society make
extra efforts to guarantee these resources to Negroes, who have been
free for over three generations? There is, of course, no answer which
will satisfy a person who raises that question. But let the average middle
class white person who reads this contemplate the following: Where
would he be today and how well would he be able to meet the needs of
his children if his parents before him, their parents, and his ancestors for
four hundred years in this country had been (a) forced to work without
pay, (b) prevented from learning to read and write, (c) prevented from
moving about at will, (d) prevented from living together as man and
wife, and (e) constantly told in ways more effective than words that they
were inherently inferior? Culture is cumulative. Special efforts to indemnify the Negro people are not a matter of guilt price or charity, they
are a simple matter of back pay.

HEALTH AND WELFARE

Physical health care is one of the few areas of welfare in which both
the executive and legislative branches of government, as well as major
private foundations and industries, have made a major commitment to
reform. A few state governments, notably New York, are among leaders
in the effort to reform the system of health care. Negroes stand to
benefit enormously from these programs. It has been estimated that
during 1967, the federally supported medical care programs of the Social
Security Act paid for one-fifth of all health care services to Americans.
One can be sure that these programs paid for a much higher share of
the health care costs for Negroes. Still, the archaic hospital system, the
rigidly middle class and bureaucratic medical practice, and the absence
of the black perspective and black professionals in all levels of the medical care system leave much to be desired in this general effort at reform.

It is in the field of social welfare, however, that the country has
demonstrated over and over again that it does not yet have the will to
reform itself. The chief institutions in the social welfare system are
federal, state, and local public welfare departments, voluntary social
agencies at all three levels, graduate schools of social welfare, and the
organized social work profession. Of the hundreds of thousands of such
institutions over the country, it is rare indeed to find a handful which are

not reflective of the racist ideology which afflicts our society. These institutions are, for the most part, insensitive to the Negro experience, imbedded as they are within the Anglo-conformity doctrine. It has been said that social work is an enterprise in which upper class persons hire middle class social workers to inflict their values on lower class clients.[16]

Social welfare, that most humanitarian of enterprises, is in as great a need for reform as the other major institutions of society if it is to meet the needs of Negro families. It is in need of both white strategies of reform by the wider society, and black strategies of reform by the Negro communities. The social welfare institutions in the wider community must become more sensitive to the needs, conditions, life styles, and response patterns of their Negro clients and potential clients. At the same time, they must incorporate in their planning, policy making, administration, and operational staffs, at all levels, sufficient numbers of Negro people to maximize this newfound sensitivity. In addition, however, the Negro people and Negro communities must begin to define, plan, control, manage, and execute the welfare programs which operate in their communities. Just as we need neighborhood levels of government in economic, political, educational, housing, and health systems, we need them in the welfare system. Our own view is that all nonfinancial social welfare programs should be controlled and administered at the neighborhood level in a multipurpose service center. The financial assistance payments should be administered directly from Washington. Other levels of government should serve coordinative roles, enabling research and evaluation, rather than administrative roles, in the social welfare field.

Service Strategy or Income Strategy

It has become rather fashionable during the last few years for certain social science-oriented reformers to call for the substitution or the abolition of the welfare system. This is often expressed in terms of substituting an income strategy for the current service strategy in social welfare. Let us give poor people money, it is said, instead of social services, and they will solve their own problems. This perspective betrays a rather limited understanding of the nature of social problems, and an even more limited knowledge of our present system of social welfare. Proponents of the guaranteed annual income for low income families often fall into this intellectual trap.

It is not true, as many experienced social workers could tell us, that

[16] Lee Rainwater, "The Services Strategy vs. the Income Strategy," *Transaction*, IV, No. 10 (October 1967), 40–41.

the country now adopts a service strategy rather than an income strategy toward low income families.[17] We have mainly an income strategy and have had it since 1935. That was the central idea of the Social Security Act, which provided for a type of guaranteed annual income for families with dependent children, with no services attached to this money at all. It was only as professional social workers and others began to see and to point out the inadequacies of this income strategy—both because of its limited amount and because some problems are not amenable to money solutions alone—that the service strategy was introduced into the federal program. Such strategy is represented by the 1962 Service Amendments to the Social Security Act. But the service aspect has had very rough sailing in public welfare programs and has not come near the level of importance of the income strategy of AFDC payments. Thus the difficulties low income families face in the ghettos of America today cannot fairly be attributed to the failure of the service strategy, for that strategy has not had sufficient support to put it to a test. Its major handicap has been that it has been tied to and hamstrung by the same regulations as govern the income strategy. Thus the income strategy, which has had longer and more generous support, has been more of a failure, if responsibility can be attributed to either of these strategies for failing to stabilize Negro family life. The cause of this failure rests only partly and, we suggest, not even mainly, in the low level of public assistance payments in the large Northern industrial states. But it rests mainly in the manner in which these funds have been administered and allocated, and in the dehumanizing effects of their administration. This failure has also been due to the almost complete absence of a family focus or philosophy in this program. It is, perhaps, characteristically American to ignore groups, including families, in social reform efforts and to concentrate on the individual. The AFDC program has been hamstrung by that philosophy and focus.

The most far-reaching and characteristic aspect of this service strategy has been the limited programs in selected communities, in which very young, upper middle class white female college graduates without any professional training have been hired by welfare departments because they scored high on examinations. They have been given caseloads of sixty low income Negro families and told to visit them once a month to see that they were not cheating the government of money and to provide casework services to them. No one, with the possible exception of politicians and social science armchair reformers, could consider this a

[17] Nathan Glazer's foreword in E. Franklin Frazier, *The Negro Family in the United States* (Chicago: The University of Chicago Press, 1966), p. xvii.

reasonable—to say nothing of maximum—effort to institute a service strategy. It is true, of course, that in some communities there have been more intensive though very limited pilot programs of casework and other services. It is equally true, however, that in most jurisdictions of the country, the service programs have been more limited and inadequate than the one we just described. And even in those pilot projects and intensive service programs, the conception of service has been restricted by the middle class, professional, psychological perspective. The fact is, however, we do not know in a professional way what services are required. We have not made sufficient efforts to find out from the people involved.

Furthermore, these monies have not been allowances to families, but allowances to individual children and adult caretakers, fluctuating wildly from one household to another, according to age and sex of the child or other criteria far less relevant—such as parentage of the child. Even after the focus on services and the interest in family stability entered the national thinking around 1962, and the Congress was persuaded to abandon the custom of requiring unemployed men to desert or divorce their wives in order for their families to be supported, only eighteen of the fifty states have adopted this provision and made it possible for such families to stay together and be supported. And these, as one might have anticipated, were not the states with the greatest need in this regard, but the large Northern industrial states, which already had much more generous welfare payment levels and policies than the other states. Not a single Southern state, for example, despite a high degree of moral indignation about Negro broken families, has taken advantage of the federally supported option to support dependent children while their father, though unemployed, remained in the home with his family. In many states, the husband and father must not only abandon his family, but must be gone for a period of time (up to ninety days in California) before the family can be considered eligible for this federal support. Thus, it is clearly not the absence of an income strategy, but the presence of a wholly inadequate and dysfunctional income strategy, which has failed to stabilize Negro family life, a task well beyond the reach of any single, simple strategy, whether income or service.

What we need is not an income or a service strategy, but both. They should be greatly expanded and focused on the family and community, not simply on the individual child or adult in a specific and rigidly defined category Beyond income and service, we need much more to solve the problems of low income Negro families and Negro communities. The other major institutions of society also need to be reformed. And

Negro people need a sense of power and control over their destinies, the conditions of their life, and the programs which operate in their communities. Under their influence, we suspect programs will go even further than income and service dispensed by the liberal white community, however generous and sensitive these dispensations might be.

Neighborhood Multiservice Center

One of the mechanisms which seems to hold promise for maximizing the control Negroes may exercise over the welfare programs which operate in their communities is the Neighborhood Multiservice Center, which has grown out of the Community Action Programs of the Office of Economic Opportunity.

The Center will not be able to function adequately in meeting the needs of families and children unless the major institutions of the larger community function adequately.

The major responsibility of the Neighborhood Service Center would be to develop and administer programs and activities designed to enhance both the structure and functioning of family life among the residents of the neighborhood and the physical, social, and emotional well-being of all children.

The primary aim of the Center should be to keep families together and able to perform the function required of them by their children and the society. Workers in this service should be selected, trained, oriented, and supported for doing whatever is necessary, constructive, ethical, and legal to help family members attain these goals. This requires a much more innovative approach than is common today, even among professional social caseworkers. Sometimes families will need a teacher, sometimes an advocate to fight for them among the institutions of the wider society; sometimes they will need an organizer, and frequently a combination of many of these. Secondly, this service should provide consumer education and training in money management and cooperative buying. Third, the family and child welfare program should provide legal assistance for families and children. The neighborhood legal services now funded by the Office of Economic Opportunity might well be located in this Center.

It should also be recognized that some families, even with substantial family allowances, counseling, and advice available from the Center, will need more concrete and direct help in order to maintain their viability and perform their functions. In this respect, Day Care Centers of sufficient scope to provide a facility for any mother who wishes to leave her children to be cared for during the day. This service should be free for families below a certain income level, say $6,000 per year, and should charge a modest fee for families earning more than that. The emphasis should be on accessibility as a meaningful child welfare resource in the community. The Day Care Centers should not be simply babysitting pools. They should provide the children with meaningful activities appropriate to their ages.

These centers should not be confined to only the poorest elements of the community but a cross section of the community. One of the great mistakes of the Office of Economic Opportunity, in our experience with local programs, has been the requirement that only the lowest income families be eligible for certain of its services. This not only divides rather than unifies the community, but the children miss the opportunity of learning from each other. And the program misses the cooperation of the more stable working class families who are often the pillars of the community.

We have urged in this chapter that the enhancement of Negro family life can best be achieved through two broad strategies, one of which must be initiated by the major economic, political, and social subsystems of the larger society, which seek to make themselves both more responsive to and more representative of the Negro people. Selected mechanisms, including economic development, special education, and housing indemnities, have been urged as means of implementing this strategy.

A second strategy involves building up institutions in the Negro community so that they may exercise greater control over the basic conditions of life which affect the people there, and manage the special health, education, and welfare services needed by the community as a regular part of its institutional life. Some mechanisms, including a Neighborhood Development Corporation and a Neighborhood Multiservice Center, have been suggested for the coordination of these efforts at neighborhood control.

We have, therefore, taken issue with two popular notions about how to strengthen Negro family life. One holds that some kind of direct intervention by the federal government to effect types of family structure is called for. The other holds that income measures alone, without other specialized social services, will solve the problems these families face. In our view, the society should provide the strategies, resources, and facilities which will enable Negro families to exercise increasingly more mastery, control, and ownership over the conditions which affect their lives and the administration of the specialized services they need.

Our central theme is that the Negro family is a subsystem of the society, dependent on and responsive to the influence of other major subsystems in that society. We have been arguing that the best way to insure
the viability of Negro family life is to insure that the major institutions of
the wider society are open and responsive to the Negro experience, and
at the same time to insure that there are strong and viable institutions
within the Negro community itself, controlled and managed by Negro
people. The implications of this view of the Negro family for social policy
and social change were touched on briefly by Nathan Glazer in his foreword to the 1966 edition of Frazier's *The Negro Family In The United
States.*

> There are parts of the society that are more legitimately subject to gov-
> ernment intervention than the family—the economy, the educational
> system, the system of police and courts and prisons—and we may hope
> to influence the family through these institutions. . . . We cannot inter-
> fere in the intimate spheres of life: we do not have the knowledge, and
> if we did, we should use it with restraint. We know that the family makes
> the social conditions. We know too that social conditions make the family.
> But it is the latter knowledge that is the basis of social policy.[18]

In a sense the kind of reformation we are urging requires a reconstruction of the whole history of the republic.

Heal Our History[19]

> Black youth, painfully embittered,
> put down our "Great Society," our
> advanced civilization, dub it a
> junkyard heaped high with mass
> produced, self diminishing things,
> skylighted by the insubstantial
> dream of the brotherhood of man.
>
> And it is our charge to relieve
> their pain to help them to believe
> again that those heretofore unrealized
> concepts on which we founded our land
> live today and bind us to a common cause.
>
> Their dark wails rise from the
> ghetto bowels of our great robot world,
> whip like lashes the sleeping American

[18] *Ibid.*, pp. xvii–xviii.
[19] Published for the first time with the permission of the author.

conscience, opens up the 300 year-old
festering sore of hate-induced violence.

We human beings are time machines
and much much more. We need the courage
to relive and forgive a hateful past,
to balance the book of heavy deeds
and then move on.

Our untended wounds are gangrene bound.
A skilled surgeon's sharp scalpel can
cleanse away the damaged tissue to
start new growth. There is no time
in our jet age world for quacks and
their quick cure schemes. Now, at
all costs, we must heal our history.
Or else our future rots in the
disease of our past.

                                        Sarah Webster Fabio

Conclusion

The report of the President's Advisory Committee on Civil Disorders concluded in 1968 that we are moving toward two societies, one white and one black, separate and unequal. This is in fact a gross understatement of the situation. We have and have always had two separate and unequal societies. What is new is a recognition on the part of the white society that these two societies exist, and a determination on the part of the black society that they should no longer exist.

While we draw upon the work of many scholars, including, particularly, E. Franklin Frazier, Talcott Parsons, Milton Gordon, and Hylan Lewis, this book is essentially a presentation of our point of view. First, we believe that Negro families have not been adequately treated by American scholars, and that as a consequence a great deal of distortion and negative evaluation have surrounded the very concept of the Negro family. In both the professional and popular literature today, the concept of "Negro family" is regarded as almost synonymous with "problem family." In the Appendix we analyze some of the factors which help to account for such a distorted view of Negro families. In Chapter 1, "A Social Systems Approach to the Study of Negro Family Life," we advance our own conception of a more adequate, general, systematic, and theoretically based approach to the study of Negro family life.

The second major element in our framework is the postulate that the history of a people plays an important part in shaping the nature of their institutions, and the conclusion that efforts to understand the nature and dynamics of Negro family life must be placed in some historical perspective. In Chapter 2, "Historical Backgrounds of the Negro Family," we present our approach to an historical perspective. In the first part of this chapter we suggest that the Negro people have a history and a heritage prior to slavery. Their forms of family life were highly complex, highly stable, well developed, mutually articulated with the wider so-

ciety, and highly functional for the economic, social, and psychological
life of the community.

We take the view that the failure to view the Negro people—and
particularly Negro family life—from the vantage point of their own independent historical milieu has distorted the context in which Negroes
are viewed and view themselves in this society. Most discussions of the
Negro family in the literature are concerned only with contemporary
conditions. Our purpose has been to show the family tradition from
which Negroes originated, not only for its sociological interest, but also
for the contribution it can make to a revaluation of the concept of the
Negro in our society. Such historical perspective can put in bold relief
the cultural discontinuity represented by the long night of terror perpetrated by the slave system and its aftermath, with crippling consequences
for the reconstruction of viable forms of Negro family life.

Pursuing this historical perspective, we describe in the same chapter
certain broad patterns of slavery, focusing particularly on some of the
distinctions between the patterns of slavery represented in the United
States and Brazil. Our view is essentially that slavery, in all the Americas,
was savage, inhumane, and crippling to continuation or redevelopment
of viable forms of family life among the Negro slaves. We seek to avoid
the impression left by some scholars and observers that slavery in Brazil
was not really slavery at all, and that consequently, Brazil is currently a
racial paradise with Negro Brazilians sharing equal rights, privileges, and
status with white Brazilians. Our study and reflections have led us to no
such conclusion. At the same time, however—and this is our major interest—there is little doubt that the system of slavery dominant in the
United States was more savage and more destructive to Negro family
life than was the system in Brazil. Accordingly, we examine some of the
forces which produced the two different patterns of slavery, describe
some of the manifestations of these differences in family life under
slavery, and speculate on some consequences of these two systems of
slavery as reflected in the current patterns of Negro family life.

The third element in our framework is the postulate that Negro family
life in the United States today is still circumscribed by powerful social
forces which prevent the Negro family from making its maximum contribution to its members, to the Negro community as a whole, and to
the wider, society. These forces are in part a legacy of slavery and in
part a characteristic of the complex social, economic, political, and technological society in which we live. This theme is the subject of Chapter 3,
"Shadows of the Plantation."

On the other hand, we show some of the ways and means by which the vast majority of Negro families have managed to develop viable forms of family life. This is the theme of Chapter 4, "Screens of Opportunity." We, therefore, take issue with those scholars and citizens who insist that the obstacles to the development of viable forms of Negro family life ended essentially with the Emancipation Proclamation, or the New Deal, or the Civil Rights Act of 1964 or 1968 and that, consequently, the job of stabilizing Negro family life is now somehow up to family members themselves, or the Negro community, or Negro leaders, or social welfare agencies. We argue that since the obstacles are systematic and pervasive, based largely on racial prejudice in the larger society, the solution must lie in a reversal of these societal trends. We suggest that the extent to which Negro families have been able to overcome the historical obstacles to stability and social achievement is directly related to the extent to which they have enjoyed a reversal of these obstacles in their current life situation.

Thus, we seek to join two current arguments among scholars and intellectuals. One argument debates whether it was slavery or contemporary discrimination which crippled the current Negro family. Moynihan, for example, emphasizes slavery, while many of his critics emphasize current discrimination. We suggest that the argument is spurious. It is both slavery and current discrimination, plus other factors, which stand in the way of Negro family achievement.

A second argument debates whether the essential problem confronting the Negro family is the Negro's economic and social position in the class structure, or prejudice and discrimination based on racial status. Civil rights activists are prone to argue that it is race, social scientists that it is social class. It is currently fashionable, for example, among scholars, particularly among white liberals, to suggest that middle-income Negroes now have all the privileges and status of middle-income whites, and that consequently the problems associated with Negro social achievement are centered in the lower classes.

Our view is that the obstacles facing the Negro family in our society are both economic and social, both class and race, as we interpret race. Of these obstacles, those associated with race are most pervasive. Reconstruction must take both these sets of forces into consideration, as well as the acculturating forces of history.

Beginning in Chapter 5, "Social Status in the Black Community," we pursue the fourth element in our over-all point of view—namely, the interrelatedness of family and societal roles. We argue that the factors which make for stability and achievement in family life are exactly those forces which make for stability and achievement in the larger society, and that a person's conception of his power and worth are mirror images of that society. While these images are sometimes deflected and distorted, they are often amazingly accurate and always effective. We show how the social forces described above, both historical and contemporary, are manifested in the Negro social class structure.

The final two chapters are devoted to our views and hypotheses about the reconstruction of Negro family life in America. We are highly critical of the tremendous concern with stability as a criteria for assessing Negro families, for we feel that viability is a more meaningful concept. Stability, as it is usually discussed in relation to Negro families refers to family structure, and more specifically the presence or absence of a husband or father in the family. In Chapter 6, "The Agony and the Promise of Social Change," we argue that the recognition and abolition of racism in the white society is the most basic change needed to enhance the viability of Negro family life. We describe some of the subtle manifestations of racism in America. Then in the final chapter, "Strategies of Social Reform," we single out some of the major institutions in the wider society that must be reformed—particularly the political, economic, education, health, welfare, religious, and communications institutions.

We also argue that Negro-owned, managed, and controlled institutions must be developed and strengthened within the Negro community itself. This point of view suggests that Negroes should own and manage the economic enterprises in the black ghettos of America. And while participating fully in the political, social, and educational systems of the total community, Negroes should have control over the operation of those institutions in the black community. This transformation of Negroes from dependent subjects in their own communities to independent managers with an important stake in their communities will require a great deal of cooperation from the white community, in the form of economic and political support as well as technical assistance. Furthermore, it will require the development of a great deal of unity and leadership within the Negro community itself.

If we are serious, as a society, about the development of the Negro potential, we must look beyond stability, law, order, and limited opportunity to a program of mass reconstruction for the Negro people, similar to what should have been done in 1867, coupled with a comprehensive and general war on poverty. The alternatives to reconstruction will be chaos and stagnation for the Negro family, the Negro community as an ethnic subsociety, and the general society of which these institutions are an inextricable part.

Appendix

The Treatment of
Negro Families in American Scholarship

Negro families constitute an important segment of social life in America. There are roughly 5 million Negro families in the United States, comprising over 90 per cent of the 22 million Negroes in the country. However, the significance of Negro families lies not in numbers, but in the crucial role Negroes have played in the evolution of our society with its many ethnic subsocieties. It would be difficult indeed to get an adequate description of American society without the representation in such a description of the Negro people. And it would be equally difficult to understand the role and place of the Negro people without an appreciation of Negro family life in America.

Yet the Negro family as an institution has been virtually ignored by students of group life in America. The principal reason for this failure seems to be associated with the fact that studies in this area, like those in other areas of human life, are as highly influenced by the political, religious, and philosophical ideologies of the authors, as by any concern with social relevance or any more general spirit of scientific inquiry. Scholars have been steered away from the study of the Negro family by their own European ethnocentrism and by the nature of their professional disciplines. When they have treated the Negro family, they have done so in a negativistic and distorted fashion for the same reasons. In this chapter we examine some of the sources of ignorance and distortion in the treatment of Negro families by American scholarship. Our hope is that we may clear the way for more accurate and meaningful perception.

There are four principal areas of scholarship which have been presented with the opportunity and, indeed, the necessity to describe and analyze Negro family life in America. These areas are: (1) studies of the family, (2) studies of ethnic assimilation in American life, (3) studies of the Negro experience, and (4) studies of social welfare problems.

On the whole, scholars in each of these areas have found it convenient to turn to matters other than the Negro family. Not that the family—or the Negro people in general—has been ignored in such studies. On the contrary, these are two of the most extensively researched and discussed areas of American life. But for reasons both historical and contemporary in nature, the two areas of study, the family and the Negro, have not come together for more than minimal consideration. The reasons lie deeper than the selective interests and rewards of individual scholars. They lie in the nature of these broad fields of study themselves. Brief reference to the history of family studies, ethnic assimilation studies, Negro studies, and social welfare studies will help to show both why Negro families have been inadequately treated and why they should receive increasing attention in all four branches of scholarship in the decades ahead.

Family Studies

It would seem most logical that studies of the American family include some reference to Negro family life. However, a recent anthology containing fifty-two family studies has only one which treats the Negro family, and that one is Frazier's, written in 1939. It is not simply that only one article is devoted exclusively to Negro families; one reads all the other articles in vain (some of which are not bound by ethnic focus) looking for any reference to Negro families as part of the general discussion of American family patterns.[1]

An equally extensive, highly respected, and widely used compendium of case studies in family law has only one paper devoted to Negro families, and that one is focused almost exclusively on the problem of illegitimacy.[2] These two volumes are unusual in giving even that amount of attention to Negro families. Two tendencies, then, are current in studies of American families. The first, and most general, is to ignore Negro families altogether. The second is to consider them only insofar as they may be conceived as a social problem. In a symposium on The Negro Family at the University of California at Berkeley a few years ago, after a nationally known sociologist referred repeatedly to the "problem of the Negro family," a Negro wife and mother rose and took him to task. "Why do you always consider us a problem?" she demanded. "I don't consider

[1] Norman W. Bell and Ezra F. Vogel, eds., A Modern Introduction to the Family (New York: The Free Press, 1960).

[2] Caleb Foote, Robert J. Levy, and Frank E. A. Sander, Case Studies and Materials on Family Law (Boston: Little, Brown and Company, 1966).

myself a problem." The sociologist was undaunted. He didn't know why she needed to be so defensive. Thus, despite the fact that the vast majority of Negro families are stable, conforming, and achieving, and cause no problems to anybody, the tendency to view them in negative terms persists. The Negro historian Benjamin Quarles recently observed that "When we pick up a social science book, we look in the index under 'Negro,' it will read, 'see Slavery,' 'see Crime,' 'see Juvenile Delinquency,' perhaps 'see Commission on Civil Disorders'; perhaps see anything except the Negro. So when we try to get a perspective on the Negro, we get a distorted perspective." [8]

Perhaps the greatest symbol of this kind of distortion in recent years is the widely read and even more widely discussed Moynihan Report. Moynihan and his staff examined the 1960 national census data and found that nearly a quarter of all Negro families were headed by females, and that nearly a quarter of all Negro babies that year were born out of wedlock. These are facts which Negroes, social workers, and students of the Negro family have been aware of and concerned about for some time. These statistics alarmed Mr. Moynihan. He concluded, quite incorrectly, that the Negro family in this country is falling apart and failing to prepare Negro children to make their way in the world. According to this view, the Negro community is being destroyed at least as much by its own family structure as by the indifferent and often hostile society around it. While his own data showed quite the contrary, Moynihan concluded that "At the heart of the deterioration of the fabric of Negro society is the deterioration of the Negro family. It is the fundamental source of the weakness of the Negro community at the present time." [4]

Because the 25 per cent of Negro families headed by females was so much higher than the proportion of white families headed by females, Moynihan paid very little attention to the fact that 75 per cent of Negro families met his criteria of stability. There are a number of methodological and substantive problems with the Moynihan report. [5] A major distortion was his singling out instability in the Negro family as the causal factor for the difficulties Negroes face in the white society. It is quite the other way round. But coming just at the time the nation was trying to find a single cause of the Watts riots, Moynihan's thesis struck a respon-

[8] Benjamin Quarles, *Jet Magazine*, XXXIII, No. 12 (December 28, 1967), p. 32.
[4] Daniel P. Moynihan, *The Negro Family: The Case for National Action* (Washington, D. C.: U. S. Department of Labor, Office of Planning and Research, March, 1965), p. 1.
[5] Lee Rainwater and William L. Yancey, *The Moynihan Report and the Politics of Controversy* (Cambridge, Mass.: The M.I.T. Press, 1967).

sive chord in the collective American breast. "... At the center of the
tangle of pathology," he concluded,

> is the weakness of the family structure. Once or twice removed, it will be
> found to be the principal source of most of the aberrant, inadequate, or
> antisocial behavior that did not establish, but now serves to perpetuate,
> the cycle of poverty and deprivation.

He could come to such faulty and inverse conclusions in part because
he had no theoretical framework to guide him in the analysis of his
statistical data, and in part because his data were limited

Another serious shortcoming of the whole report was the tendency,
common among liberal social scientists, to compare Negroes with whites
on standardized objective measures which have been demonstrated to
have meaning only in the white, European subculture. Many statistical
studies which compare Negroes and whites fall into the almost inevitable
position of characterizing the Negro group as deviant. If all a study can
describe about Negro family life is what it simultaneously describes
about white families, it cannot tell us very much about Negro family life.
Moynihan compounded this error, however, by his failure to take into
account two very important aspects of the Negro experience: social class
and social caste.

Simple white-Negro comparisons on almost any set of standardized
variables will necessarily produce distortions, for they ignore the important dimension of social class. The white sample will contain large
numbers of middle and upper income families and the Negro sample will
be dominated by low income families. Using statistics for the same year
Moynihan found that 25 per cent of Negro families were broken, Lee
Rainwater has shown that if one considers only Negro families with
family incomes of $3,000 or above, this proportion dropped from 25 per
cent to 7 per cent, while for Negroes earning less than $3,000, it rose to
36 per cent.[6] But while income level explains a great deal of the original
racial differential, it does not explain it all. For at all income levels, the
rate of broken families is higher among Negroes. Thus among white
families earning $3,000 or under, the rate is 22 per cent—considerably
less than the 36 per cent for Negro families. And among white families

---

[6] For a critique of the Moynihan report see William Ryan, *The Nation*, November
22, 1965; Benjamin F. Payton, *Christianity and Crisis*, December 13, 1965; Herbert
Gans, *Commonweal*, October 15, 1965; Hylan Lewis, Agenda Paper, White House
Planning Conference (unpublished); and Laura Carper, *Dissent*, March–April, 1966.
Each of these papers is reprinted in Lee Rainwater and William L. Yancey, *op. cit.*

earning $3,000 and over, it drops to 3 per cent, less than half the Negro rate.

This brings us, then, to the second major variable overlooked by Moynihan, despite his own analysis of this factor elsewhere in his report. We refer to the importance to the Negro experience in America of the caste-like barriers which exclude Negro families from so many of the resources of the society. Even when the income *levels* are similar for the white and the Negro samples, the two groups are not comparable. For we know that even in the low income category of under $3,000, the mean incomes for white families falls considerably toward the top of that range, while the mean income of Negro families is considerably lower. A white family with an income of $2,750 and a Negro family with an income of $1,500 are both under $3,000 and both undoubtedly lower class, but they do not have the same resources and options available to them. Even if two groups of white and Negro families were matched with exactly the same income, education, and occupation, they would still not be comparable. For the Negro group must reflect its experience with the caste barrier as well as its distinctive history, both of which set the conditions for growing up black in white America. Thus, white-Negro comparative studies may be very important for certain purposes, but they are wholly inadequate for understanding processes of causation and other dynamics of Negro family life, particularly if they are conducted without a general theoretical framework.

The low income Negro family faces three insidious problems. One is poverty, the other is prejudice, and the third is historical subjugation in his own country because of his race. The low income white family faces only one of these problems, and in this respect is better off then even the middle class Negro family—contrary to the implications of the Moynihan report. For the middle class Negro makes considerably less money than the middle class white, and in addition, must face the color bar in ways unknown to the experience of his white counterpart. However powerful the variable of social class, it does not obliterate and, indeed, was not invented to account for the racial factor.

But those very social scientists who insist that Moynihan's only sin was that he ignored social class are themselves guilty of ignoring even more powerful definers of the conditions facing Negro families in this country. Negro family life in America is circumscribed by a complex set of social conditions which shape the family in various ways. The Moynihan report is only a more recent and popular example of studies which do not take cognizance of these complexities. For now, however, the question is, how did American scholarship come to provide such a distorted perspective on Negro family life? Reference to the historical development of American family studies provides at least part of the answer.

Family sociology in America was born in the late nineteenth century when social Darwinism held sway.[7] During this period the focus was not on contemporary family life at all, but on earlier more primitive forms. The underlying assumption was that contemporary European family forms represented a natural evolution and had reached a certain stage of perfection. The idea was to search among primitive peoples for the earlier forms of family life, so that the evolutionary process could be traced and the sources of such perfection established. Scholars argued about whether original family relationships were monogamous or polygamous, and found evidence for both in historical documents and oral traditions. They were concerned with whether earlier forms of family structure had been essentially matriarchal or patriarchal, and again found evidence for both.

However vigorously scholars pursued the study of the natural evolution of the family, and however vehemently they argued among themselves, it is strikingly clear that there was no room in such scholarship for concern with Negro family life. For in the United States in the latter part of the nineteenth century, the Negro family had no recognized institutional existence. Freshly released from slavery, the Negro people were struggling to find a place in the wider society, with various degrees of help and obstruction from that society. The dominant focus was on politics and economics in the most basic sense, with no appreciable concern for social integration in any form, and certainly none for family integration. Both Negroes and whites were concerned mainly with survival—the survival of the Negro people, the survival of the southern way of life, and the survival of the republic.

Because there was almost no focus on contemporary family life, and because the Negro people, as a free people, were considered to be extremely contemporary, it is little wonder that Negro family life was so completely ignored. And if some scholars saw that the origin of man was somewhat bound up with the origin and development of group life as represented by the family, it would certainly be the origin and development of the white man which would be studied, and not that of the "primitive" black people in their midst. For in the late nineteenth century, whatever the contribution of the abolitionists, the Civil War victors, and the reconstructionists, none of these liberal groups succeeded in

[7] Bell and Vogel, pp. 3–5.

comprehending the essential humanness shared by black and white people alike. All of "the liberals" proceeded on the assumption that the black people was another people, quite apart from the rest of society, though deserving of special help and a certain, though limited, degree of freedom.

A second phase of family studies, stimulated by conditions of *poverty*, focused on the conditions of life faced by contemporary families. These studies grew out of the early twentieth century liberal humanitarian movements, and are represented by the studies of Roundtree and the Webbs of England. Many surveys were conducted to document the conditions of "life and labor" of the working classes in the cities of Europe and America. Such studies were continued in the United States, particularly as economic adversity struck the industrial communities of America, which were being peopled by immigrant families from Europe.

While earlier family studies had focused on primitive groups, these focused on poverty groups and were almost exclusively concerned with economic conditions affecting family life. No attention was paid to the broader set of relationships between family life and community life, or to the place of family life in the wider society. These studies concentrated on the urban poor and consequently ignored Negro family life, for around the turn of the century Negroes were still not an urban industrial force. They were essentially rural peasants located in the deep South.

In many respects, many of the studies of family life conducted during this period were predecessors of some of the current commentary on Negro families. They depended on secondary rather than on first-hand data and were usually statistical in form. Moreover, they concentrated on various forms of deviant behavior which were believed to be results of breakdown in family life. These included divorce rates, crime rates, illegitimacy rates, death rates, and various health statistics. There are indeed some striking parallels between those early poverty studies focused on other ethnic minorities and current studies focused on Negroes.

The 1920s ushered in a third phase of family studies. Poverty seemed somewhat under control, or at least it was pushed from the headlines by the burgeoning prosperity. Scholars of family life began to turn their attention to some of the problems faced by *middle class families*. This period of inquiry may be termed the psychological phase, for many of these studies were concerned with the dominant themes of "adjustment" and "individual happiness." Despite the growth of the middle class in America, economic well-being was not sufficient to guarantee these psychological values. Middle class families began to discover that they had problems of personal—and particularly sexual—adjustment. The study of family life shifted dramatically during this period to the study of middle class family life, and the problems of psychological functioning associated with these families. Not only Freud, but also the social psychological studies of George H. Mead and the sociological studies of Ernest W. Burgess reflected this concern.

Again, Negro families were left out. For while they were becoming increasingly urban after the great migrations of 1914 to 1918, and while they were indeed concentrated in industrial towns and cities of the South and North, the industrial poverty phase of family studies had passed. The new thing was to study the problems of family life among the middle classes, and Negroes, alas, were not yet middle class in any appreciable numbers. Furthermore, and not unrelated to this fact, they were not yet perceived as having psychological and sexual problems to the extent and degree of refinement that white middle class families had them. The European emigrants had discovered that neither a certain degree of assimilation nor economic well-being solved all the problems of existence and family life. Native whites made a similar discovery, thanks to the insights of psychoanalysis. But Negroes were not yet to be admitted into these private circles of family life education lectures, private psychiatric treatment, and studies of family structure and function. For Negroes were still engaged in the struggle for economic survival, and students of family life had already passed through this stage, along with the more prosperous white segments of the society.

The years 1930 to 1940 were the golden age for studies of Negro life; the best studies of Negro family life available today were done during that period. These were years of tremendous political activity. For the first time in nonwar years, what happened in Washington vastly affected every segment of American life. For the first time since Reconstruction, Negroes became an important political force. Negroes were now so transplanted from the rural South and so concentrated in key industrial areas they could not be ignored in the political efforts to save American society from the economic disaster ushered in with 1929. Consequently, as the eyes of the nation turned to a reconstruction of the whole society, including the Negro elements, scholarship turned in a similar direction. Students of family life thus discovered the Negro family.

If the first factor which accounts for this discovery is broadly social—in the sense that the whole society, including all of its important elements, was in trouble and deserved to be studied—the second factor was the emergence of Negro scholars, who could not ignore the Negro family precisely for the same reasons that white scholars could and did. It was during these years, with generous support from white institutions, that Negro scholars, sometimes in active collaboration with white scholars, produced some of the most important studies of Negro family life. Chicago was the focus of sociological inquiry during this period, and from there arrived E. Franklin Frazier's study of *The Negro Family in Chicago*,[8] to be followed toward the end of the decade by his *The Negro Family in the United States*.[9] A few years later there appeared the monumental study of Drake and Cayton, *Black Metropolis*,[10] which has large sections on Negro family life. In addition, the comprehensive series of studies on Negro youth commissioned by the American Council on Education[11] has not since been equaled. These studies, conducted in each of the major sections of the country, developed a great body of information on Negro family life. In addition to his work with the American Council on Education, Charles S. Johnson conducted a long series of studies of Negro life in rural America, making a significant contribution to the study of family life among Negroes.[12]

Thus during this period a handful of Negro social scientists, including W. E. B. DuBois, Charles S. Johnson, Allison Davis, St. Clair Drake, Horace Cayton, E. Franklin Frazier, and Ira Reid, joined by a dozen or so white scholars centered mainly around Chicago, including Louis Wirth, Munro Edmonson, John H. Roehr, Robert E. Park, John Dollard, Burleigh B. Gardner, Marx R. Gardner, and W. L. Warner, produced the bulk of social science scholarship about Negro family life.

But in the period running roughly from 1940 to 1960, students of American society had other matters demanding their attention. There was the war to explain, the unprecedented industrialization, the accompanying bureaucratization of society. Along with this, there was the new psychoanalytic revolution, a new and growing prosperity, social class considerations, mental health, and large interest in child rearing practices in the American family. Consequently, it was only with the new emphasis

[8] E. Franklin Frazier, *The Negro Family in Chicago* (Chicago: University of Chicago Press, 1932).

[9] ———, *The Negro Family in the United States* (Chicago: University of Chicago Press, 1939).

[10] St. Clair Drake and Horace R. Cayton, *Black Metropolis*, rev. ed. (New York: Harper & Row, Publishers, 1962).

[11] Allison Davis and John Dollard, *Children of Bondage* (New York: American Council on Education and Harper & Row, Publishers, 1940). Other studies in this series are: E. Franklin Frazier, *Negro Youth at the Crossway* (1940); Charles S. Johnson, *Growing up in the Black Belt* (1941); W. Lloyd Warner, Buford H. Junker, and Walter A. Adams, *Color and Human Nature* (1941); Ira De Augustine Reid, *In a Minor Key: Negro Youth in Story and Fact* (1940).

[12] Charles S. Johnson, *Shadow of the Plantation* (Chicago: University of Chicago Press, 1934).

on poverty ushered in during the early 1960s that social scientists again discovered the Negro family. Now they became increasingly aware that not only war and prosperity, but poverty as well, seemed destined to be fixed factors in our social life. The incongruity of it all forced a reexamination, both of the social fabric of the larger and now international society and of the inner workings of our own pluralistic society.

When we took a fresh look at poverty, we observed that Negroes were conspicuous among the poor, though they constituted less than a third of the total poor people in this country. But by now we were armed with statistical techniques which helped us to see that Negroes were over-represented among the poor. We therefore focused on them, and searched for explanations. By now we also knew the connections between family life and the broader social context, including economic, political, and educational advancement.

It is perhaps a peculiarly American quality to look for single causes of complex phenomena. It was amazingly convenient to explain poverty by ignoring the total poverty picture and explaining only Negro poverty, for in this way one could avoid some of the more troubling aspects of the Negro experience, aside from poverty—namely, persistent prejudice and discrimination based on race. Seeking to explain only *Negro* poverty, one could conveniently ignore the mass of causal factors and focus on the Negro people themselves, their leadership, their psychological motivation and aspirations, their family structure, and, in a flash of superficial enlightenment, their history of slavery. The Negro family, therefore, came in for some scholarly attention. But this attention has been directed to only that "half" of Negro families in the lower class, and even more specifically, that "third" of Negro families below the poverty line, or that "quarter" of Negro families headed by women, or that "tenth" of Negro families with illegitimate children, or that even smaller proportion of Negro families which combine these three conditions and are supported by public welfare.

For it must be said with all candor that the social scientists who have recently discovered the Negro family have not yet produced a study of that 75 per cent of Negro families who have stable marriages, or that half of Negro families who have managed to pull themselves into the middle class, or that 90 per cent of all Negro families who are self-supporting, or that even larger portion who manage to keep out of trouble, often despite the grossest kinds of discrimination and provocation. It would be very instructive indeed to know how two thirds of all Negro families with less than $2,000 annual income in 1966 could manage to hold themselves together and meet the American test of family stability. For surely that is the statistic which needs explaining, rather than the minority of poor families where the man disappears in order to let the family survive economically. In addition, some understanding of how this majority of Negro families manages can help provide clues for the rehabilitation of other families, and at the same time can enlighten the society about the problems these Negro families still face.

The major reason for this selective focus on the negative aspects of Negro family life is that scholars do not yet seem to be interested in the Negro family as an institution for its own sake, and for what an understanding of it can tell us about our society. Studies so far which have focused on Negro family life in the lower class, problem-ridden sectors are not concerned at all with Negro family life. They are concerned, instead, with poverty, family breakdown, and illegitimacy, and somehow tie these phenomena to the Negro experience. This seems to obviate, for a time at least, the urgent need to explain these phenomena in the larger white society, where they are far more numerous. Perhaps if it can be said convincingly enough that people are in these conditions because they have been enslaved and still have a slave mentality, and because they have been discriminated against because of their race—all of which are true enough—then scholars and social reformers can avoid, for a few more years, looking for causes of these phenomena in the normal workings of our society—particularly in the workings of the upper reaches of our financial, industrial, military, educational, political, and religious institutions. This can postpone, for a time, the possible revelation that these pathologies may be endemic to our society, and are therefore normative and structural—not merely functions of individual, psychological, and subcultural hangups.

Fortunately, there is already emerging a small but growing literature on Negro families which takes these families seriously in their own right and does not treat them essentially as deviants from white norms. Outstanding among this new literature is the work of Jessie Bernard,[13] Hylan Lewis and his associates,[14] Lee Rainwater and his associates in St. Louis,[15] Joan Gordon in Harlem,[16] and a number of unpublished works.

[13] Jessie Bernard, *Marriage and Family among Negroes* (Englewood Cliffs, N. J.: Prentice-Hall, Inc., 1966).
[14] Hylan Lewis, "Changing Perceptions of Race, Class, Culture, and Social Welfare." Paper presented at Institute on Research toward Improving Race Relations, Airlie House, Warrenton, Va., August 1967. See also Lewis's introduction to Camille Jeffers' *Living Poor* (Ann Arbor: Ann Arbor Publishers, 1967), and Elliott Liebow, *Tally's Corner* (Boston: Little, Brown and Company, 1966).
[15] Lee Rainwater, "Crucible of Identity: The Negro Lower-Class Family," *Daedalus* (Winter 1966).
[16] Joan Gordon, *The Poor of Harlem: Social Functioning in the Underclass* (New York: Office of the Mayor, Interdepartmental Neighborhood Service Center, July 31, 1965).

Ethnic Assimilation Studies

A second stream of scholarship within which one might have anticipated some attention to Negro family life is that body of literature devoted to analyzing the process and problems associated with the assimilation of the various ethnic minorities into what is considered the mainstream of American values and behavior patterns. Much of that literature has focused on family life in an effort to chart the growing disparities in the values and behavior of family members of succeeding generations. Yet, except in minor respects, the Negro family has been conspicuously absent from such considerations. A brief reference to the historical developments in this field of American scholarship will indicate both how and why this has been so.[17]

At the time of the American Revolution, the largely white Protestant population of the United States had already absorbed large numbers of other northern European peoples. These included, particularly, Germans, Scotch-Irish, Frenchmen, Dutchmen, Swedes, Swiss, and Poles. Although at the time Negroes made up nearly a fifth of the population—a much greater proportion than today—they were given no consideration as a significant element to be assimilated into the mainstream of American society. This omission is largely a result of the slave status of the vast majority of Negro people at that time, but must also be attributed, in part, to the fact that even the nonslave-holding peoples of the North, who were in fact dominant, did not consider Negroes, whether slave or free, as part of the human race. For to be human was to be northern European.

The dominant thinking and research on assimilation during this period reflected an overwhelmingly and unabashedly English bias. Most scholars unhesitatingly assumed the desirability of maintaining English institutions, the English language, and English cultural patterns. The questions for investigation had to do with how other peoples could or did become assimilated to these values. According to Milton Gordon, this "Anglo-conformity doctrine" has been "the most prevalent ideology of assimilation goals in America throughout the nation's history."[18]

By the last decade of the nineteenth century, however, the steady stream of immigrants from the southern European countries had begun to

[17] This discussion is drawn from the work of Milton Gordon, *op. cit.*
[18] Gordon, *op. cit.*, p. 89.

stimulate large-scale concern on the part of citizens and scholars with racism in America.

> Previously vague and romantic notions of Anglo-Saxon peoplehood, combined with general ethnocentrism, rudimentary wisps of genetics, selected tidbits of evolutionary theory, and naive assumptions from an early and crude imported anthropology produced the doctrine that the English, Germans, and others of the "old immigration" constituted a superior race of tall, blond, blue-eyed "Nordics" or "Aryans," whereas the peoples of eastern and southern Europe made up the darker Alpines or Mediterraneans—both "inferior" breeds, whose presence in America threatened either by intermixture or supplementation, the traditional American stock and culture.[19]

While these people could not be eliminated from the society, or conveniently ignored—they were too numerous, too valuable, and, politically, too powerful—the dominant elements bent their efforts toward converting them into Anglo-Saxon Americans. A great number of rather repressive measures were sanctioned in efforts to "Americanize" these "inferior" peoples.

The southern Europeans in America have been the object of extensive studies of ethnic assimilation. There was no room, however, in this phase for studies of Negro families, for how could one study the impact of the New World on value changes within the family and between the generations, if there was no baseline for comparison in the old country? And how could one study the process of acculturation if not much was actually taking place? As for the "old country" for Negroes, Africa did not exist in these assimilation studies, nor indeed did Africa exist very much in American thought, except perhaps in the dark reaches of the collective unconscious. For whatever might have been the efforts to anglicize other non-English peoples, there was no massive efforts to do so with Negroes.

From the end of the eighteenth century onward, the Anglo-conformity phase had to share the stage with a somewhat competing philosophy, commonly known as the "melting pot" thesis. This thesis held that it was not necessary, maybe not possible, and perhaps not even desirable for all peoples to become anglicized. The notion arose that many diverse peoples had cultural contributions to make to America, and that all might be poured into a common pot to be processed into a new type of human element. Perhaps the outstanding exponent of this point of view was the

[19] Gordon, *op. cit.*, p. 97.

American historian, Frederick Jackson Turner. In a series of writings beginning in 1893, Turner devoted a long and distinguished scholarly career to expounding the melting pot thesis.[20] His central argument was that the dominant influence in shaping American institutions and democracy was not our English or European heritage, but the experiences created by the western frontier, which acted as a solvent for the national heritages of the many nationality groups which came to people the new country.

Ralph Waldo Emerson heralded this philosophy in 1845 when he wrote in his journal

> . . . so in this continent—asylum of all nations,—the energy of the Irish, Germans, Swedes, Poles, and Cossacks, and all the European tribes—of the Africans, and of the Polynesians, will construct a new race, a new religion, a new state, a new literature, which will be as vigorous as the new Europe which came out of the melting pot of the Dark Ages. . . .[21]

Thus Emerson had a place for the Negroes in his melting pot. But his lead was not pursued, not even by himself.

A third important contributor to this evolving melting pot philosophy was an English-Jewish writer, Israel Zangwill, whose play, The Melting Pot, became a success in 1908. Zangwill also gave passing attention to the Negroes. "Englishmen, Germans, Frenchmen, Slavs, Greeks, Syrians, Jews, Gentiles, even the black and yellow races, were specifically mentioned in Zangwill's rhapsodic enumeration. And this pot patiently was to boil in the great cities of America."[22] Again, however, not many scholars followed Zangwill's lead. The pot did not boil for Negroes. And the process by which it did not and the dynamics of Negro family life during that long period from the end of slavery to the mid-twentieth century has still to be chronicled.

Perhaps the sociologist Ruby Jo Reeves Kennedy made the most perceptive contribution to the melting pot thesis when she coined the phrase "triple melting pot." In her study of intermarriage in New Haven from 1870 to 1940, she found that while marriages took place increasingly across nationality lines, they tended to be restricted within one of the three major religious groups—Protestants, Catholics, and Jews. She

---

[20] For a discussion of this thesis of Frederick Jackson Turner see Gordon, op. cit., pp. 117–20.

[21] Gordon, op. cit., p. 117. Quoted from Stuart P. Sherman, Essays and Poems of Emerson (New York: Harcourt, Brace & World, Inc., 1921), p. xxxiv.

[22] Gordon, op. cit., p. 121. See also Israel Zangwill, The Melting Pot (New York: The Macmillan Company, 1909).

therefore urged the abandonment of the original single melting pot thesis and the substitution of a triple melting pot thesis.[23]

It would have been possible in 1940 for Mrs. Kennedy to have looked beyond or even within New Haven and discovered that there were more than three separate tracks to this melting pot, for Negroes continued to marry among Negroes, often across religious lines. Out west, Orientals practiced the strictest endogomy, and Mexicans in the southwest showed a similar tendency. But scholarship is often blind to that which is not encompassed within its study sample, and invalid generalizations are perpetrated for a whole country. But once the notion was seriously advanced that there was not a single melting pot, it was not long before a more general ideology of culture pluralism, without a fixed number of elements, gained recognition in American scholarship.

Toward the latter part of the nineteenth century, this pluralist movement was led by social workers, usually middle and upper class Anglo-Saxons who went to "settle" in the slums of major American cities. The settlement houses fostered an appreciation of the immigrant's native cultural heritage and of his efforts to maintain some of this heritage in the institutions he created in America. Jane Addams was prominent in this phase of assimilationist ideology. Perhaps the classic statement of this position, however, came from Horace Kallen, an American Jew who was a Harvard-educated philosopher. Early in 1915 he published two articles in *The Nation* in which he set forth his philosophy and description of ethnic group life in America:

> . . . He was impressed by the way in which the various ethnic groups in America were coincident with particular areas and regions, and with the tendency for each group to preserve its own language, religion, communal institutions, and ancestral culture. All the while, he pointed out, the immigrant has been learning to speak English as the language of general communication, and has participated in the over-all economic and political life of the nation.[24]

Kallen argued that this process was for the good of both the ethnic groups and the general society, and described this as "cooperation of cultural diversities, as a federation or commonwealth of national cultures." To him, these group cultures represented the essence of democracy, for "democracy for the individual must, by extension, also mean

[23] Ruby Jo Reeves Kennedy, "Single or Triple Melting Pot? Intermarriage Trends in New Haven, 1870–1940," *American Journal of Sociology*, XLIX (1944), 331–39.
[24] Gordon, *op. cit.*, pp. 141–42. A discussion of Kallen's work appears in Gordon, pp. 141–54.

democracy for the group." For a period of forty-five years, while teaching at the New School for Social Research in New York, he was the leading exponent of cultural pluralism in America.

In modern times, cultural pluralism has become an accepted philosophy from which have sprung theoretical formulations about group life in America. Contemporary sociologists also include the Negro people in their treatment of this theme. Two prominent works in this vein, both prize winning essays, are *Beyond the Melting Pot* by Nathan Glazer and Daniel P. Moynihan,[25] and *Assimilation in American Life* by Milton M. Gordon.

Race Relations Studies

The third field of American scholarship in which one might have expected a continuing focus on Negro family life is that which focuses on the Negro people in American society. Along with the study of the American family, studies of the American Negro have been abundant, particularly since the middle of the twentieth century. Yet few of these studies have concerned themselves specifically with Negro family structure and function. In an extensive bibliography of works on the Negro published since 1954, Elizabeth W. Miller has listed some 4,000 entries, only fifty of which can be construed as focusing on Negro family life, and even then, this category overlaps with that of child rearing.[26]

One reason Negro family life has occupied such a minor place in all the Negro studies is that most of these studies are not of Negroes at all, but of the relations between Negroes and whites, or the attitudes of whites toward Negroes or vice versa, or of the Negro protest movement and other efforts to integrate into white institutions. In short, studies of the Negro have blended into the prevailing ideology in our society that Negro life is something to be avoided, overcome, escaped, and ignored. Thus, aside from the handful of sociologists mentioned above, we must look largely to Negro writers like Richard Wright, Langston Hughes, Ralph Ellison, James Baldwin, Gordon Parks, Ann Petry, Margaret Walker, Pauli Murray, Dorothy West, and a few white novelists for intimate glimpses of Negro family life.

The second factor which helps to account for the absence of the Negro family from American social science literature is the relative paucity of

[25] Nathan Glazer and Daniel Patrick Moynihan, *Beyond the Melting Pot* (Cambridge, Mass.: The M.I.T. Press and Harvard University Press, 1963).

[26] Elizabeth W. Miller, *The Negro in America: A Bibliography* (Cambridge, Mass.: Harvard University Press, 1966).

Negro scholars and the selectivity of their scholarly interests. One searches the social science journals in vain for a steady stream of contributions by Negro social scientists. It is our view that if there were more Negro social scientists, there would be more systematic studies of Negro life—from the inside, so to speak—not simply studies of race relationships. And if there were more studies of Negro life, there would be more studies of Negro family life. It is a hypothesis which fortunately we shall be able to examine empirically over the next decade. For social scientists in the great universities are beginning to discover Negroes again, not only as subjects or objects of study, but as objects of education as well, including education at the highest levels of graduate study.

A final reason to be specified here why Negro family life has been relatively absent from studies of Negroes in America has to do with the nature of the disciplines involved in such studies. These are principally sociology, economics, political science, and social psychology—all of which have in common a heavy reliance on statistical techniques, large-scale survey methods. But most important, insofar as they have focused on the Negro experience or race relations in America, they have been *ad hoc* studies without a limiting range of guiding and overarching theories. This last characteristic is the most serious and crippling. For while it is true that the methodological tools most in vogue for social science during recent years do not lend themselves to the study of family life, it is a more searching indictment that these disciplines have had so few theories to guide their studies of the Negro situation. Had they had such overarching and comprehensive theories of group life, it might have been clearer to them that some glaring omissions were being made in their researches regarding Negro family life.

Studies in Social Welfare

The field of social welfare where social work is the major profession might also be looked to as a source of knowledge about the structure and function of Negro family life in America. The major portion of professional social work activity centers on families experiencing one kind of problem or another, and indeed, the major portion of the teaching curriculum in professional schools of social work has reflected this family focus. But despite this professional concern with families, social work scholars have almost ignored the family as a field of studies. Most of social work research is focused on social workers, their agencies, and their attitudes toward a variety of objects, including their clients; a few studies have enquired into the orientations and problems of foster parents and adoptive parents. But, with the conspicuous exception of an imaginative series of studies by Geismar and his associates,[27] the social work literature is barren of research-based knowledge of families. And if the family in general has been ignored by social work scholars, the Negro family has been even more ignored. For there is a strong belief among social work scholars that there is nothing special about Negro family life which cannot be surmised from studies of other low income and lower class families.

This tendency has been fortified by the nature of the professional orientation of social work scholars. Their major reference group has been the social sciences, particularly psychology and sociology. They have, therefore, adopted both the theoretical and methodological perspectives of the other disciplines and have confined themselves largely to the same kind of substantive studies.

For a number of reasons, then, Negro family life has been virtually ignored by the four major areas of American scholarship which have legitimate claim to this aspect of American life—the field of American family studies, the field of ethnic assimilation studies, the field of American Negro studies, and the field of social welfare. While each of these fields of scholarship has its own peculiar historical development, each also has three factors in common. A ready response to the popular, the fad, the current national ideology; an ethnic limitation, in the sense that each field has not been consistently open, inviting, and rewarding to Negro scholars; and most critical of all, an abundance of empirical observations and a shortage of generalizing theories to guide research. In addition, scholars in these disciplines have obviously been guided by their own ethnocentrism and intellectual commitment to peoples and values transplanted from Europe. Consequently, they have not been able to see that the subject of the Negro family is a natural child of theirs to be nurtured and developed. Instead, they have treated this area as a stepchild, foster child, or worse.

Perhaps the major contribution of the Moynihan report is that it brought to the attention of scholars, of planners, as well as of the general public, the fact that Negro families are an important part of the national life. It has already stimulated other scholars to undertake studies in this important area.

Hopefully, among the series of studies on Negro family life which will

[27] Ludwig L. Geismar and Beverley Ayres, *Measuring Family Functioning: A Manual on the Method for Evaluating the Social Functioning of Disorganized Families* (St. Paul: Family Centered Project, Greater St. Paul Community Chest & Councils, 1960).

be ushered in during the late 1960s and 1970s, there will be studies focused not only on poor Negroes from broken families, but on middle class and even upper class Negro families who have other kinds of problems and achievements.

One of the major purposes of this volume is to suggest that such studies should be conducted with historical perspective, in the context of the broad range of social forces affecting family life, with some explicitly stated theoretical framework and with methods both comprehensive and flexible enough to capture the complexity of the Negro experience in America.

Index

About the Authors

Andrew Billingsley, Ph.D., is Professor and Chair of the Department of Family and Community Development at the University of Maryland, College Park. He was previously President and Professor of Sociology at Morgan State University, Vice President and Graduate Professor of the Social Sciences at Howard University, and Assistant Chancellor and Associate Professor of Social Welfare at the University of California at Berkeley. Dr. Billingsley is also consultant to the National Urban League and director of a national study on family support programs conducted by black churches. Dr. Billingsley is considered by his colleagues to be one of the leading sociologists in the nation. In addition to *Black Families in White America*, he is author of several other books, including *Children of the Storm* and *Black Families and Their Struggle for Survival*, and more than two hundred articles, reviews, and technical papers. His work is widely quoted by other social scientists, professionals, and policymakers. Dr. Billingsley is currently completing work on a new book, *Climbing Jacob's Ladder: Black Families in White America Revisited*, to be published by Touchstone Books, a division of Simon & Schuster Inc.

Amy Tate Billingsley operates a private consulting firm. She currently serves as Exhibits Manager and Marketing Consultant for a national consortium of historically black colleges and universities (N.A.F.E.O.). She is President of the national black MBA (Masters of Business Administration) association.